DAY BY DAY WITH AMY BOLDING

DAY BY DAY WITH AMY BOLDING

by

AMY BOLDING

BAKER BOOK HOUSE
Grand Rapids, Michigan

Library of Congress Catalog Card Number: 68-29785

PHOTOLITHOPRINTED BY CUSHING - MALLOY, INC.
ANN ARBOR, MICHIGAN, UNITED STATES OF AMERICA
1 9 6 8

This book is dedicated to Mr. Cornelius Zylstra, without whose help I could never have written this book. He not only is my editor but I count him a friend.

Contents

January:

A Month of Beginnings

January 1

"But as it is written, Eye hath not seen nor ear heard, neither have entered into the heart of man, the things which God hath prepared for them that love him." — I Corinthians 2:9

We have come to a new year; a year to invest in happiness, a new year to invest in service and love. Let us forgive all that is in the past, and look forward to a bright handful of tomorrows.

Isn't it fun to have a surprise! It makes a day brighter. We like so much to have surprise parties for those we love. God has a wonderful year of surprises awaiting those who love him.

We will enjoy these things which God has prepared for us more if we lay aside all littleness that may have kept us from doing our best in the past and determine to give our best in the year ahead. Shall we resolve to do so?

> To be of greater service, Lord,
> A closer student of Thy Word;
> To help to bear a brother's load
> And cheer him on the heavenly road;
> To tell the lost of Jesus' love,
> And how to reach the home above;
> To trust in God whate'er befall,
> Be ready at the Master's call
> For any task that He may give;
> And thus through all the year to live
> For Him who gave Himself for me
> And taught me that my life should be
> A life unselfish, not self-willed,
> But with the Holy Spirit filled.

Prayer: Dear God, help us to accept with gratitude the measure of our days. Help us with grace to accept each day as a gift and use it to prepare for the eternal. We ask in the name of the giver of all days. Amen.

January 2

"Thou wilt show me the path of life: in thy presence is fulness of joy; at thy right hand there are pleasures forevermore."
— Psalm 16:11

We have taken only one step on the road of our new year. How exciting! God's tomorrow has become God's today! The things which last week we planned to do next year are now ready to be started, for "next year" has become today. There is so much hopefulness in this day, so much promise, and so much excitement. It is time to begin what we had looked forward to doing. We are inevitably and steadily marching forward on this pathway of life. Let us walk carefully, for our footsteps cannot be retraced. Let us accept with joy the path before us.

Plan that today will be better than the days that have passed. Plan that the footstep you leave behind will guide someone who will follow.

> One small life in God's great plan,
> How futile it seems as the ages roll,
> Do what it may, or strive how it can,
> To alter the seep of the infinite whole!
> A single stitch in an endless web,
> A drop in the ocean's flow and ebb!
> But the pattern is rent where the stitch is lost,
> Or marred where the tangled threads have crossed;
> And each life that fails of its true intent
> Mars the perfect plan that the Maker meant.
>   — Susan Coolidge

Prayer: As we start the pathway of a new year, dear Father, help us to submit our lives to thy will. Realizing our own helplessness, may we put our trust completely in thee. Help us to seek thy purpose for us and triumph in giving ourselves to the fulfilment of that purpose. Amen.

January 3

"We will keep his commandments, and do those things that are pleasing in his sight." — I John 3:22

> Have Thine own way, Lord!
> Have Thine own way!
> Thou art the Potter;
> I am the clay.
> Mold me and make me
> After Thy will,
> While I am waiting
> Yielded and still.

God made the world after a divine plan, and for a divine purpose. In fact, he has a plan and purpose for each life. We cannot know God's plan and purpose for our life in advance, but we can trust that it is perfect and correct. In this confidence it is ours to keep his commandments and be pleasing to him.

We might think of ourselves as a vessel being fashioned and designed for his purpose. When we grow rebellious the design becomes blurred and ugly. We must learn to live with our past mistakes, but also ever to strive to make each day better as we submit to the Master's touch.

> Where deeds of mine can help
> To make this world a
> Better place for men to live in,
> Where word of mine can cheer
> A despondent heart or brace
> A weak will,
> Where prayer of mine can serve the
> Extension of Christ's kingdom
> There let me do and speak and pray!

Prayer: Almighty Father, we stand in need of protection from the enemies standing round about us. Help us ever to determine to keep thy commandments and in keeping them to live a better life of service and love. Amen.

January 4

"Therefore if any man be in Christ, he is a new creature: old things are passed away; behold, all things are become new."
— II Corinthians 5:17

> Today another challenge comes,
> In accents loud and clear:
> How am I going to spend my life
> Throughout the coming year?
> Shall I for self and pleasure live,
> And listless pass the days?
> Or shall I live for Christ, the Lord,
> And render Him my praise?
> Lord, I would spend this year for Thee,
> So, help me as I try;
> My Saviour's smile — the glorious prize
> Awaits me bye and bye.
> — Marie L. Olson

We may classify people into three groups. First we think of the people who have to be pushed or shoved along. They never have enough energy to get busy and do worthwhile things on their own. They remind us of a rowboat without anyone to row or push it along — useless unless helped by others.

Then there is a group of people who remind us of a sailboat. It moves along very well when the wind is blowing in a favorable direction. These people like to be with the crowd and work as the crowd works. They must have wind for their sails if they are to accomplish anything.

The people who make the world a wonderful place to live and work are like the man described in the Scripture verse: "He is a new creature." Through storm or calm they go right on doing what they feel is right. For them each new day is a day for service for God and man.

We choose the kind of people we will be.

Prayer: Father, as the winds of life buffet me about, help me, that I may be led of thee to be firm and true to thy kingdom work. Inspire me to love those about me in such a way that they too will want to be a new creature in Christ. Grant thy special blessing upon those who are slow or who are going only with popular currents. Help them to trust in thee. For in the name of the one who makes us new we pray. Amen.

January 5

"Then they willingly received him into the ship: and immediately the ship was at the land whither they went." — John 6:21

I was sitting in the car after church — just watching people as they left. Then I saw a young couple come out of the door. They were holding hands, and from the way they looked at each other I knew they must be in love. The boy was a stranger to me, but I had known the girl, a college senior, since she was very small.

As I watched them with warmth in my heart, I suddenly remembered. That same young girl had called the week before to tell me that as soon as graduation was over she was going to a foreign land to be a missionary helper for two years.

My heart felt heavy. She would go for the two years when most girls are having a good time, choosing husbands, and getting married. I knew too that her parents were not happy about her decision. Then the thought of today's Scripture verse came to my mind. With Christ as her traveling companion the time would seem short. She would be a blessing to many people and there would still be young men in America when she returned. In fact, the one who was holding her hand might not mind waiting for her return.

The sea of life grows smooth when we have Christ as our traveling companion.

> Others may do a greater work,
> But you have your part to do;
> And no one in all God's heritage
> Can do it so well as you.

Prayer: Dear Lord, bless those who are serving thee, whether here at home, or far away. In Jesus' name we pray. Amen.

January 6

"Order my steps in thy word: and let not any iniquity have dominion over me." — Psalm 119:133

When I was a child my parents tried to teach me what was right and what was wrong. I did not always do just the right thing, and at times I was punished for disobedience. Then suddenly I was grown up, and when a question of right or wrong arose I had to make the decision myself. Even in adulthood I found that one is punished if one chooses the wrong path. More and more, as I developed as a Christian, I found it best to ask God to order my steps — I found it best to depend upon him for guidance. When my steps were ordered by the Lord I found my life happier and more complete. You, too, will find this to be true.

> He does not lead me year by year
> Not even day by day,
> But step by step my path unfolds,
> My Lord directs the way.
> Tomorrow's plans I do not know
> I only know this minute!
> But He will say, "This is the way,
> By faith now walk ye in it."
> And I am glad that it is so;
> Today's enough to bear.
> And when tomorrow comes, His grace
> Shall far exceed its care.

Prayer: Dear Father, exceeding and abundant are thy gifts to us each day. Help us to be grateful for thy blessings; for thy guiding hand along life's way. We rejoice in the glorious hope we have for tomorrow; for the promises of thy sufficiency and care. For we pray in the name of Christ. Amen.

January 7

"Herein is love, not that we loved God, but that he loved us, and sent his Son to be the propitiation for our sins."

— I John 4:10

Josephine Skaggs, a missionary in Nigeria, was told by a friend to "slow down." She replied: "It isn't what we do that hurts us; it's what we can't do. It is the knowledge that over the next hill there are multitudes who would respond, as others have, if we could but go to them. But there aren't enough hours in the day, nor is there enough strength in the human frame to meet their appalling needs."

This missionary loves so much that she is literally wearing out her body in her zeal to tell others about Christ's love. God has such a wonderful love for a lost world that he made a way of redemption for us. He literally poured out his love for us. God is able to save from the uttermost and to the uttermost.

Oh what love! How can we "slow down" — or sit still?

If I have moved a single grain of sand
This day to help my fellow man,
If I have brought one stray into the fold,
Or sent a ray of hope to one lonely soul
Like a sunbeam in a prison cell;
Or on the desert sands a water well
To quench his anguish on the way of life,
Or ease his heartbreak in the battle strife —
This day is not lost.

— Patricia Soito

Prayer: Father, we thank thee for the wonderful people of the earth who are willing to spend their lives in service far from home. Bless them today. We ask in Christ's name. Amen.

January 8

"Two are better than one; because they have a good reward for their labor. For if they fall, the one will lift up his fellow: but woe to him that is alone when he falleth; for he hath not another to help him up." — Ecclesiastes 4:9, 10

Ralph Waldo Emerson wrote: "The glory of friendship is not the outstretched hand, nor the kindly smile, nor the joy of companionship; it is the spiritual inspiration that comes to one when he discovers that someone else believes in him and is willing to trust him with his friendship."

We should try *to be* a helpful friend. To be a good friend one must have clean thoughts and noble purposes. If we deal justly with those around us, tell the truth, and show fine conduct, people want us for their friends.

We should strive *to have* good friends. They offer encouragement when we are discouraged; they offer to share our joys when we are glad. They keep life from being barren and lonely.

> Some folks hunger for a friend,
>   For friends make life worthwhile;
> And other hearts are hungry
>   For just a pleasant smile.
> Kind words and deeds have wondrous power
>   To save a soul from sin;
> To drive the threatening clouds away
>   And let the sunshine in.

Prayer: For our friends we are grateful. Send us out to be more friendly to those in need of help. May people never reach out in vain asking our friendship. We ask in the name of the greatest friend man has known. Amen.

January 9

"If thou turn away thy foot from the sabbath, from doing thy pleasure on my holy day; and call the sabbath . . . the holy of the Lord . . . and shalt honor him, not doing thine own ways, nor finding thine own pleasure, nor speaking thine own words: then thou shalt delight thyself in the Lord. . . ." — Isaiah 58:13, 14

We should plan for Sunday to be different from all the other days in the week. If we truly love God and delight in serving him we will observe Sunday as he asks us to. Sunday should be a day for worship, a day for resting, a day for fellowship with friends in the Lord's house. Sunday should be a day of helpfulness to others.

Sunday should be the day we are quiet and listen to God speak. We will be thankful for his blessings if we have a quiet time to meditate on them.

In many ways we disregard God's will for this one day in seven. In early days of America, without the aid of modern refrigerators, the housewife prepared the food on the day before. She, too, rested on Sunday.

God gave us Sunday as a precious jewel hanging on the chain of the week. We should guard the way we use it.

17

Safely through another week
God has brought us on our way;
Let us now a blessing seek,
Waiting in His courts today;
Day of all the week the best,
Emblem of eternal rest:

While we pray for pardoning grace,
Through the dear Redeemer's name,
Show thy reconciled face;
Take away our sin and shame:
From our worldly cares set free,
May we rest this day in Thee.

— John Newton

Prayer: Father, how grateful we are that we can say, "Thy word is a lamp unto my feet, and a light unto my path." If we have been heedless in thy house, forgive us and make us true worshipers of thy son. We ask in Jesus' name. Amen.

January 10

"I press toward the mark for the prize of the high calling of God in Christ Jesus." — Philippians 3:14

Many years ago, in the early years of West Texas, people sometimes lived in dugouts. These were rooms dug down in the ground and covered over, with only a door leading outside. One day the teacher of a small one-room schoolhouse noticed the beginning of a snow storm. She dismissed school and told the children to hurry home as fast as they could. Three little children, who lived in a dugout two miles from the school, started for home. When it seemed to them they would never find their home because the snow was so thick, the little one began to cry from exhaustion and cold.

The two older ones were holding her hands and almost carrying her along. They, too, felt lost and helpless but wanted to be brave for her sake.

"Look! I see a light," one of them cried. Sure enough, they could see a faint light. "We will try to reach that light."

So they kept going with the faint glow of the light to guide them. Soon they reached home, guided by the light hanging high on their windmill. Their anxious mother had climbed to the top and hung a lighted lantern there.

Many people are near their goal in life but no one lights a lantern for them, and they falter on the way. Sometimes just a kind word of encouragement will help a fellow traveler.

Prayer: Help us, O God, to consecrate our lives to the giving of light to those who are in darkness. Let thy presence go with us today. We pray in the name of our Lord and Saviour. Amen.

January 11

"Behold that which I have seen: it is good and comely for one to eat and to drink, and to enjoy the good of all his labor that he taketh under the sun all the days of his life, which God giveth him: for it is his portion." — Ecclesiastes 5:18

We must admit we are inadequate without God. With God life is a big adventure. With him as our partner we need not be afraid. The person trusting in God is eager to see what is around the corner. He does not look forward with fear but with expectation of God's blessings.

It is wonderful when as children of God we can see all the beauties of life God has planned and prepared for us and be blind to a few discomforts along the way, knowing that God has a portion for us and it is good. The children of Israel were fed manna every day when they needed it. They found water when it was needed. All was provided by God who watched over them and cared for them. Do we not worship the same God? Is he not just as good and powerful today? He will provide for us.

> In heavenly love abiding,
>   No change my heart shall fear,
> And safe in such confiding,
>   For nothing changes here.
> The storm may roar without me,
>   My heart may low be laid;
> But God is round about me,
>   And can I be dismayed?
>   — Anna M. Waring

Prayer: O God, make us aware that each day is a precious gift from thee. Help us to reflect our love for thee in our relationship with our fellow men. May each day of our life have meaning for us and be spent in helping others. For it is in the name of Christ we pray. Amen.

January 12

"For the which cause I also suffer these things: nevertheless I am not ashamed: for I know whom I have believed, and am persuaded that he is able to keep that which I have committed unto him against that day." — II Timothy 1:12

In a youth camp I sometimes visit there is a swimming pool. The pool is divided into two parts by a rope. One part is shallow and the other part is deep. The lifeguard decides the part in which a child will be allowed to swim by whether or not the child knows how to dive. If a child can get on the diving board and dive into the deep water, he is considered ready for the deep part of the pool.

Will we go through life paddling around in shallow water — or will we launch out into the deep and try for big things? Some of us are afraid to try big things, fearful that we may fail. Others jump out into life and try over and over, trusting God to help them. If we take God with us we will find the deep water easier to conquer. We should never leave home in the morning without asking God to guide our steps that day. We should never come face to face with a major decision without asking God to help us make the right choice.

> It's glorious just to walk with God,
>   In fellowship so sweet;
> To revel in his presence as
>   Our souls the Saviour meet.
>
> His blessed Word is practical,
>   But it must be applied
> In ordinary daily tasks
>   Or else Christ is denied.
>
> Our lives are to embody him,
>   And live him forth each day,
> That all may see the difference in
>   The world's and Jesus' way.
>
> It is our wondrous privilege
>   God's temple here to be:
> The Spirit's living, earthly house
>   Where men, our Lord, may see.
>   — J. T. Bolding

Prayer: Merciful Heavenly Father, give us wings that will lift us above the common things of earth into realms of heavenly places. Help us have courage to attempt big things. We ask in Jesus' name. Amen.

January 13

"And we know that all things work together for good to them that love God, to them who are called according to his purpose."
— Romans 8:28

Confucius said: "The gem cannot be polished without friction, nor man perfected without trials."

There are times when we think we have our life all planned, all cut out according to a certain pattern. Then tragedy or change comes and we find it necessary to go in another direction. At such a time we must remember the Scripture and know that Romans 8:28 is still in effect. It is still true: "All things work together for good to them that love God." God directs us — sometimes gently, sometimes roughly — but always he is pushing us toward his purpose for us.

> God grant that I may find my task,
> And have the grace to do it well;
> And leave behind a stepping-stone,
> To earth's triumphant citadel.

> Keep firm my faith and strong my grasp
> On true perspective and the goal;
> That I may toil and weary not,
> And be the captain of my soul.

> Let not the lure of fame or greed,
> Make one dark blot upon my line;
> That each day's work be clean and good,
> In keeping with Thy will and mine.

> God, grant that I may find my task,
> And have the grace to do it well;
> And leave behind a stepping-stone,
> Complete, unmarred, celestial.

— Alex Hoe

Prayer: Make us diligent toilers in thy vineyard. For in Christ's name we pray. Amen.

21

January 14

"For all flesh is as grass, and all the glory of man as the flower of grass. The grass withereth, and the flower thereof falleth away: But the word of the Lord endureth forever."

— I Peter 1:24, 25a

This time of year the yards are brown and ugly; no green grass or blooming flowers are to be seen. Often we look out on ground covered with rain or snow, with a dream in our hearts of spring when the grass will be green and flowers blooming bright and beautiful.

Life is like that. Many times we look out at a dark day and feel that all is lost. We forget that spring always comes. We must remember that God's word endures forever and is filled with promises of his springtime for us. He has never made a cloud so dark but that in time the sun shone through.

We were attending a party; people were laughing and talking. Everyone seemed to be happy and everything seemed to be wonderful. Suddenly there was a great roaring noise. A long train was passing by on the tracks near the house. The talking stopped; people could only look at each other; the party seemed ruined. Suddenly the train was past and all was gay again. So it is with life. None of the bad things last forever; they pass away, and love, hope and faith abide.

Prayer: Lord, cheer and comfort our hearts today. Lift us out of sorrow. We pray in the name of Christ. Amen.

January 15

"Watch therefore: for ye know not what hour your Lord doth come." — Matthew 24:42

On a corner in West Texas there is a small house where children wait for the school bus. Billy is always the one who peeps out into the wind to see if the bus is coming. When he sees it far down the road he signals the others to gather up their books and be ready. If some child has not arrived yet, he pleads with the bus driver to wait just a moment for the late one. The children all laugh about Billy being so anxious about them. One day Billy was ill and could not go to school. The children in the little shelter felt lonely and cold. They missed Billy's ordering them about and being so concerned about them. The bus came and sounded the horn before they realized it was even near.

We take God's loving care for us so much for granted that we often forget to say thanks. Then one day when we are not watching, a dark shadow comes over our life and we realize how much God's love and protection means to us.

> The Lord has promised good to me,
> His Word my hope secure;
> He will my shield and portion be,
> As long as life endures.

Prayer: We thank thee, our Father, for the glorious gifts thou dost so bountifully bestow upon us. In Christ's name we pray. Amen.

January 16

"But these are written, that ye might believe that Jesus is the Christ, the Son of God; and believing ye might have life through his name." — John 20:31

Books are written for many purposes. When I was a child I thought the First Reader was about the most important book in my life. As a teen-ager I often walked a mile to the public library in order to read and be with the books. John wrote his Gospel for a special purpose — to help people believe in Jesus Christ. That which you read may bless or curse you the rest of your life. Be very careful how you spend your reading time.

Richard Le Gallienne, an English author, said of books: "They are the immortal nightingales that sing forever."

Provide good reading for those who are your responsibility.

When you provide a Bible for someone you may be the means of changing the whole way of life for that person.

When you provide a book of inspiration about some great character you may encourage a genius.

"Books are the ever-burning lamps of accumulated wisdom," says G. W. Curtis.

THE BIBLE CONTAINS:

The mind of God, the state of man, the way of life, the doom of sinners, the happiness of believers.

> Read it to be wise.
> Believe it to be safe.
> Practice it to be holy.

It gives the light to direct you, food to support you, and comfort to cheer you.

Prayer: Hide thy word in our hearts, O Lord, and fill us with thy love. In Christ's name. Amen.

January 17

"Wherefore take unto you the whole armor of God, that ye may be able to withstand in the evil day, and having done all, to stand." — Ephesians 6:13

One of my friends gave a party. I felt hurt because I did not receive an invitation. A few days after the party she asked me, "Why didn't you come?"

"I was not invited," I replied tartly.

A few days later the invitation came. The letter had been missent to another address and I received it too late. The hurt I had felt in my heart had made a scar which did not heal quickly.

Someone hurts your feelings — so you want to give up and hide. That is not the way. Put on the whole armor of God and let the darts be bent as they push against it. There are goals in life to be reached. They cannot be reached if we do not have an armor against the bad and unhappy things we encounter along the way.

Most people at some time or other feel lonely, apprehensive, or uneasy. Put on your armor against these feelings.

Happiness is a sweet spring flowing from your devotion to God. The firmer is your devotion to God the stronger is your armor.

The grandstand is always full of people who criticize and tell the players how to play; but the ball game is won by the ones on the field, those putting forth the effort to win. Remember the ones who throw the darts are usually not in the game. Let their darts bounce off your armor, and stride forth with a firm determination to win.

Prayer: Father, set our hearts aglow with the warmth of thy love. Infuse us with joy and peace. We pray in the name of Christ our Lord. Amen.

January 18

"Therefore let no man glory in men. For all things are yours; whether Paul, or Apollos, or Cephas, or the world, or life, or death, or things present, or things to come; all are yours; and ye are Christ's; and Christ is God's." — I Corinthians 3:21-23

24

Drop a pebble in the water,
    And its ripples reach out far;
And the sunbeams dancing on them
    May reflect them to a star.

Give a smile to someone passing,
    Thereby make his morning glad;
It may greet you in the evening
    When your own heart may be sad.

Do a deed of simple kindness;
    Though its end you may not see,
It may reach, like widening ripples,
    Down a long eternity.

— Joseph Morris

"For all things are yours." What wonderful words! Yet to make all things ours we must live for the good of others. In the beginning of the world "God saw that it was good." We still live in a world that has much good in it. It is up to us to go out and make it ours. We must believe that there is still good to be found and accomplished in the world. Believing this we must make the good things ours — ours to enjoy, to give to others, to share with the sad, to enlighten the ignorant, to teach the unlearned, to lift up all those we meet.

To really make the world ours we must give ourselves completely to the Christ who paid the ransom for our sins.

Prayer: Make our lives today hospitable, and appreciative. Through Christ our Lord we pray. Amen.

January 19

"For he that will love life, and see good days, let him refrain his tongue from evil, and his lips that they speak no guile: Let him eschew evil, and do good; let him seek peace, and ensue it."
— I Peter 3:10, 11

When I have lost my temper
    I have lost my reason, too,
I am never proud of anything
    Which angrily I do!
In looking back across my life
    And all I've lost or made,
I can't recall a single time
    When fury ever paid.

25

I have learned by sad experience
That when my temper flies,
I never do a worthy deed, or wise.

We should start each day with joy in our hearts and we should try to retain this spirit throughout the day. If we let someone make us angry and cause us to say ugly words we take away not only our own joy but the joy of others as well.

Perhaps when we grow angry with someone we have not stopped to consider that person's problems. He may be laboring under a heavy load and in need of a lift — not an angry word.

The Indians had a saying: "Never judge another until you have walked a week in his moccasins."

Sometimes we grow angry and say unkind words. We intend to ask forgiveness in a few moments, or at the end of the day. And then we forget or neglect doing so. Why not ask forgiveness at once. Why take the chance of leaving someone hurt and disappointed from our quick temper? Why hurt him at all?

Some people want to master a trade. Others want to develop a skill — or master an art. But we should all want to master our tempers.

Prayer: Bless us now, O God. Fill our hearts with prayer and meditation. We ask in Jesus' name. Amen.

January 20

"... And have put on the new man, which is renewed in knowledge after the image of him that created him."
— Colossians 3:10

People seem to want to be like the crowd. If some terrible crime is reported in the paper, in a few days there will be reports of similar crimes committed by people who were weak and acted on the power of suggestion. Christians must strive to be carbon copies of Christ, not of the world.

When we attempt to be carbon copies of some person we admire, or maybe even someone we fear, we too should ask the question, "Will I be willing to pay the price?" Jesus asked the disciples if they were able to suffer as he would suffer.

For many years all the young Baptist ministers tried to copy the late Dr. George Truett. But they could not in their preaching reach the heights that he reached. There was a reason unknown to most of them. They had not gone to the depths in suffering as he had gone. He had accidentally shot a friend on a hunting trip. From that day forward his life was more fully dedicated to service.

It is hard for parents to make their children see that some popular youth is not worthy of imitation. A parent knows that a wild youth will in all probability come to a sad end, but it is hard to make children realize that. They see the future only as the present looks. We must ever hold up the ideals and image of the one who created us.

Whom shall we take as an example — for ourselves, for our children?

Prayer: Father, let thy love be our companion on this pilgrimage of life. Strengthen our hearts with faith. We ask in the name of Christ. Amen.

January 21

"I can do all things through Christ which strengtheneth me."
— Philippians 4:13

There are times when we need strength from above, not for some giant problem but just for the everyday, petty annoyances of life.

We have a friend who has his office in his home. He spent a tidy sum of money having a beautiful sign made and painted, and placed in his front yard. All went well until a family with five small children moved across the street. All through the day the children would run across the street and climb the man's sign. They got the letters all dirty and caused the sign to wobble from their weight. Our friend repeatedly had to take of his valuable time to go out and persuade the children to leave. He was a Christian and did not want to act unkindly. So as often as he went out he asked God to give him grace to act kindly but firmly. Only love of God and strength from above kept him from having an open feud with the children and their parents.

There are times when we must ask for strength to meet petty annoyances. If allowed to control our thoughts they can make us unhappy. Sometimes we have to ask God to make us deaf to the sound of a neighbor's barking dog when we need our sleep. Perhaps at times like these we should quote our Scripture for today.

Prayer: Lift us today, out of petty, trifling things; make us more like Christ our Saviour. For in His name we pray. Amen.

January 22

"And there we saw the giants, the sons of Anak, which come of the giants; and we were in our own sight as grasshoppers, and so we were in their sight." — Numbers 13:33

We should see our difficulties as opportunities for exercising faith in God. When we are like the Israelites, seeing only the giants, we are defeated. We must see the power of the God we serve.

It is a great tragedy to stand before a difficulty unprepared. Then we think only of dodging trouble, forgetting that dodging may bring even greater trouble.

One beautiful spring morning when my sister was driving to work a bee flew into her car. She became frightened and tried so hard to dodge the bee that she wrecked her car. If she had just driven along very quietly, the bee might have found a place to alight, and she would have avoided a large repair bill.

Do you fix your eyes upon God when troubles come? Be positive. Know that He is able to conquer the giants — and then trust Him to do so. Have faith in God.

> Simply trusting ev'ry day,
> Trusting through a stormy way;
> Even when my faith is small,
> Trusting Jesus, that is all.
>
> Brightly doth His Spirit shine,
> Into this poor heart of mine:
> While He leads I cannot fall;
> Trusting Jesus that is all.
>
> Singing if my way is clear;
> Praying if the path be drear;
> If in danger, for Him call;
> Trusting Jesus, that is all.
>
> Trusting Him while life shall last,
> Trusting Him till earth be past;
> Till within the jasper wall:
> Trusting Jesus, that is all.
>
> Trusting as the moments fly,
> Trusting as the days go by;
> Trusting Him what e'er befall,
> Trusting Jesus, that is all.

— E. **Page**

Prayer: God of grace, may we find comfort in trusting thee today. We pray in the name of Jesus. Amen.

January 23

"And call no man your father upon the earth: for one is your Father, which is in heaven. Neither be ye called masters: for one is your Master, even Christ." — Matthew 23:9, 10

Who is the master of your life?

The great preacher, Billy Sunday, used to say: "Wrong thinking makes everything wrong. Right thinking makes everything right." When we forget who is Master of our lives we are thinking wrongly.

Many people plan someday to give their heart to Christ but they think there are still many years ahead in which to make the Christ the Master of their lives. We have only today. There is no promise of tomorrow; so we must pick a master worth serving today. "Choose you this day whom you will serve."

It is truly wonderful to have Christ as the head of our lives. When problems arise and we seem to stand alone we need only to remember that Christ is our Master. Then we will not feel alone. He is a master worth serving. He can meet our every need.

Prayer: Fill us with a desire to serve men far and near. Bless our efforts as we try to serve. We pray in the name of Christ. Amen.

January 24

"When thou shalt besiege a city a long time, in making war against it to take it, thou shalt not destroy the trees thereof by forcing an ax against them: for thou mayest eat of them, and thou shalt not cut them down (for the tree of the field is man's life) to employ them in the siege." — Deuteronomy 20:19

How we all admire a tree grown straight and tall! But we seldom stop to think of the many years it takes a tree to grow and develop.

One spring we had an unusually large number of bad windstorms. A young apricot tree just outside our back door was especially windblown. Some days it seemed as if we would have to cut the lush green top out in order to save our prized tree from blowing down altogether. My husband took soft rags and ropes and anchored it to stakes. With the ropes to help anchor it, the tree finally came through the windy season without losing its bushy green top.

29

Many a child stands straight and tall morally because his parents have anchored him against worldly winds. They have taught him God's will for his life as we find it in the Bible. With the Bible as a guide, people are anchored to withstand the strong winds of temptation or adversity.

Jan was a Christian young woman working at a strange new job far away from home. She was tempted, from loneliness, to go out with the wrong crowd. One evening as she was dressing to go out she remembered a Scripture text often quoted by her mother: ". . . think on these things" (Philippians 4:8).

Jan called and broke the date. She went to church instead. There she met the kind of young people with whom she had grown up. Soon she was happy with Christian friends.

Prayer: Our Father, help us at all times to realize we are by thy grace made sons and heirs to heaven. Fill us with thy love and spirit. We ask in Christ's name. Amen.

January 25

"Keep thy heart with all diligence; for out of it are the issues of life." — Proverbs 4:23

Good habits in day-to-day living help make one's life a real success. It is not often that one great, good act performed on the spur of the moment makes a successful life. Successful living involves doing the best you can each and every day.

Happiness comes from a number of things added together to make a pleasant whole. (1) First we must all have something to do. An idle person is never very happy or even nice to have around. (2) Then we need something, or someone, to love. A life lived entirely for self is very empty indeed. Seek for someone to love. It may be a child down the street, a member of your own family, or some unfortunate person in a rescue mission. Love someone. When we are busy, when we love someone, we still need another step to make us truly happy. (3) We need something to look forward to.

All three things may seem to be small things, but they add up to a whole that spells usefulness and contentment. So, develop the habit of feeling that your job is important. Remember that those you love are helped and encouraged by your love. Always look forward to a brighter tomorrow; it might turn out to be the most dramatic day of your life.

Prayer: Father, give us sincere and humble purpose as we seek to walk in thy will today. We pray in the name of Jesus. Amen.

30

January 26

*"The Lord bless thee, and keep thee: The Lord make his face
to shine upon thee, and be gracious unto thee: The Lord lift
up his countenance upon thee, and give thee peace."*

— Numbers 6:24-26

Driving down the street I often look at a sign which reads:
"A Wonderland of Comfort."

We are all looking for a wonderland of some kind. God has
promised that if we follow him he will give us a wonderland of
peace.

People who are financially able often build cabins on lakes or
in the woods just to have a quiet place where they can get away
from the noise and worry of the world. If you are a Christian
you do not have to build a retreat away from home. You can
learn to retreat into your own mind with happy, pleasant thoughts,
knowing who is in charge of your life.

Someone asked President Harry Truman how he managed to
carry the heavy load of the last days of World War II. He replied,
"I have a foxhole in my mind."

When you feel upset and your load seems unbearable, try
entering the wonderland of peace by silently quoting verses of
Scripture to yourself. Try thinking of some special blessing God
sent you in days gone by. Soon you will be at peace and things
will be bright.

One night at church I was almost in tears, just sitting there
feeling sorry for myself. A small child went upon the stage to
quote some Scripture. She started, "Ask and ye shall receive. . . ."

"You foolish woman," I thought. "You have forgotten to ask."
I entered the wonderland of peace and became calm and happy.

Prayer: Eternal God, make thy face to shine upon us today.
We have been bought with a price; make us ever mindful of our
duty as Christians. We ask in the name of Jesus. Amen.

January 27

*"They were armed with bows, and could use both the right
hand and the left in hurling stones and shooting arrows out of
a bow. . . ."* — I Chronicles 12:2

Some people practice overcoming the handicaps of life until
they are very good at some things. The warriors in our verse
of Scripture could use both hands in fighting. In life the person

who wins is the one who fails to look at handicaps but determines to fight with both hands.

Lucian Thomas is a business man who was hurt in a car wreck during his college days. He loved sports very much, but the wreck left him to live out his days in a wheel chair. Did he quit? No, each year during the football season he is wheeled out on the playing field and he makes an award to some worthy boy. He uses his quick mind to make money which he shares with some fine active boy who needs a boost.

> If you talk about your troubles
> And tell them o'er and o'er,
> The world will think you like them,
> And proceed to give you more.
>
> — *Pittsburgh Post*

Prayer: Father, let us think of our joys in life. Make our joys like wings to lift us above worldly problems. We ask in the name of Christ. Amen.

January 28

And Achish said, Whither have ye made a road today?
— I Samuel 27:10

If at the close of each day someone asked us, "Whither have ye made a road today?" what would be our answer?

Have we put forth an earnest effort to make the way easier for someone in need of help? Have we been cheerful when in the company of those who were sad?

Jesus each day faced a hard road — a road of persecution and trouble. Yet he made the road a brighter and better one for all he touched.

We must never feel that we are a completed person. There always should be the effort to build our lives a little better and a little nearer to God.

> I'm going by the upper road.
> For that still holds the sun:
> I'm climbing through night's pastures
> Where starry rivers run:
> If you should think to seek me
> In my old dark abode,
> You'll find this writing on the door:
> "He's on the Upper Road."

Prayer: Eternal Father, give us a missionary spirit. Fill us with joy as we help others along the way. We pray in the name of Christ our Lord. Amen.

January 29

"The hills melted like wax at the presence of the Lord, at the presence of the Lord of the whole earth." — Psalm 97:5

There are times when we make a foolish mistake or feel we have blundered. Then we go home and keep going over and over our mistakes and blunders. We repeatedly ask ourselves, Why? Or, we think about some problem we expect to arise, and foolishly imagine all the troubles we will have because of the problems. Such things are making mountains out of mole-hills. How often people lie awake at night and climb mountains of trouble! On the other hand, when the light of day comes, our mountains often become molehills and are soon forgotten.

We should look at those mountains, those mistakes and blunders, and ask our Heavenly Father to help them melt like wax. Talk them all over with him, then forget them and relax.

> Said the Robin to the Sparrow,
> "I should really like to know
> Why these anxious human beings
> Rush about and worry so."
>
> Said the Sparrow to the Robin,
> "Friend, I think that it must be
> That they have no Heavenly Father
> Such as cares for you and me."
>
> — Elizabeth Cheney

Prayer: Father, receive and bless our lives today. We wish to consecrate ourselves to thee. We ask in the name of Christ. Amen.

January 30

"There is therefore now no condemnation to them which are in Christ Jesus, who walk not after the flesh, but after the Spirit. For the law of the Spirit of life in Christ Jesus hath made me free from the law of sin and death." — Romans 8:1, 2

Race riots in Los Angeles cost over one hundred million dollars, and took thirty-two lives. All was lost because people forgot authority and went wild. They followed a crowd and forgot law and order.

33

Children who are not made to obey authority grow up to be lawbreakers, heart-breakers and burdens to society.

A man I know was an adopted child. As he grew up his parents never corrected him. Others in the family begged them to think what they were doing to themselves and the child, but they resented advice. The boy grew to be a man and he was often in jail, but his father paid his fine and got him out. He married and divorced two wives. He brought children into the world who had to be cared for by others. His parents took the attitude that the world had mistreated him and because of that he was in so much trouble. But actually the parents mistreated him by not making him respect authority from the time they adopted him until he was grown.

"He that spareth his rod hateth his son; but he that loveth him chasteneth him betimes" (Proverbs 13:24).

A good proverb for adults to follow is this: "Never bolt the door of tomorrow by failure to use authority today."

Prayer: Father, make us good and worthy parents. We thank thee for our children. Use them, dear Lord, in thy service. Through Christ we pray. Amen.

January 31

"Not that I speak in respect of want: for I have learned in whatsoever state I am, therewith to be content."

— Philippians 4:11

"Better is little with the fear of the Lord than great treasure and trouble therewith." — Proverbs 15:16

My friend Julia was ill and cross. Nothing seemed right to her. After a long talk she promised me she would work in her yard for an hour each morning. Soon she was so fascinated with things growing under her care that she forgot to be cross and complaining.

I heard about a man in our city who was laid off from work because of a disability. He got tired of staying in the house and complaining; so he started making doll houses in his garage. Soon he had more orders than he could fill.

Home is the place where we must look for the treasure of contentment and fulfillment. God knew in the beginning that man would need a home and a companion. We often forget how wonderful home is until we have to be away for a long time.

Then we remember, and wish we could relive the days we spent in complaining.

Our homes should be fragrant with the breath of happy events taking place right there, and happy things we plan to do in our own domain.

> Some day I'll stop seeking
>   Hillsides far apart,
> When I learn that peace abides
>   Only in my heart.
>
> — Edna Becker

Prayer: Father, we thank thee for our blessings today. We pray through Jesus. Amen.

February:

Thoughts on Love

February 1

"He that dwelleth in the secret place of the Most High shall abide under the shadow of the Almighty." — Psalm 91:1

> No coward soul is mine,
> No trembler in the world's storm-
>   troubled sphere.
> I see heaven's glories shine,
> And faith shines equal, arming me
>   from fear.
>
> Oh God within my breast,
> Almighty, ever-present Deity!
>   Life — that in me has rest,
> As I — undying Life — have power in
>   Thee!
>
> — Emily Bronte

A little baby rests comfortably and securely on his mother's breast. A little chicken hides under its mother's wing and is safe from harm. How safe we, as God's children, should feel if we abide under the shadow of the Almighty!

Our problem is not in the power of our refuge, but in our failure to dwell in the secret place of the Most High. His protecting care is ready for our weakness. Let us take refuge there, and abide there.

If we abide in God's love we will find it easier to shut our eyes to the slights and blows of the world upon us. We will be able to say, "I am trusting in God. He will make all things right in his time."

Prayer: Father, may we turn our complaints into praise and find joy in thy purpose for our lives. Through Christ we pray. Amen.

February 2

"Blessed is the man that trusteth in the Lord, and whose hope the Lord is." — Jeremiah 17:7

Our Pilgrim Fathers are a wonderful example of people who had hope for the future. They had much to fear but they had faith in God. This gave them strength to overcome difficulties and to conquer in a strange land.

God was as near to the Pilgrim band in America as he had been in the homeland. He had as much power as he had in

England or Holland: They had but to trust and ask for help. And they were blessed.

We too have the assurance that if we go forth each day with trust in God he will help us meet our problems. And we will be blessed.

A small child standing on a bench and jumping off to be caught in his father's arms is not at all afraid. He knows his father will catch him and hold him safely. So we too should jump out into life each day without fear, for we with Paul, "Know in whom I have believed and am persuaded he will keep that which I have committed unto him against that day."

Prayer: O Blessed Lord, make thy truth to shine about us. Help us to know and understand thy love for us. We pray in the name of the one who was all truth. Amen.

February 3

"And God said, Let us make man in our image, after our likeness: and let them have dominion over the fish of the sea, and over every creeping thing that creepeth upon the earth."
— Genesis 1:26

What a piece of work is man!
How noble in reason!
How infinite in faculty!
In form and moving how express and admirable!

In action, how like an angel!
In apprehension, how like a god!
The beauty of the world!
The paragon of the animals.

— Shakespeare

You are somebody because you were made in the image of God. Only man was given the breath of God to make his life immortal. Only man was given dominion over the fish of the sea, and over every creeping thing.

What a responsibility! You are somebody, therefore you should act like somebody.

Tom was the only son of a mill owner. His father was very strict with him and always taught him that he was to grow up to take his place in the little town as a leader. While Tom was away in college he was out one night with a girl of doubtful character. When she wanted to go to a place of which Tom knew God would not approve, he seemed to hear his father saying:

"You are somebody; you can't do that." He returned the young woman to her dormitory and never went out with her again. His father's faith in him meant more than the pleasures of a few moments.

Prayer: Fill us with a whole-hearted desire to live and act like a Christian should. May the love of Christ constrain us from evil. We ask in Jesus' name. Amen.

February 4

"It is good for me that I have been afflicted; that I might learn thy statutes." — Psalm 119:71

People in the West smile when you mention the highway called Route 66. This is a coast-to-coast highway. Part of the way it is divided and very good. Just when a driver leans back and feels all is perfect there is sure to be a detour. You cannot go far on Route 66 without coming to a detour. Life is like that highway. We feel all is perfect; the way is smooth; we are happy; we relax. Then adversity strikes and we must go over some rough roads.

Often as we travel the detour we can look across and see the highway. It looks finished and ready for use, and we wonder why it is not open. So in life we have troubles and look back at the good days, and we wonder why we could not have gone on in the same comfortable path. But we must not forget that detours are for our safety.

So also we are safe in the storms God sends us. In fact they are for a purpose. Often the purpose is to bring us into closer fellowship with God; to realize our dependence upon him.

When we are temporarily having trouble and adversity we might remember Milton who, though blind, yet saw Paradise. Beethoven was deaf, yet wrote beautiful harmonies. Adversity is something to be overcome. Contrary winds are to be faced. We can overcome if we put our trust in God. It is good for us to be afflicted so that we may be brought closer to the God we worship.

Prayer: Graciously help us to face our trials with peace of mind and faith in thee. We ask in the name of Christ. Amen.

February 5

"How God anointed Jesus of Nazareth with the Holy Ghost and with power: who went about doing good, and healing all that were oppressed of the devil; for God was with him." — Acts 10:38

Abraham Lincoln used to say he always plucked a thorn and planted a rose wherever he thought a rose would grow.

John Wesley said:

> Do all the good you can,
> By all the means you can,
> In all the ways you can,
> In all the places you can,
> At all the times you can,
> To all the people you can,
> As long as ever you can.

Different people have different ways of doing good but we should all try to live by John Wesley's motto and do all the good we can.

Recently a friend of mine lost her father. As she talked about her loss she kept telling me how many trees her father had planted in his lifetime. "He always said someone would enjoy them." That was his way of making the world a better place.

If you feel despondent and discouraged, go out and do a kind deed for someone. The day will become brighter. This is a cure for blue days. You cannot go far in doing things for others and not feel the love of God reflected in their gratitude. Just giving someone a ride or running an errand may make his day brighter — and yours.

The Scripture says that Jesus went about doing good and then mentions that God was with him. God will be with us if we do all the good we can.

Prayer: Give us today a sense of thy presence. Give us a desire to help others. We pray in Jesus' name. Amen.

February 6

"There is a friend that sticketh closer than a brother."
— Proverbs 18:24

One cannot always choose his surroundings or even his vocation in this world. But one can choose his friends. We should test people's attitudes toward the things which are high and holy before we take them to be our close friends. What kind of influence does a friend have on your life? Does an evening spent with your "friend" make it hard for you to say your bedtime prayers? If that be true, then change friends.

A young man was with a group one night, not knowing how rough and wild they were. Before the evening was over they had robbed a store. The bewildered young man was caught with the group and sent to prison. His life was ruined because he chose the wrong friends for one evening.

There are many faithless friends in this world, but it pays to stay close to the "Friend that sticketh closer than a brother." He will not lead one astray, but will always be there in time of need.

> I am a part of all whom I have met,
> So friend, of me, you are a wholesome part;
> Our precious visits, lingering with me yet,
> Are flowers in the garden of my heart.
> — Charles Elmer Chapler

Prayer: O Lord Jesus Christ, make us worthy of our friends. Help us always to serve the friend who sticketh closer than a brother. We pray through Christ our Lord. Amen.

February 7

"Therefore all things whatsoever ye would that men should do to you, do ye even so to them: for this is the law and the prophets." — Matthew 7:12

The law of society today seems to be, "Don't get involved." If you stop at a wreck — you may have to take off from work to testify at a trial. If you go to a neighbor's home to help in trouble — you may be sued. So, just don't get involved.

That is not the way Christ would have us live. He said that we should treat others as we would like to be treated. That can only mean becoming involved when we see a case of need. When we see a child being abused, is it too much to notify the authorities? When we see someone needing a boost to get a job, can't we say a helpful word? What if Christ had looked down on a sinful world and said, "I just don't want to get involved"?

If it were not for the fact that some are willing "to get involved" there would be no orphans' homes, no hospitals, no places of charity where the hungry may be fed and clothed. Do get involved. Christ did!

Prayer: Father, may we maintain enthusiastic devotion to our task as thy children. May we become so enthusiastic we will strive to be a blessing to others. In thy holy name we pray. Amen.

February 8

"Whose voice then shook the earth: but now he hath promised, saying, Yet once more, I shake not the earth only, but also

heaven. And this word, yet once more, signifieth the removing of those things that are shaken, as of things that are made, that those things which cannot be shaken may remain.''

— Hebrews 12:26, 27

Thinking of God shaking the earth and removing those things that are shaken reminds me of a story I heard of a truck driver who parked a large truck in a dry river bed. Since the truck was hard to start he left it running while he went to lunch with some other workers. When he returned the vibrations of the running truck on the quicksand had caused the truck to sink hopelessly into the sand.

We look at the wars and crime going on around us and we feel so hopeless. Yet the last part of verse 27 assures us there are things which cannot be shaken but will remain. The sun, moon and stars will always be shining someplace. There always will be a harvest time and planting time. There always will be the Word of God — perhaps hidden in our hearts, but we can depend upon it. Jesus will always be near for those who have trust and believe. Because Christ cannot be shaken there always will be love. Christ can understand any language and can be near us in any land.

Perhaps we have been too satisfied with our modern world and God is shaking us up for our own good, to bring us back to a realization of his power and rulership.

Prayer: Father, give us the kind of faith which the happiest believers exercise. We pray in the name of Christ. Amen.

February 9

"And he said unto them, When ye pray, say, "Our Father which art in heaven, Hallowed be thy name. Thy kingdom come. Thy will be done, as in heaven, so in earth. Give us day by day our daily bread.

And forgive our sins; for we also forgive everyone that is indebted to us. And lead us not into temptation; but deliver us from evil.'' — Luke 11:2-4

We made a phone call to our daughter's home twelve hundred miles away. A baby sitter answered the phone. We were so disappointed! We should have called person-to-person. So it is with our prayers, We want to talk person-to-person to our Father in heaven. No one else can do our praying for us. Someone else may pray for our well being, but that will not take the place of our own talk to God about our problems.

These are the gifts I ask of thee,
    Spirit serene —
Strength for the daily task;
Courage to face the road;
Good cheer to help me bear the traveler's load;
And for the hours of rest that come between,
An inward joy in all things heard and seen.
These are the sins I fain would have thee
    take away —
Malice and cold disdain;
Hot anger, sullen hate;
Scorn of the lowly, envy of the great;
And discontent that casts a shadow grey
On all the brightness of a common day.

                — Henry Van Dyke

Prayer: Dear Lamb of God, we thank thee for all the burdens you have borne for us. We thank thee for the privilege of prayer. We pray in the name of Jesus. Amen.

February 10

"But seek ye first the kingdom of God, and his righteousness."
                — Matthew 6:33

All through life we are choosing between things we consider to be major and minor. Some people choose to live in what we call major cities; others prefer the small town. Some choose to major on a good education, while to some a good job at the moment seems major.

Housewives will make out a list of things they want to accomplish in a day. Then they will work on what they consider the major items first.

Many college young people start school with one major, then change to another. There is one major in life we should never change. Christ and His kingdom should always be first in our plans and thoughts. If we major on Christ's kingdom the other things in life will just naturally fall in place.

My grandaughter has a puzzle with a cat's face on it. When she works the puzzle she first looks through all the pieces for the face, then she soon has the other parts in place around the face. If we can keep the kingdom of God major in our plans and lives, the minor things will fall into place.

Prayer: Father, thou knowest what is in our hearts. Teach us to choose the better thoughts. We pray in Christ's name. Amen.

February 11

"And be ye kind one to another, tenderhearted, forgiving one another, even as God for Christ's sake hath forgiven you."
— Ephesians 4:32

A little, golden-haired girl passed by a house on the way to the seashore. On the porch sat an elderly man. Often she took time to stop and talk a few moments. Sometimes if she found an interesting seashell, she would give it to the man. Several years went by. Even though she grew older she never forgot to be friendly to the lonely man. One day he died and when his will was read a large amount of money was left for the girl. She had been his only bright spot for a number of years.

We should make a list of things in our hearts that we will remember to do. One should be to treat aged people with kindness. They are often lonely and a kind word is a ray of sunshine.

We should always be ready to make an apology. An apology offered often saves a friendship. After all, God knows who is right or wrong and that is all that matters.

Remember, if you are angry and write a letter, destroy it as quickly as possible. It could carry a poisoned dart.

When someone is starting a scandal and you can do something to stop it, do your best to save a reputation.

You will never regret helping a wayward child find himself. Often he only needs a little understanding and confidence.

You will never regret serving God, and living in such a way as to honor him.

Prayer: Father, unto thy name be glory and praise and honor. We offer our love to thee today. In thy holy name we pray. Amen.

February 12

"The steps of a good man are ordered by the Lord: and he delighteth in his way." — Psalm 37:23

Abraham Lincoln was born February 12, 1809. He led our country in a wonderful way during the Civil War. The following words were spoken or written by him.

"I am not bound to win, but I am bound to be true. I am not bound to succeed, but I am bound to live up to what light I have. I must stand with anybody that stands right; stand with him while he is right and part with him when he goes wrong."

46

"I desire so to conduct the affairs of this administration that if at the end, when I come to lay down the reigns of power, I have lost every other friend on earth, I shall at least have one friend left, and that friend shall be down inside of me."

"I have been driven many times to my knees, by the overwhelming conviction that I had nowhere else to go. My own wisdom, and that of all about me, seemed insufficient for that day."

> He liveth long who liveth well!
> All other life is short and vain;
> He liveth longest who can tell
> Of living most for heavenly gain.
>
> He liveth long who liveth well!
> All else is being flung away;
> He liveth longest who can tell
> Of true things truly done each day.
> — Horatius Bonar

Prayer: O Lord, walk with us today. Lead us to serve thee aright. Refresh us and make us better men and women. We ask through Christ, our Lord. Amen.

February 13

"For I the Lord thy God will hold thy right hand, saying unto thee, Fear not; I will help thee." — Isaiah 41:13

Many people live in a state of anxiety all the time. Some are afraid they will lose their jobs or their business. Some women are afraid they will lose their beauty or their husbands. We fear war; we fear robbers; we fear drunk drivers. Parents worry about their children. If one is quiet and likes being at home they try to push him out into society. If a child is too loud they try to quiet him.

This is indeed an age of anxiety. But it need not be if our hope is in the Lord. He has promised to hold our hand and to help us over the trying fears of everyday life.

Let us be done with fear. Why not read the verse above and believe in God's promise? It is better to live in a constant state of hope, expecting the best, than to develop a life of worry.

> A little boy once played so loud
> That the Thunder, up in a thunder-cloud,
> Said, "Since I can't be heard, why, then
> I'll never, never thunder again."

And a little girl once kept so still
That she heard a fly on the window-sill
Whisper and say to a lady bird —
"She's the stillest child I ever heard!"
　　　　　　　　　— James Whitcomb Riley

Prayer: Teach us, our Father, to be kind and patient. Give us power in our lives through love and worship. We ask in the name of Jesus. Amen.

February 14

"Greater love hath no man than this, that a man lay down his life for his friends." — John 15:13

". . . Having loved his own which were in the world, he loved them unto the end." — John 13:1

Man is made for love. But there are many shadows and many difficulties in the way of loving and being loved.

When we think of love we usually think of the love of Christ for his redeemed ones. Then we often think next of the love of mother and father for their children, and of children for their parents.

When we think of February 14 we usually think of the love of sweethearts — love of a woman for a man or love of a man for a woman.

God knew the human need for all these different kinds of love — and gave his blessing to them. He sprinkled love in the hearts of man and woman that the world might be a better place in which to live.

But let us never forget that he made the supreme example of love by giving his Son.

God, give me love; I do not only pray
　　That perfect love may be bestowed on me;
　　But let me feel the lovability
Of every soul I meet along the way.
Tho it be hidden from the light of day.
　　And every eye but Love's, Oh! I would see
　　My brother in the monarch and the bee —
In every spirit clothed in mortal clay.

Give me the gift of loving! I will claim
　　No other blessing from the Lord of Birth,
For he who loves needs no high-sounding name,

Nor power, nor treasure to proclaim his worth;
His soul has lit at Life's immortal flame
A lamp that may illumine all the earth.

— Elsa Barker

Prayer: Our Father, the author and giver of all good gifts, look upon us with compassion and forgive our ungratefulness. We ask in the name of Jesus. Amen.

February 15

"I am not ashamed, for I know whom I have believed and am persuaded that he is able to keep that which I have committed unto him against that day." — II Timothy 1:12

". . . And, lo, I am with you alway even unto the end of the world." — Matthew 28:20

Somewhere there waiteth in this world of ours
For one lone soul another lonely soul,
Each choosing each through all the weary hours
And meeting strangely at one sudden goal,
Then blend they like green leaves with golden flowers,
Into one beautiful and perfect whole;
And life's long night is ended, and the way
Lies open onward to eternal day.

— Edwin Arnold

Even the bravest hearts are sometimes lonely, longing for a companion to hear their troubles and share their sorrows. The gospel of Christ would be empty indeed if it had no message for the lonely people of our world.

Loneliness is like an animal lying in wait in the shadows, ready to jump out and frighten even the bravest. Sometimes it comes because we have lost a dear one, a companion or child. To love is to run the risk of losing. So we all at times go through a lonely period.

But Jesus promised to be with us at all times. He is with us when we are young and look out on the throngs we must meet and associate with to make life a success. He is with us when we are old and feel life is passing us by. He is with us in the thick of the battle, when we feel we are standing alone against a multitude of problems. God is with his children no matter from what vantage point we look at life. We need not be afraid.

Prayer: Father, may we keep our hearts with all diligence. Let the beauty of thy love dwell in us. We pray in the name of one who was always lovely, Christ our Saviour. Amen.

February 16

"I am sure that neither death, nor life . . . will be able to separate us from the love of God in Christ Jesus our Lord."
— Romans 8:38-39

"So you have sorrow now, but I will see you again and your hearts will rejoice, and no one will take your joy from you."
— John 16:22

In our work we attend many funerals and see the reaction of many people to loss and grief. One can almost tell how close a person walks with God by his reaction to grief. A strong Christian knows that love stands at the gateway of death and opens the door to a fuller happier life for the one called to go.

"Death is swallowed up in victory" (I Corinthians 15:54).

There is comfort in knowing someone has been relieved of suffering and pain.

True, a house is lonely when a loved one goes away. Jesus knew this would be true so he gave us the promise found in John 16.

> He leaves our hearts all desolate,
>   He plucks our fairest sweetest flowers;
> Transplanted into bliss, they now
>   Adorn immortal bowers.
>
> The bird-like voice, whose joyous tones,
>   Made glad those scenes of sin and strife,
> Sing now an everlasting song,
>   Around the tree of life.
>
> — John L. McCreery

Prayer: Father, give us the knowledge today that in thy grace there is sufficiency. We pray through Christ our Lord. Amen.

February 17

"I can do all things through Christ which strengtheneth me."
— Philippians 4:13

> "I Can't" lacks in nerve; he's too faint of heart
> To pitch in like a man and do his part;
> He has none of the spirit that fights and wins;
> He admits he is beaten before he begins.
>
> "I Can't" sees as mountains what bolder eyes
> Recognize as molehills; ambition dies

And leaves him complaining in helpless wrath
When the first small obstacle blocks his path.

"I Can't" has a notion that, out of spite,
He's being cheated of what's his right.
The men who succeed by hard work and pluck
He envies and sneers at as "fools for luck."

"I Can't" is a loafer, who won't admit
That his life's the mess he has made of it;
The treasure that's sparkling beneath his eye
He thinks he can't reach — and won't even try.

"I Can't" has a feeling the world's in debt
To him for the living he has failed to get.
But, given a chance to collect, he'll rant
About past failures and whine, "I can't."

— Doris Beason

I sat at home for months after a sick spell saying to myself:
"I can't." But at last Mr. "I Can" took hold of my mind, and I
decided to try going out again. Imagine my surprise when my
old friends remembered and seemed glad to see me. Their encouragement and kindness gave me courage to stop hiding behind, "I can't."

We should always encourage people, whatever their problems.
If we believe we can, then half the battle is won. If someone
else says, "You can do it," a lot more of the struggle is won; and
the first thing we know, a victory is won.

Prayer: Father, help us to find joy and fellowship in praise to
thee this day. In Christ's name. Amen.

February 18

*"That you being rooted and grounded in love, may have power
to comprehend with all the saints what is the breadth and length
and height and depth, and to know the love of Christ which
surpasses knowledge, that you may be filled with all the fullness
of God."* — Ephesians 3:17-19

When we think of God's love we think of something measure-
less. What a thrill to think of the duration of his love — throughout all eternity, forever and forever! My bank account will run
out and have to be replenished — but not so God's love. Then
there is the width and breadth of God's love. How wide he

51

made it in John 3:16! It is wide enough to include all who want to be included, from the least to the greatest.

We have different ways of measuring human love but no measuring rod will stretch far enough to measure God's love for his children.

"I love you, Mother," said little John.
Then, forgetting his work, his cap went on.
And he was off to the garden swing,
And left her the water and wood to bring.

"I love you, Mother," said rosy Nell —
"I love you better than tongue can tell";
Then she teased and pouted full half the day,
Till her mother rejoiced when she went to play.

"I love you, Mother," said little Fan;
"Today I'll help you all I can;
How glad I am that school doesn't keep!"
So she rocked the baby till it fell asleep.

Then, stepping softly, she took the broom,
And swept the floor and dusted the room.
Busy and happy all day was she,
Helpful and happy as child could be.

"I love you, Mother," again they said,
Three little children going to bed;
How do you think that mother guessed
Which of them really loved her best?

Prayer: Help us to show our love for thee this day as we help others. In Jesus' name we pray. Amen.

February 19

"He that hath an ear, let him hear what the Spirit saith unto the churches; To him that overcometh will I give to eat of the tree of life, which is in the midst of the paradise of God."
— Revelation 2:7

Are you optimistic enough to believe there are better days ahead? If you are, life will be sweet and complaints few. Happy people are the ones who can overcome outer hardships with inner joys.

Sometimes we may feel we are climbing on the rough side of life. But if we are filled with the inner joy of trust in God we will overcome the ups and downs of everyday living. We will then look forward to the joys of life in the paradise God has prepared for us.

I knew a woman whose husband had a heart attack. He lost his job as a result. Then when it looked as if they had no way to go but up, her only son had a nervous breakdown and was hospitalized for months. As a result of the loss of job and financial strain of a long hospital stay they were forced to move out of their spacious home into a small apartment. Through all this the woman, a devout Christian, went right on going to church and kept a radiant smile on her face for the world to see. She knew that God was in control.

> Be it healthy or be it leisure,
>   Be it skill we have to give,
> Still in spending it for others
>   Christians only really live.
>
> Not in having nor receiving,
>   But in giving, there is bliss;
> He who has no other pleasure
>   Ever may rejoice in this.

Prayer: Fill us with a yearning for a sweeter communion with thee. We pray in Christ's name. Amen.

February 20

"And he shall speak great words against the most High, and shall wear out the saints of the most High, and think to change times and laws: and they shall be given into his hand until a time and times and the dividing of time.

But the judgment shall sit, and they shall take away his dominion, to consume and to destroy it unto the end."

— Daniel 7:25, 26

Usually the person who manipulates things behind the scenes does a great deal of work. We think, for example, of the stage hand in a play and the social chairman for an organization. There are many people who work behind the scenes. God is behind the scenes of our life all our days. He understands why some things happen and others fail to happen.

The person behind the scenes is usually rather popular. Men curry his favor because they want his influence. They try to get close to him just to know what is going to happen.

Why then do we so often fail to get close to God? We could

understand the changes in life and meet them better if we were close to the one who is behind the scenes of all things. As the Scripture indicates, sometimes the times are seemingly in the hand of others. But only for a period does God allow Satan to rule. We can be sure that in his time God will take away Satan's dominion.

Prayer: May we worship thee with power and understanding. We thank thee Father, for the blessings thou dost shower down upon us. In the name of the great Redeemer we pray. Amen.

February 21

"And ye have forgotten the exhortation which speaketh unto you as unto children, My son, despise not thou the chastening of the Lord, nor faint when thou are rebuked of him: For whom the Lord loveth he chasteneth, and scourgeth every son whom he receiveth." — Hebrews 12:5, 6

> Dare to do right; dare to be true;
> You have a work that no other can do.
> Do it so kindly, so bravely, so well
> Others shall hasten the story to tell.

"I hate to think what that child will be when she grows up." I made that comment as some company with a very unruly child left my home. Not once during all her naughty behavior did her mother correct her and really mean it. I certainly wanted to, but I was not the parent. The privilege should have been hers.

Sometimes it seems pretty rough when we feel God's chastening hand on us; but we emerge better children and more useful to the world. A parent who truly loves his child wants that child to obey certain rules of behavior and thus grow up to be well adjusted in society.

God wants his children to mature by living by a certain set of rules too. We are to be Christlike in all we do. It is easy enough to know what God demands by reading the New Testament.

God is gracious and kind to those who try to live as Christ lived, to those who seek to win others. He gives us many glorious promises if we live by this pattern.

Prayer: Father, help us to find thy gracious guidance for our lives. We pray in the name of Jesus Christ. Amen.

February 22

"If thou wilt not observe to do all the words of this law that are written in this book, that thou mayest fear this glorious and fearful name, THE LORD THY GOD. . . ."

— Deuteronomy 28:58

Different names invoke different feelings in us. We honor and worship the name of our God. When the name of The Father of Our Country is mentioned we think with a thoughtful heart of one who left a comfortable home and led hungry men to fight for freedom.

What do men think when your name is mentioned? Do they have pleasant thoughts and feel glad they know you? Or are they cold and unresponsive?

We are the ones who give people the feeling they have about our name. We cannot all be leaders of our country but each of us can fill his own corner in the very best possible way. We cannot all be known far and wide but we can be known by those near at hand as good or bad, as standing for right and wrong.

> Lord of the Universe! shield us and guide us,
>   Trusting Thee always, through shadow and sun!
> Thou hast united us, who shall divide us!
>   Keep us, O keep us the *many in one!*
>   Up with our banner bright,
>   Sprinkled with starry light,
> Spread its fair emblems from mountain to shore,
>   While through the sounding sky
>   Loud rings the Nation's cry, —
> *Union and liberty! One evermore!*

— Oliver Wendell Holmes

Prayer: We thank thee, Father, for those great men who have in the years of our history made our nation great. We pray in the name of the greatest of all, our Saviour and Lord. Amen.

February 23

"For what shall it profit a man, if he shall gain the whole world, and lose his own soul?" — Mark 8:36

With a limited amount of money to spend I take my time when I go shopping. I try to make sure I get the full value in my purchases. When I get home and look over what I have bought I like to feel my money was well spent.

As we go through life we have only one soul. We have

only the promise of the present. The past is forever gone; the future is uncertain. Each day we should make sure we spend our time in the most profitable pursuits. Each day is a precious jewel in the chain of our lives and we should get the full value from it.

> Open the door of your hearts, my lads,
>> To the angel of Love and Truth
> When the world is full of unnumbered joys,
>> In the beautiful dawn of youth.
> Casting aside all things that mar,
>> Saying to wrong, Depart!
> To the voices of hope that are calling you
>> Open the door of your heart.
>> — Edward Everett Hale

Prayer: O God of truth and holiness, come into our hearts today. Lead us into the better way of life. May we seek and find the pearl of great price. We pray in Jesus Holy name. Amen.

February 24

"Who when he had found one pearl of great price, went and sold all that he had, and bought it." — Matthew 13:46

Wasn't it fun as children to look for pretty pebbles! (For some of us it still is.) Sometimes we would trade with each other. In our childish hearts we just knew that some day we would find a pebble that would turn out to be a diamond or some other jewel.

Jesus told the story of a man who was searching for something: "Again, the kingdom of heaven is like unto a merchant man, seeking goodly pearls" (Matthew 13:45).

All mankind goes through life seeking something. Some only look for insignificant little pebbles; but others seek a pearl of great price. Some seek financial security; some seek social popularity; some seek fame. All are good, but they are still only as pebbles on the beach compared to the pearl of great price.

A man whose daughter was seriously ill offered the doctor a large sum of money if he would cure her.

"The one who can cure her now demands no money," the doctor told him. "You must pray and ask God to heal her."

How often we let the little, brightly colored pebbles of the world keep us from accepting the pearl of great price! Jesus stands ready to offer us a place in the kingdom if we only accept. We do not have to haggle in a foreign market place as the merchant did. We are offered eternal life as a free gift. Yet many hold out their hand to the world and say, "Fill it with pebbles; the pearl looks too small."

Prayer: Give us today true penitence in our hearts. We are ashamed of our negligence and sin. Let us turn to ways of peace. In Christ's name we pray. Amen.

February 25

"Whatsoever thy hand findeth to do, do it with thy might; for there is no work, nor device, nor knowledge, nor wisdom, in the grave, whither thou goest." — Ecclesiastes 9:10

How can you make your life count? Begin where you are with what you have today!

We all like to dream of the big things we are going to accomplish some day while we neglect doing the things at hand.

Don't be guilty of saying, "Oh, I am just an inconsequential person."

God made all men important. All have something to do. So our main task is to get busy. As we work at the tasks at hand we find other opportunities opening up for us. We find we can do something a little harder than we thought we could, and we grow.

So you feel small and lost in this vast world? Well, how about a snowflake? Yet we would not want to do without them. They add together and make our winter beautiful; they prepare the soil for the next season. So God has many tasks for the people who may feel they are inconsequential. Put your hand to the task at hand.

> Let us do our work as well,
>   Both the unseen and the seen;
> Make the house where Gods may dwell,
>   Beautiful, entire, and clean.
>
> Else our lives are incomplete,
>   Standing in these walls of Time,
> Broken stairways, where the feet
>   Stumble as they seek to climb.
>
> Build today, then, strong and sure,
>   With a firm and ample base;
> And ascending and secure
>   Shall tomorrow find its place.
>   — Henry Wadsworth Longfellow

Prayer: May we be ever conscious that "there is none other name under heaven, that is given among men, wherein ye must be saved." We pray in the name of Jesus. Amen.

February 26

"Boast not thyself of tomorrow: for thou knowest not what a day may bring forth." — Proverbs 27:1

We put off many good things until tomorrow — and then we are sad and disappointed when tomorrow never comes. Today is ours; we should accomplish all the good we can while we have the opportunity.

We often have good intentions for tomorrow. Felix did too. He sent Paul away and thought he would hear more about Christ at a convenient season. That tomorrow never came.

People often fret and lose sleep over problems they expect to arise tomorrow. We fret as if God were not going to be there tomorrow to help us meet our problems and provide a way out for us.

Some parents are so busy they neglect spending time with their children, planning to spend time with them tomorrow. Too often that tomorrow never comes. Before they realize it the children are grown and the happiness of enjoying them as they grow is gone.

Do the things today you have been putting off for tomorrow.

Lord, for tomorrow and its needs I do not pray;
Keep me, my God, from stain of sin just for today.

Let me both diligently work and duly pray;
Let me be kind in word and deed just for today.

Let me in season, Lord, be grave, in season, gay;
Let me be faithful to thy grace just for today.

So for tomorrow and its needs, I do not pray;
But keep me, guide me, love me, Lord, just for today.

Prayer: Today let us remember that in thee we live and move and have our being. Renew our spiritual lives. We ask in the name of Jesus. Amen.

February 27

"He that findeth his life shall lose it; and he that loseth his life for my sake shall find it." — Matthew 10:39

The above Scripture is the best recipe for happiness to be

found. As we live for others life becomes worthwhile and we feel whole and complete.

Men are always looking for the radiant life, the joyful life, the truly happy life. Few find it. Those who spend life seeking just what they want for themselves have very little true happiness.

I remember visiting in a beautiful home when I was young. I felt out of place. I was the mother of three small children; my husband was a poor young pastor. The cost of the clothes our hostess wore would have fed us for many weeks. She took us about her house showing off her treasures and accomplishments. I was glad when the time came for us to go. After we left my husband remarked, "What an empty life to have only dishes and silverware to live for."

We can make our lives happy and beautiful by living for others. I know a lady who has no children at home; yet she runs the Sunbeams in her church for the small children. She makes the children happy and gives the mothers a few moments rest.

We can be like the Dead Sea, take all we can get for ourselves — and be stagnant and useless. Or we can be like the mighty Mississippi River, giving to all along the way — carrying loads for others. Happiness comes from giving; so we must see how much of ourselves we can give away.

Prayer: Father, make our lives beautiful and fruitful. Make us happy in our daily tasks as we serve thee. In the name of Christ we pray. Amen.

February 28

"And Moses took the bones of Joseph with him; for he had straitly sworn the children of Israel, saying, God will surely visit you; and ye shall carry up my bones away hence with you."

— Exodus 13:19

It is sometimes hard to get people traveling on the train or bus to check their baggage. Some want it where they can "get at it" during the entire trip. A boy I knew taking his first bus trip failed to check his bag. He carefully placed it on the shelf over his head. At one of the bus stops he got off to look around. When he arrived home he reached for his bag — and it was not on the shelf. The bag was never found. The boy determined that if he ever took another trip he would check his baggage.

We all take out into the world with us each day things we

might better check. For example, we would do well to check and forget many frets and worries. Why don't we "take them to the Lord and leave them there"?

If we ask God to work out our problems and then go on about our work we may rest assured he will work them out for us.

There are, however, some things we should take along and never check: a happy smile, a cheerful word of greeting, a helping hand for those about us. These are so easily carried along. Let's keep them with us.

> Build a little fence of trust
> Around today;
> Fill the space with loving deeds,
> And therein stay.
> Look not through the sheltering bars
> Upon tomorrow;
> God will help thee bear what comes
> Of joy or sorrow.
> — Mary Frances Butts

Prayer: Our Heavenly Father, we desire an abundance of thy grace. Use us to advance thy kingdom. We pray in the name of our Lord. Amen.

February 29

"And there came a leper to him, beseeching him kneeling down to him, and saying unto him, if thou wilt, thou canst make me clean.. And Jesus, moved with compassion, put forth his hand, and touched him, and saith unto him, I will; be thou clean."
— Mark 1:40, 41

How good it feels when one is ill to have a cool hand rubbed across the brow! How comforting is the touch of a mother to a disturbed child! There are numerous places in the Bible where the touch of Jesus is mentioned. Little children came just to feel his touch. Jesus said, "Let them come."

The touch of a friend means a lot in time of bereavement. The clasp of a hand on Sunday makes one feel warm and happy inside. The touch of a sweetheart or loved one brings joy and peace.

This world today needs the touch of the hands of Jesus. He is not here in physical body to give that touch, but he has you here to work for him. Let us be his hands. Let us go out and help the sick and lonely.

There are days so dark that I seek in vain
For the face of my Friend Divine;
But though darkness hide, He is there to guide
By the touch of His hand on mine.

Oh, the touch of His hand on mine,
Oh, the touch of His hand on mine!
There is grace and power, in the trying hour,
In the touch of his hand on mine.

There are times when tired of the toilsome road,
That for the ways of the world I pine;
But He draws me back to the upward track
By the touch of His hand on mine.

When the way is dim and I cannot see
Thro' the mist of His wise design,
How my glad heart yearns and my faith returns
By the touch of His hand on mine.

— Jessie Brown Pounds

Prayer: Touch us today with thy hand of love. Cleanse us from
our sins. We ask in the name of Jesus. Amen.

March:

Good Ways to Live

March 1

"If thou wilt be perfect, go and sell that thou hast and give to the poor, and thou shalt have treasure in heaven: and come and follow me." — Matthew 19:20

> Bear on! Our life is not a dream,
> Though often such its mazes seem;
> We were not born for lives of ease,
> Ourselves alone to aid and please.
> To each a daily task is given,
> A labor which shall fit for Heaven;
> When Duty calls, let Love grow warm;
> Amid the sunshine and the storm,
> With Faith life's trials boldly breast,
> And come a conqueror to thy rest.
> Bear on — bear bravely on!

How often as a child I heard the old saying, "It takes a sacrifice to satisfy."

It does take a sacrifice to get the things we want. Jesus told the young ruler he would have to sacrifice earthly riches if he were to have treasure in heaven. Instead, the young ruler foolishly sacrificed eternal life with Christ in order to satisfy his love for money.

A good student sacrifices time he might spend in fun and pleasure, so that he may prepare himself for a life of service. Good parents sacrifice going out too often at night so that they may make a better home for their children. All of life is a choice and we must sacrifice in order to have the best.

Christ sacrificed his life for us. He sacrificed the glories of Heaven for a season in order that we might share Heaven with him. He sacrificed himself for us.

Sometimes Christ does not ask us to go and sell what we have. At times he asks us to give ourselves. He asks us to go and tell the story. He asks us to seek the lost sheep and bring them into the fold. He asks us to comfort the ones in sorrow. Is it too much to spend time for Christ when he did so much for us?

Prayer: We thank thee for our assurance of immortality. In the name of Christ we pray. Amen.

March 2

"And the king sat upon his seat, as at other times, even upon a seat by the wall: and Jonathan arose, and Abner sat by Saul's side, and David's place was empty." — I Samuel 20:25

David's place was empty because he was afraid of the king. We often leave our places empty in the house of our King, because we are indifferent or lazy.

There is a place in the church for everyone. There is a place of service for all, if it is just to be present to encourage those who lead. How often as a teacher I have felt ready to quit! Then some pupil would express love and gratitude for my work. I started up afresh, ready to work.

Sometimes we attend the services and yet are absent in thought and spirit. How cold the services seem on days like that! We should try never to let our places be empty in the House of God.

> Do thy little; do it well;
> Do what right and reason tell;
> Do what wrong and sorrow claim;
> Conquer sin and cover shame.
> Do thy little, though it be
> Dreariness and drudgery;
> They whom Christ apostles made
> Gathered fragments when he bade.

Prayer: Father, may we help all humanity toward the attainment of true brotherhood as we fill the place assigned to us in thy kingdom's work. We ask in the name of Jesus. Amen.

March 3

"And now they sin more and more, and have made them molten images of their silver, and idols according to their own understanding, all of it the work of the craftsmen: they say of them, Let the men that sacrifice kiss the calves." — Hosea 13:2, 3

In some respects the road of sin is like a freeway. Getting on the freeway is much easier than getting off. It is so easy to miss an exit, especially when one is speeding along, hardly conscious of what lies ahead.

The freeway of sin is described in the above Scripture. Once having entered the road of sin, it was easy for Israel to keep going, sinning "more and more."

Occasionally one is forced from a freeway by an accident, perhaps a tragic one, which blocks all oncoming traffic. Sometimes God also uses a tragedy in our lives to steer us from the freeway of sin, back to the narrow road of the Christian life.

The freeway of sin is crowded. Millions are gliding along without realizing where they are going. They sin "more and more." What they do not know is that even though the Christian travels the narrow road, it can be one filled with joy and happiness.

Prayer: Everlasting God, who art always ready to hear us when we pray; we thank thee for all thy providential care. May thy Holy Spirit fill our lives and lead us in service for thee. We pray in the name of Christ. Amen.

March 4

"For he that hath, to him shall be given: and he that hath not, from him shall be taken away even that which he hath."
— Mark 4:25

In the Scripture text Jesus is talking about his followers hearing the gospel and growing in the knowledge of the truth.

In our day we need to be careful what we hear and what we read, for poison can enter our minds and hearts by the wrong speakers and the wrong books.

Bunyan said, "Satan enters in at the ear-gate." But so can truth.

If we lend our ears to false teachers and God-dishonoring speech, we will soon scorn the truth and despise Christian teachings. We will find ourselves drifting off after these wrong teachings, and then after evil companions and deeds. If we love the truth and obey it, our power of understanding will be greater and our knowledge increased. And we will "walk in the truth."

> Lulled in the countless chambers of the brain,
> Our thoughts are linked by many a hidden chain;
> Awake but one, and lo! what myriads rise!
> Each stamps its image as the other flies.
>
> — Pope

Prayer: Give us today a new vision of thy truth. We confess our sin and ask for forgiveness. Create in us a clean heart. In the name of Christ we pray. Amen.

March 5

"And Jesus answering said unto them, Have faith in God."
— Mark 11:22

Many lives have been saddened because people placed their faith in the wrong people, or the wrong business venture. Many lives have been saved because someone had faith in another and encouraged him. Faith is something unseen, yet having a great influence on people.

67

A boy was out with the wrong companions one night. As they sat in the car planning to commit a crime he kept hearing his mother say: "Son, I have faith that you will do right."

So he said to the boys, "Let's drive up on the mountain and look down at the lights of the city. The view is just grand from up there. We don't really want someone's old hub caps anyway."

While they were on top of the mountain looking and guessing which lights were where, the boy promised himself he would never be caught out with that crowd again. He did not want to betray his mother's faith in him.

Have faith in God when your pathway is lonely,
He sees and knows all the way you have trod;
Never alone are the least of His children;
Have faith in God, have faith in God.

Have faith in God when your prayers are unanswered,
Your earnest plea He will never forget;
Wait on the Lord, trust His Word and be patient;
Have faith in God, He'll answer yet.

Have faith in God though all else fail about you;
Have faith in God, He provides for His own;
He cannot fail though all kingdoms shall perish,
He rules, He reigns upon His throne.

— B. B. McKinney

Prayer: Renew a right spirit within us we pray in the name of our Lord and Saviour Jesus Christ. Amen.

March 6

"I must work the works of him that sent me, while it is day: the night cometh, when no man can work." — John 9:4

When I drive about our city after dark and see the thousands of cars on the streets I often wonder if people know it is dark. The night was designed by God to be a time of rest, and cessation from the toil of the day.

Jesus knew there would come a dark time for him when his work on earth would be finished. He determined to accomplish his purpose before that night came.

We often drift through our days as if we have forever to accomplish the task given us. But we, too, will face a dark time when we can work no more. We should determine each day to work all we can for God, and to pass on the torch of the gospel so that it will keep burning long after we are gone.

If you have not gold and silver
   Ever ready to command;
If you cannot t'ward the needy
   Reach an ever-open hand;
You can visit the afflicted,
   O'er the erring you can weep;
You can be a true disciple
   Sitting at the Saviour's feet.

If you cannot be the watchman,
   Standing high on Zion's wall,
Pointing out the path to heaven,
   Offering life and peace to all;
With your prayers and with your bounties
   You can do what Heaven demands,
You can be like faithful Aaron,
   Holding up the prophet's hands.

Do not, then, stand idly waiting
   For some greater work to do;
Fortune is a lazy goddess —
   She will never come to you.
Go and toil in any vineyard,
   Do not fear to do or dare;
If you want a field of labor,
   You can find it anywhere.
                                  — Ellen H. Gates

Prayer: Our Father, we come to thee this happy day and ask that
thou fill our lives with thy presence. For it is in the name of
Jesus our Lord we pray. Amen.

March 7

*"And he shall be as the light of the morning, when the sun
riseth, even a morning without clouds; as the tender grass spring-
ing out of the earth by clear shining after rain."*
                                  — II Samuel 23:4

Isn't it wonderful to get up on a spring morning and discover
something beginning to grow in the garden? It fills us with cheer
to see little green shoots peeping out of the ground. We are reminded afresh that God is in charge of the world and will make
things right in their season.

Sometimes we miss the beauty of the morning. We begin the
day grumbling or cross. We should be happy and thankful

from the depths of our hearts for the chance of a fresh start each day.

>Some one started the whole day wrong —
>   Was it you?
>Some one robbed the day of its song —
>   Was it you?
>Early this morning some one frowned;
>Some one sulked until others scowled;
>And soon harsh words were passed around —
>   Was it you?

>Some one started the day aright —
>   Was it you?
>Some one made it happy and bright —
>   Was it you?
>Early this morning, we are told,
>Some one smiled and all through the day
>This smile encouraged young and old —
>   Was it you?

Prayer: Kindle our hearts with love and grace today. May we ever be aware of thy desire to give us bountiful blessings. We pray through the name of Christ. Amen.

March 8

"When I was a child, I spake as a child, I understood as a child, I thought as a child: but when I became a man, I put away childish things." — I Corinthians 13:11

Some people seem to grow up faster than others. I know a fourteen-year-old girl who helps cook, clean house and care for several smaller children.

"Why is she so much more dependable than other girls that age?" a friend asked.

"Because something has been expected of her," was her mother's reply.

God expects His children to grow up and take responsibility. He has lots of work He wants us, as his children, to help accomplish. We should jump right in and try our best to serve. We may make mistakes, people may ridicule us, but with the help of an all-knowing Heavenly Father we cannot fail.

>For life seems so little when life is past,
>And the memories of sorrow flee so fast,

And the woes which were bitter to you and to me,
Shall vanish as raindrops which fall in the sea;
And all that has hurt us shall be made good,
And the puzzles which hindered be understood,

And the long hard march through the wilderness bare
Seems but a day's journey when once we are there.

— Susan Coolidge

Prayer: Through this day may the thought of thy nearness to us be in our consciousness. May we be ready to do thy will. We ask in the name of Jesus. Amen.

March 9

"Thy word is a lamp unto my feet, and a light unto my pathway." — Psalm 119:105

I met a stranger in the night,
Whose lamp had ceased to shine.
I paused and let him light
    His lamp from mine.

A tempest sprang up later on
And shook the world about.
And when the wind was gone,
    My lamp was out.

But back to me the stranger came —
His lamp was glowing fine!
He held the precious flame,
    And lighted mine!

— Lon Woodrum

The Word of God is the greatest lamp we can light for others. The Gideon organization places Bibles in many public places, hotels and motels. The stories they can tell of people who have found God in moments of lonely despair would fill many books. We can all pass on the torch of hope by quoting a Scripture verse, or writing one, to someone.

I knew a man once who was losing his eyesight. He memorized all the Scripture he could each day so that he would still have the light of God's Word when the dark settled down on him. He was an inspiration to others, never complaining, just getting ready. We do not know when there will come a dark time in our life; so we should have a store of memory verses for comfort and strength at all times. We can never give away too many verses of Scripture, for they will always come back to us in time of our own need.

Prayer: Make our lives beautiful and fruitful in thy service to-day. Through Jesus Christ we pray. Amen.

March 10

"Therefore I say unto you, Take no thought for your life, what ye shall eat, or what ye shall drink; nor yet for your body, what ye shall put on. Is not the life more than meat, and the body than raiment? Behold the fowls of the air: for they sow not, neither do they reap, nor gather into barns; yet your heavenly Father feedeth them. Are ye not much better than they?"
— Matthew 6:25, 26

Ted was a young business man. He had invested in the stock market and made good. He was very closefisted with his family, and his wife always had to wait a long time for any improvement she wished to have made in the home. One day Ted was stricken with an illness and carried to the hospital. His mother and wife lovingly and faithfully took turns nursing him. As days grew into weeks and weeks into months he despaired of his life. One day he noticed his mother coming in shivering. Her coat was threadbare and she wore no gloves.

"Mother, I am ashamed to have you go cold." He took his check book from the night stand, and as he handed her a check he said, "Take this as payment for some of the many times you have been a free baby sitter for us. Go and buy yourself a good coat and gloves."

Later he also gave his wife a generous check and told her to buy Christmas gifts for the children. She was overjoyed and began to plan for a happy holiday.

When Ted went home after three months in the hospital he was different. His home was a happier place because he started to live every day, not just plan to live for some day when he had conquered the world.

Prayer: Let thy grace be our guide and make our hearts living altars of thy love. For Jesus' sake. Amen.

March 11

"This one thing I do, forgetting those things which are behind, and reaching forth unto those things which are before, I press toward the mark for the prize of the high calling of God in Christ Jesus." — Philippians 3:13, 14

Young people of each generation ask questions about things which bother them. Where did we come from? Why are we here? Where are we going?

The Bible is the source of answers to these questions. Paul tells us that the basic goal in life is getting to know Christ. Other goals become useless and vain when Christ is left out. "Seek ye first the kingdom of God and his righteousness, and all other things will be added unto you." God wants us to pursue that goal willingly.

No one forces us to follow Christ. It is a voluntary goal. His spirit enables us to heed an upward calling. His spirit gives us strength to try for greater things in life.

Prayer: O King of all the earth, grant unto us thy blessings this day. Direct our ways in thy service. We ask in the name of Christ our Lord. Amen.

March 12

"The path of the just is as the shining light, that shineth more and more unto the perfect day." — Proverbs 4:18

Often in life we are faced with a decision between two pathways. If we take one, will it perhaps lead to fame and fortune? Or, if we take a different one, will it perhaps lead to contentment and peace?

A boy about to go overseas to the war front asked his father for advice. The father replied, "Son, always remember two can be a majority as long as one of the two is God."

Often in dangerous places wondering what to do and who to trust, the son would remember his father's statement and he would silently ask his "partner" which pathway to follow.

All pathways lead eventually to life after death. We must choose the path of salvation if we would spend eternity with God.

Which path will you choose?

> One is walking with me over life's uneven way,
> Constantly supporting me each moment of the day;
> How can I be lonely when such fellowship is mine,
> With my blessed Lord divine!

> — Harold Lillenas

Prayer: Bless, we pray thee, our home today. Make us more mindful of thy great blessings. We pray through Jesus. Amen.

73

March 13

"But he that knew not, and did commit things worthy of stripes, shall be beaten with few stripes. For unto whomsoever much is given, of him shall be much required: and to whom men have committed much, of him they will ask the more."
— Luke 12:48

Little Joe wanted a dog very much. "You may have a dog but you will be responsible for taking care of him," his mother told him.

At first Joe was very good about seeing to it that the dog was fed and given all the attention he needed. When the newness wore off he began to neglect the dog. One day the gate was carelessly left open and the dog ran into the street and was killed.

God gives each person something for which he is accountable. We are accountable for our thoughts and our desires; for our money and our children. We are accountable for all of life that God has given to us. When we are tempted to be slow and negligent in making the most of what we have we should remember the verse above.

> What, my soul, was thy errand here?
> Was it mirth or ease?
> Or heaping up dust from year to year?
> Nay, none of these.
> — Whittier

Prayer: Let us work no ill to our neighbor. For Christ's sake. Amen.

March 14

"By this shall all men know that ye are my disciples, if ye have love one to another." — John 13:35

"Let love be without dissimulation. Abhor that which is evil; cleave to that which is good. Be kindly affectioned one to another with brotherly love; in honor preferring one another."
— Romans 12:9, 10

One of the most beautiful things in our world is to see a happy Christian family showing love for each other.

> Love wore a threadbare dress of grey
> And toiled upon the road all day.
>
> Love wielded pick and carried pack
> And bent to heavy loads the back.

Though meager fed and sorely tasked,
One only wage love ever asked —

A child's sweet face to kiss at night,
A woman's smile by candle-light.

Love for others, as Christ wanted us to have, will transfigure and glorify our lives.

A man standing inside a cold house was scraping frost from the window.

"Why scrape the frost away?" another coming in asked.

"So I will be able to see out."

"Build a warm fire in the room and the frost will soon disappear," his companion told him.

When we find our life all frosted over and fail to see our blessings, we need to build a warm fire of love in our hearts.

Prayer: As we contemplate the unsearchable riches of Christ's love, may we be thankful and joyful. In his name we pray. Amen.

March 15

"For even when we were with you, this we commanded you, that if any would not work, neither should he eat."

— II Thessalonians 3:10

Each day we read in the newspapers stories of people who do not want to work, to serve, or be of use in the world. At times mobs of people run wild, looting and burning the property of others. They have forgotten that true happiness and contentment comes from honest labor.

People who refused to work were known also in the days of Paul and he gave his solution to the problem: . . . if any would not work, neither should he eat."

In the early days of our country when men had to work long hard hours to build houses and plant crops, the rule of no work, no eat, had to be used again.

Jesus grew up in a carpenter shop. He knew what it was to work. He glorified work by his example.

Parents have an obligation to teach their children to work — to teach children there is joy in work. There is no medicine for the human mind and body like honest work.

The heights of great men reached and kept
Were not attained by sudden flight,
But they, while their companions slept,
Were toiling upward in the night.

Prayer: Thank thee, Father, for the ability to work. Reveal to us thy desires for our lives. In Christ's name we pray. Amen.

March 16

"A good man out of the good treasure of the heart bringeth forth good things: and an evil man out of the evil treasure bringeth forth evil things." — Matthew 12:35

". . . Wherefore think ye evil in your hearts?" — Matthew 9:4

A new family moved into our neighborhood. The house had been vacant for some time and the yard was waist high in weeds from a month of rains. Almost as soon as the moving van had been unloaded, the children, four teen-agers, were out hoeing and pulling weeds. Next day I looked out and their yard was all smooth and ready for planting a lawn.

As people, we often let our hearts get all grown up with weeds of jealously, greed, anger, hate and just general dissatisfaction. We can weed these things out of our hearts by getting busy thinking good thoughts, doing kind deeds for others. Already I have almost forgotten what my new neighbor's yard looked like before they moved in. So we as people need to weed out the ugliness from our hearts and forget it. Others will notice the change too. And so will God.

> I will start anew this morning
> With a higher, fairer creed;
> I will cease to stand complaining
> Of my ruthless neighbor's greed;
> I will cease to sit repining
> While my duty's call is clear;
> I will waste no moment whining
> And my heart shall know no fear.

Prayer: Take from our hearts all envy and jealousy. Make us mindful of thy love. Fill our hearts with expectation of better things to come. In Jesus' name we pray. Amen.

March 17

"Let the words of my mouth, and the meditation of my heart, be acceptable in thy sight, O Lord, my strength, and my redeemer." — Psalm 19:14

> A room of quiet,
> A temple of peace,
> The home of faith

Where doubtings cease;
A house of comfort
Where hope is given,
A source of strength
To make earth heaven;
A shrine of worship,
A place to pray —
I found all this
In my church today.

— Lennie Todd
(from *Decision* Magazine)

We should worship God every day. Especially are we blessed when we go to a designated place to worship.

I remember as a small child worshiping in a school building. Yet we were happy with the simple worship service in humble surroundings. We felt very fortunate on the days the minister could be there to break the bread of life. Now I worship each Sunday in a very modern and expensive building. But worship must, and can, come from the heart no matter the time or place.

To worship God we must love him and admire the things which he created. To worship we must give our interest, our enthusiasm, and our wholehearted devotion. Then the place makes little difference.

Prayer: Father, bestow upon us strength for our daily tasks. Give us quiet in the midst of tumult. Fill our hearts with hope for a bright future. We ask in the name of Jesus. Amen.

March 18

"I returned and saw under the sun, that the race is not to the swift, nor the battle to the strong, neither yet bread to the wise, nor riches to men of understanding, nor yet favor to men of skill; but time and chance happen to them all." — Ecclesiastes 9:11

Isn't it fascinating to go into a jewelry store and see all the different kinds of time pieces — watches, clocks, and even sundials of all descriptions. Yet no matter how intricate, or how beautiful, all can only number twelve hours for half-a-day.

In Strasbourg Cathedral there is a clock which preaches a sermon each hour. At the first quarter glad Childhood emerges and strikes the bell; at the second quarter rosy Youth comes forth; at the third, sober Manhood lifts his robust arm; and at the last quarter, feeble and decrepit Old Age life wearily his hammer to strike. When he has finished, Death lifts his arm and strikes the hour.

Put yourself in one of the four groups. How much time do you have left? No one knows except God. So we should all ask the question, "What am I doing with my life?"

Look at the timekeeper of life. No prayer, no entreaty, no skill of physicians, can stop the clock. We must do the best we can with our lives today.

> Time, like an ever-rolling stream,
> Bears all its sons away.
> — Isaac Watts

Prayer: Make us worthy of thy great love. We thank thee for thy unnumbered blessings. In Christ's name. Amen.

March 19

"And when they had platted a crown of thorns, they put it upon his head, and a reed in his right hand: and they bowed the knee before him, and mocked him, saying, Hail, King of the Jews!" — Matthew 27:29

Each day we crown Christ in our lives. When we are disobedient and selfish we crown him with a crown of thorns. If we worship him and follow his leading we crown him with a crown of glory.

In Matthew 21:9 we read how the multitudes went before Christ and cried out praises to his name. Yet just a few days later they were ready to crucify him.

Do we praise Christ today — and tomorrow crown him with thorns? We must remove from our lives the things which keep us from crowning him Lord of lords and King of kings. He is always ready to forgive us our past mistakes and help us do better in the future.

> The king of a wonderful castle am I,
> It needs constant watching and care;
> To keep it so free from all that's impure,
> That Jesus my temple may share.
>
> I'm a king! I'm a king!
> To rule o'er my life victorious;
> My Savior I'll take, He'll never forsake;
> With Him my triumph is glorious.
> — Emma Virginia Miller

78

Prayer: Father, we need thee through all our days. Hear us as we lift our hearts in prayer to thee. Continue to help us with our problems from day to day. We ask in the name of Christ our Lord. Amen.

March 20

"Thy word have I hid in mine heart, that I might not sin against thee." — Psalm 119:11

The young mother smiled as she emptied the pockets of a very dirty pair of blue jeans and prepared them for the washing machine. She found pretty rocks, string, nails and a broken pencil. The little boy doubtless felt he would sooner or later have need of the things he had collected in his pocket.

Think of your life as a pocket. Are you collecting things you will need in the future? Are you storing up strength for the time when trials will come? Can there be anything better to have for future use than verses of God's word memorized and ready to recall when we need help.

> Some scraps of song and bits of rhyme,
> I have tucked away
> In the pockets of time
> So a certain feeling of wealth still clings
> When they are empty
> Of other things.
> And with my tears a joy will mingle
> As I repeat each rhyme and jingle.
> — Bess Foster Smith

Prayer: Father, smile on our activities today. Make us successful in our undertakings. We pray in the name of Jesus. Amen.

March 21

"Simon Peter said unto him, Lord, whither goest thou? Jesus answered him, Whither I go, thou canst not follow me now; but thou shalt follow me afterwards." — John 13:36

Life is an adventure! We know not today what tomorrow will bring forth. Life is marvelous in its variety and scope. Life is awesome and at times fearsome.

As we pass through the adventures of every day here we should be ever mindful of the much greater adventure which awaits us after death and spend time preparing for it.

When our family is to take a vacation away from home we spend time in preparation. We anticipate what we will need on the trip and plan to take along things to make our trip happy and successful.

As we prepare for the adventure of all adventures we must above all be sure that we have faith in our Lord Jesus. We must have convictions for right living and we must have love for our fellow man.

> My faith is all a doubtful thing
>   Wove on a doubtful loom,
> Until there comes, each showery spring,
>   A cherry tree in bloom.
>
> And Christ, who died upon a tree
>   That death had stricken bare,
> Comes beautifully back to me
>   In blossoms everywhere.
>
>   — David Morton

Prayer: We beseech thee, that we may improve in our service to thee. Consecrate us anew in thy will. We pray in Jesus' name. Amen.

March 22

"For, lo, the winter is past, the rain is over and gone; The flowers appear on the earth; the time of the singing of birds is come, and the voice of the turtle is heard in our land; the fig tree putteth forth her green figs, and the vines with the tender grape give a good smell." — Song of Solomon 2:11, 12, 13

Early this morning I went into my back garden and gathered tomatoes and okra. I admired the pretty red crepe myrtle blooming, and I stopped to smell the fragrant honeysuckle. I pulled a weed that had dared to grow among the ferns.

God's world must be to him somewhat like a spring garden. There are people who sparkle and are a joy to behold, and there are people who just plod along making the wheels of industry and life turn smoothly. Then, sad to say, there are those who are misfits in society. They prey off others and only cause others and themselves sorrow and trouble.

Yet God is constantly caring for his garden. He waters, he plants, he transplants, he thins out, he destroys the wicked — all in his own good time.

> A garden is a lovesome thing.
>   God wot!
>   Rose plot,

> Fringed pool,
> Ferned grot,
> The veriest school
> Of peace; and yet the fool
> Contends that God is not.
> Not God! In gardens!
> When the eve is cool?
> Nay, but I have a sign;
> 'Tis sure God walks in mine.
> — Thomas E. Brown

Prayer: Let thy love grow in our hearts as flowers in a garden. We ask in his Holy name. Amen.

March 23

"I can of mine own self do nothing: as I hear, I judge: and my judgment is just; because I seek not mine own will, but the will of the Father which has sent me." — John 5:30

In our space age we read and hear a great deal about being in orbit. Christ pointed out the right orbit for himself and for us when he said, "I seek not mine own will, but the will of the Father."

Sometimes we see people who just cannot seem to get into orbit. They are at outs with all they meet and with whom they try to work. They need Christ. When we, as Christ did, seek to do the will of the Father then other things just naturally work out. I have bowed my head many times at the typewriter and asked God to lead me. In a flash my thought became clearer and I was able to go on working.

Try talking to God all through the day as problems arise, and as occasions for thanksgiving come. You will find yourself in perfect orbit with him for a guide and confidant.

> Does life seem a fret and tangle,
> Has everything gone wrong?
> Are friends a bit disloyal
> And enemies full strong?
> Is there no bright side showing?
> Then — as a sage has said:
> "Just polish up the dark side
> And look at that instead."

Prayer: With joyful hearts we yield and dedicate our lives to thee. Use us to thy glory. We pray in the name of Jesus. Amen.

March 24

"Cast away from you all your transgressions, whereby ye have transgressed; and make you a new heart and a new spirit: for why will ye die, O house of Israel?" — Ezekiel 18:31

One time we moved into a new house and there, nestled quietly in the kitchen sink, was a disposal. I quickly learned how to dispose of all the kitchen garbage. I enjoyed peeling vegetables and fruits for the refuse was quickly gone, down the disposal. How wonderful it would be if people could cast away all the wrong and ugly in their lives and see and feel them no more! There is only one way all our mistakes can be forgiven and forgotten. That is by believing in Jesus Christ and asking him to blot out our mistakes.

Prayer: Make us our Father, the tender objects of thy solicitude and care. We are weak, wilt thou make us strong. We ask in the name of Jesus our Lord. Amen.

March 25

"And now also the axe is laid unto the root of the trees: every tree therefore which bringeth not forth good fruit is hewn down, and cast into the fire." — Luke 3:9

In the first church my husband ever pastored there was an elderly lady who liked to quote Scripture. At times she would get her Scripture and her proverbs mixed. One day in a testimony meeting she stood and glibly quoted: "Every tub must stand on its own bottom."

After services my husband, who was very young and not trained in "The Art of Winning Friends and Influencing People," told her there was no Scripture such as she had quoted. After a few sessions with a concordance and Bible he failed to convince her and she went right on happily quoting it when she felt someone in the church was not fully aware of his personal responsibility.

We are all responsible for our actions. When the great day of judgment comes each will be asked to give an account of his own life.

"Your task — to build a better world," God said.
    I answered, "How?
This world is such a large, vast place,
    So complicated now!
And I so small and useless am —

There's nothing I can do!"
But God, in all his wisdom, said,
"Just build a better you!"

— Dorothy R. Jones

Prayer: May thy will be done in our lives. May we be gracious to those about us who need help. We pray for the sake of Christ. Amen.

March 26

"Bring ye all the tithes into the storehouse, that there may be meat in mine house, and prove me now herewith, saith the Lord of hosts, if I will not open you the windows of heaven, and pour you out a blessing, that there shall not be room enough to receive it." — Malachi 3:10

We are all human in the fact that we want more than just the plain pie of everyday living. We want meringue on top. We want as much as our friends have, or maybe a little more.

A little girl was moving. She had not seen the house they were moving to, since it was in a distant city. In her heart she had a dream. She wanted a house with flowers growing in the yard. When they had traveled a long way to the new home she became very eager to get there.

"When the car turned into the driveway at the back there were just flowers and flowers," she told friends later. She had the topping on her pie.

The poet Lowell wrote; "We have a little room in the third story (back), with white curtains trimmed with evergreen, and are as happy as two mortals can be."

If we will just read and heed the Scripture for today we will find we have an abundance of extra blessings poured out upon us.

God has his best things for the few
Who dare to stand the test;
He has his second choice for those
Who will not have his best.

Prayer: Open the windows of heaven and pour out upon us thy bountiful blessings, we pray. Grant that we may live closer to thee today. In his name we pray. Amen.

March 27

"And when he had apprehended him, he put him in prison, and delivered him to four quaternions of soldiers to keep him; intending after Easter to bring him forth to the people."
— Acts 12:4

The above Scripture is the only place in the Bible where the word Easter is used. The name Easter was given to the Passover time later by the Christians.

The Passover was a Jewish festival celebrating the deliverance of the Israelites from bondage in Egypt. The observance of the Passover, for Jews, begins on the evening of the 14th of Nisan (first month of the religious calender, corresponding to March and April) and lasts seven days.

Easter is our chief Christian celebration. We count it the anniversary of the resurrection of Jesus Christ.

> The world cannot bury Christ.
> The earth is not deep enough for His tomb;
> The clouds are not wide enough for His winding sheet.
> He ascends into the heavens,
> But the heavens cannot contain Him.
> He still lives — in the church which burns unconsumed
>   with His love;
> In the truth that reflects His image;
> In the hearts which burn as He talks with them by the
>   way.

Prayer: Help us today to lift the burdens of those we meet. May we bring hope to the despairing and joy to the sad. In Jesus' holy name we pray. Amen.

March 28

"Remember now thy Creator in the days of thy youth, while the evil days come not, nor the years draw nigh, when thou shalt say, I have no pleasure in them. — Ecclesiastes 12:1

What a disappointment I felt when I met a former school friend, after many years, and that friend failed to remember me. We had shared many good times together and I could not see how she could have forgotten our girlhood.

How ashamed God must be of his children when they get all involved with the world and forget him! He must be sad many times as he sees us rushing madly after pleasures of the world and neglecting to worship or work for him.

God gave each person a memory. If our memory is filled with good experiences we find them to be a well-spring for a radiant life. Good memories feed the heart and help it glow with joy and satisfaction.

Memories brighten the atmosphere when we are with friends. They inspire us when we are alone and meditating.

> "I am a part of all whom I have met"
> So, friend of mine, tho' you are far away,
> Between us may stretch mountain, plain or sea,
> Yet by my side you walk and talk each day,
> Because you are a precious part of me.
>
> — Charles Elmer Chapler

The most wonderful thing to remember is our Creator and the great things he has done for us.

Prayer: Let grace be our guide today. Write thy will upon our remembrance. Fill our hearts with thy love. In the name of Jesus we pray. Amen.

March 29

"All things are possible to him who believes." — Mark 9:23
"But Jesus took him by the hand and lifted him up, and he arose." — Mark 9:27

The deaf and dumb boy was healed when Jesus took him by the hand. What a wonderful moment in his life that must have been! All of us remember times in life when we have felt very near to God. Some of us have experienced times when we felt a miracle had been performed. We reach out in times of darkness and we find God has reached out to help us.

Mrs. Peter Marshall tells the story of an exceptional hour in her life. When the day came that she and her great preacher husband knew that death had marked him they were sad. After they had gone to bed in their separate twin beds and the lights were out, she was overcome with the prospect of his death and conpulsively reached out her hand through the darkness across the space which separated her from her husband. And, she tells us, as her hand reached out through the darkness, it touched her husband's hand! He was reaching toward her.

> No service in itself is small;
> None great, though earth it fill;
> But that is small that seeks its own,
> And great that seeks God's will.

Then hold my hand, most gracious God.
Guide all my goings still;
And let it be my life's one aim,
To know and do thy will.

Prayer: Gracious God, we thank thee for all the hours of our lives. May we make them count in thy service. In Jesus' name we pray. Amen.

March 30

"How God anointed Jesus of Nazareth with the Holy Ghost and with power: who went about doing good, and healing all that were oppressed of the devil; for God was with him."
— Acts 10:38

Jesus has been called "the first philanthropist." Jesus came to earth for a purpose and he sought to accomplish that purpose. He seemed to have one great aim in life: to go about doing good — to redeem the lost world from eternal punishment.

It is human to want a measure of popularity. Some seek this one way and some another. I can think of no better way than to follow Jesus' example and, "go about doing good."

A new man came to our church one time. He had some wealth and he started entertaining the people he felt were most influential and could help him gain popularity. He gave expensive gifts to community leaders. When he failed to become as popular as he expected he complained, "They do not appreciate what I did for them."

Real abiding popularity will come when we go about doing good just for the sake of helping others.

Prayer: Father, we adore and praise thy name. We thank thee for sending Christ to make a way of redemption. In his name we pray. Amen.

March 31

"He is not here: for he is risen, as he said. Come, see the place where the Lord lay." — Matthew 28:6

"And if Christ be not raised, your faith is vain; ye are yet in your sins." — I Corinthians 15:17

Many years ago a man made a speech against the Christian religion. He felt he had successfully proved that faith in Christ was only a product of the imagination. At the close he asked if anyone wanted to comment on his message.

A young minister arose and went to the platform. He turned and faced the audience. Calmly but firmly and with evident conviction he said, "Brothers and sisters, Christ is risen!"

Out in the audience someone replied, "Verily he is risen."

The meeting closed and the flowery eloquence of the atheist had availed him nothing. Christ is risen. He lives in the hearts of his followers today.

> Low in the grave He lay — Jesus my Saviour!
> Waiting the coming day — Jesus my Lord!
> Up from the grave He arose,
> With a mighty triumph o'er His foes;
> He arose a Victor from the dark domain,
> And He lives forever with His saints to reign.
> He arose! He arose! Hallelujah! Christ arose!
>
> — Robert Lowry

Prayer: Let us stand today in the glory of our God. Fill our souls with a spirit of gratitude for our many blessings. We pray in the name of Christ our Saviour. Amen.

April:

Showers of Blessings

April 1

". . . All power is given unto me in heaven and in earth. Go ye therefore, and teach all nations, baptizing them in the name of the Father, and of the Son, and of the Holy Ghost . . . and, lo, I am with you alway, even unto the end of the world."

— Matthew 28:18, 19, 20

By nature and by practice far
  How very far from God!
Yet now by grace brought nigh to Him
  Through faith in Jesus' blood.

So nigh, so very nigh to God,
  I cannot nearer be;
For in the person of His Son
  I am as near as He.

So dear, so very dear to God,
  More dear I cannot be;
The love wherewith He loves the Son —
  Such is His love to me.

Why should I ever fearful be,
  Since such a God is mine?
He watches o'er me night and day
  And tells me "Mine is thine."

We have the promise that Christ is with us always only if we receive him as Saviour and Lord.

Many people want God to be near when they are in trouble, or in need of his help; yet they do not wish to give him their heart and life in service.

Would you be powerful? Would you be useful? Would you be happy? Then meet the conditions which assure you Christ will be with you, "even unto the end of the world."

Prayer: Give us more power today to become servants of thine. We pray in the name of Jesus. Amen.

April 2

"And I say also unto thee, That thou art Peter, and upon this rock I will build my church; and the gates of hell shall not prevail against it." — Matthew 16:18

What do I think of when I say "my church"?

Do I think of a place of brick, mortar, steel and plaster? Yes. But I think also of a quiet place of reverence and meditation, a place where I can go and get away from the world, a place to commune with God. Yes, my church is a place of quietness and peace; but it is much more!

The church is a group of people. It is made up of people who have given their hearts to Christ and are banded together to work to bring in his Kingdom. It is people who have helped to make it grow with money, prayers, labor and love.

My church is the bride of Christ. In Revelation 21:9 we read: ". . . Come hither, I will show thee the bride, the Lamb's wife."

> The Church's one foundation Is Jesus Christ her Lord;
> She is His new creation By Water and the Word;
> From Heav'n He came and sought her To be His holy bride;
> With His own blood He bought her, And for her life He died.
>
> Elect from every nation, Yet one oe'r all the earth,
> Her charter of salvation, One Lord, one faith, one birth;
> One holy name she blesses, Partakes one holy food,
> And to one hope she presses, With ev'ry grace endued.
>
> Yet she on earth hath union With God the three in One,
> And mystic sweet communion With those whose rest is won:
> O happy ones and holy! Lord, give us grace that we,
> Like them, the meek and lowly, On high may dwell with Thee.

> — Samuel J. Stone

Prayer: Father, we thank thee for a church building in which to worship. We thank thee for an organized church to which we may belong. Truly we wish to dwell in the house of the Lord and inquire after knowledge in his temple. Through Jesus we pray. Amen.

April 3

"And David had success in all his undertakings; for the Lord was with him." — I Samuel 18:14

Real success in life comes only through faith in God. This equipped him for service. Many times we are not willing to pay the price.

David had some characteristics which made him successful, even when the king sent him away on hard missions.

He had no place in his life for revenge. Many people ruin their lives because they want revenge on someone.

Our task as Christians is even greater than the task assigned David. We might follow his example getting ready.

Above all, in tribulation he kept his faith in God. David had a magnanimous spirit. He was also resourceful. As Christians we too often go on year after year in the same old rut. We should think of new ways to witness.

David depended upon God for success. David was filled with humility. Too often we get excited over our own importance. Humility is a mark of greatness.

> Oh, not for more or longer days, dear Lord,
>   My prayer shall be —
> But rather teach me how to use the days
>   Now given me.
>
> I ask not more of pleasure or of joy
>   For this brief while —
> But rather let me for the joys I have
>   Be glad and smile.
>
> I ask not ownership of vast estates
>   Nor piles of gold —
> But make me generous with the little store
>   My hands now hold.
>
> B. Y. Williams

Prayer: Dear Lord, the strength of our lives, help us not to be afraid of the world and the evil therein. Let us put our trust completely in thee. In Christ's name we pray. Amen.

April 4

"Pride goeth before destruction and a haughty spirit before a fall." — Proverbs 16:18

We say a man has too much pride when he is filled with a feeling of self-importance. Pride is repeatedly and severely condemned by God as a serious sin.

The man too full of pride is an unhappy man. He is sensitive. He imagines people are slighting him. A proud man treasures up fancied injuries. Pride is self-destructive.

I knew a boy who was always pampered by his parents. As a young child he could always get his way if he tried. When he started to school he was a problem to his teachers because he expected to be "it" in all the activities. Often he was deceitful because he thought it would get him the things he wanted. When he was grown he secured a good position but was unable to keep it because he expected too much attention. He drifted from job to job always blaming others for his failure. He went through life an unhappy man.

> He that hath light within his own clear breast
> May sit in the center and enjoy bright days;
> But he that hides a dark soul and foul thoughts,
> Benighted walks under the midday sun;
> Himself is his own dungeon.

> — Milton

Prayer: Give us patience with all those who need help. If we have wronged anyone accept our repentance and forgive us. We pray in the name of one who could do no wrong. Amen.

April 5

"Thou hast proved mine heart; thou hast visited me in the night; thou hast tried me, and shalt find nothing; I am purposed that my mouth shall not transgress." — Psalm 17:3

To live is to be tested. No man has ever gone through life without some trials and times of testing.

I have a very dear friend who has worked for the same firm since he was twelve years old. Now at forty he is discouraged because others come into the firm and are promoted ahead of him. Because he loves his work and has a family to support he hesitates to quit and look for other employment.

We have all gone through times when we feel someone else is getting the breaks while we lag behind. What if everyone quit when such times came along? There would be chaos in the business world.

If we contribute to life the best we can each day then when times of testing come we are better able to meet them.

We have a little saying in our family, "A tempest in a teapot, it will soon pass."

When we take the tempest in a teapot attitude we can look over problems better and realize they will soon be past.

> There's only one method of meeting life's test:
> Jes' keep on a strivin' an' hope for the best;
> Don't give up the ship an' quit in dismay;

'Cause hammers are thrown when you'd like a bouquet.
This world would be tiresome we'd all get the blues
If all the folks in it jest held the same views;
So finish your work, show the best of your skill,
Some folks won't like it, but other folks will.

Prayer: Walk with us today and help us to avoid the mistakes of yesterday. In Jesus' name we pray. Amen.

April 6

"Let your light so shine before men, that they may see your good works, and glorify your Father which is in heaven."
— Matthew 5:16

I know a lady who collects antique lamps. She has over four hundred lamps of various descriptions. Some are valuable and some are just common. Some are very pretty and some are ugly and crude. To her they all have a history and a meaning. She would not part with a single one.

We are Christ's lamps. He commissioned us to shine before the world and point men to him. If we are followers of Christ we must make our presence felt by letting our Christian light shine.

His lamp am I, to shine where He shall say;
    And lamps are not for sunny rooms,
    Nor for the light of day;
    But for dark places of the earth;
    Where shame, and crime and wrong have birth;
    Or for the murky twilight gray
    Where wandering sheep have gone astray;
    Or where the light of faith grows dim,
    And souls are groping after Him . . .
So may I shine — His light the flame —
    That men may glorify His name.

Prayer: Dear Lord, our light and our salvation, strengthen our lives today. May we seek after thee and be conscious of thy presence. In the name of our Lord Jesus we pray. Amen.

April 7

"But my God shall supply all your need according to his riches in glory by Christ Jesus." — Philippians 4:19

An elderly farmer was riding with us one day. We passed a country store where a number of men were playing dominoes on the front porch.

95

"Look at them!" our friend exclaimed. "I have worked and saved all my life while they drifted about too lazy to work. Now the government taxes me to pay them for sitting around."

Almost any place we look today we see people who want to be fed and housed without working for it. People who are willing to work hard have a right at times to feel frustrated.

Our nation is shocked at acts of violence and destruction carried out by the unemployed. The sage of old said, "An idle mind is the devil's workshop."

God promises to supply our needs. But God usually has a condition going along with his promises and we are to meet the conditions. Paul stated God's condition thus: "For even when we were with you, this we commanded you, that if any would not work, neither should he eat" (II Thessalonians 3:10).

> In the carboniferous era
> We were promised abundance for all
> By robbing individual Peter
> To pay collective Paul.
>
> Although we had plenty of money
> There was nothing that money could buy,
> And the gods of the copybook heading said,
> "If you don't work you die."
>
> — Kipling

Prayer: We thank thee dear Father, for the joy of work. We thank thee for the rest that comes after a day of work well done. We pray in the name of Jesus. Amen.

April 8

"I am the bread of life; he who comes to me shall not hunger and he who believes in me shall never thirst." — John 6:35

We all recognize the need for physical food. We will work long hours for small pay, if necessary, in order to buy food. Few of us realize the necessity for spiritual food.

Jesus said, "I am the bread of life." He becomes our bread of life when we believe in him as our personal Saviour and Lord.

Sometimes people do not have enough physical food to divide with a needy friend or brother. This is never true with spiritual food. The more we share it with others the richer and fuller our own lives become.

A small child was converted one night in a revival service. The father of the child was not a Christian, but he was at the

96

services that night. After the child felt the cleansing love of Christ she turned away from the altar and went to her father. She did not say a word, but just took his hand and gently led him to the altar. To have the bread of life is to want to share it with others.

> Break Thou the bread of life, dear Lord, to me,
> As Thou didst break the loaves beside the sea;
> Beyond the sacred page I seek Thee Lord;
> My spirit pants for Thee, O living Word.

> — Mary Ann Lathbury

Prayer: Father, help us to place our hand in thine and walk in faith this day. Help us always to believe that all things work for good to thy children. In Christ's name we pray. Amen.

April 9

"He who loves his life loses it, and he who hates his life in the world will keep it for eternal life." — John 12:25

A story came to us from the Vietnam war of a young soldier who threw himself upon a grenade in order to save his men. He literally gave his life for the men with him.

Jesus sought to make his followers realize that to serve God they were to give their lives in service for others.

Many times Jesus stated the principle of dying to live. The only way we can be fruitful is by giving up our lives in service.

> Must Jesus bear the cross alone,
> And all the world go free?
> No: there's a cross for everyone.
> And there's a cross for me.

> The consecrated cross I'll bear,
> Till death shall set me free;
> And then go home my crown to wear,
> For there's a crown for me.

> — Thomas Shepherd

If a grain of wheat fall into the ground it will live again — and bring forth fruit.

Prayer: Father, we direct our prayer to thee today and look up to thee for guidance. Bless our loved ones and make them happy. We ask in the name of Jesus. Amen.

April 10

"Now then we are ambassadors for Christ, as though God did beseech you by us: we pray you in Christ's stead, be ye reconciled to God." — II Corinthians 5:20

When I was a child my mother often sent me on errands. I was really an ambassador for my mother. As a wife I am, at times, an ambassador for my husband when he cannot attend some meeting. My most important place as an ambassador is to be an ambassador for Christ, to tell the story of salvation to those who do not know His love.

> I am a stranger here, within a foreign land;
> My home is far away, upon a golden strand;
> Ambassador to be of realms beyond the sea,
>   I'm here on business for my King.
>
> My home is brighter far than Sharon's rosy plain,
> Eternal life and joy thro'-out its vast domain;
> My Sov'reign bids me tell how mortals there may dwell,
>   And that's my business for my King.
>
> This is the message that I bring,
> A message angels fain would sing:
> "Oh, be ye reconciled,"
> Thus said my Lord and King,
>   "Oh, be ye reconciled to God."

— E. T. Cassel

Prayer: Father, make us worthy ambassadors in thy service. We offer this petition in the name of Jesus. Amen.

April 11

"Sufficient unto the day is the evil thereof." — Matthew 6:34

"Thy shoes shall be iron and brass; and as thy days, so shall thy strength be." — Deuteronomy 33:25

We should not be burdened today with the past. We should cast all our past cares upon God who forgives our sins. And then we should confidently and courageously press on to the future.

Our anxiety today cannot change our tomorrow. So why fret. Let us commit our ways unto the Lord and live as abundantly as possible today.

> Could we but lift tomorrow's veil
>   And read there all our trouble,

Today's sweet joys would fade away,
　　And all our sorrows double.

We'll have enough of pain today,
　　Don't look ahead to borrow.
For God has hung a friendly veil
　　Between us and tomorrow.

Yes, God has kindly hid from us
　　Each pain or heavy trial,
And bids us trust to Him alone,
　　Each joy or self-denial.

"Give us this day our daily bread,"
　　Then crave not more, my brother:
Be thankful for the loaf you have,
　　And then He'll give another.
　　　　　　　　　　— D. Y. Bagby

Prayer: Father, we praise thee for all thy mercies. Fellowship with thee brings us so much joy and so many blessings. Through Jesus Christ we pray. Amen.

April 12

"And Abram said unto Lot, Let there be no strife, I pray thee, between me and thee, and between my herdmen and thy herdmen; for we be brethren." — Genesis 13:8

How sweet it is to visit in a home where the children play happily together, and where the mother and father show love and affection for each other.

　　　　There is beauty all around,
　　　　When there's love at home;
　　　　There is joy in every sound,
　　　　　　When there's love at home.
　　　　Peace and plenty here abide,
　　　　Smiling sweet on every side,
　　　　Time doth softly, sweetly glide,
　　　　　　When there's love at home.

A large family I know has one child with bad eyes. As a consequence she often stumbles and is very hard on her shoes. When she has to have shoes before the others they do not act jealous. They smile and say, "Sister is harder on her shoes than the rest of us."

Right-thinking people want home to be a foretaste of heaven.

That can only be accomplished by all the members in a family loving each other; by all members of a family thinking of others first.

Prayer: Grant us the ability to face life's tasks with joyful hearts. May we earnestly endeavor to live in peace and harmony with those round about us. In Christ's name we pray. Amen.

April 13

"Give me thine heart." — Proverbs 23:26

"Give me thy heart," says the Father above,
No gift so precious to him as our love,
Softly he whispers wherever thou art,
"Gratefully trust me, and give me thy heart."

Every living person has a precious gift to bestow on someone or something. It is the gift of his heart! Young people look for a worthy lover to whom they may give their heart. Older people often bestow their hearts upon a cause. We must have something upon which to bestow our affections.

The heart is a precious gift. Christ gave his all on Calvary in order to make our hearts pure. We owe our hearts to Christ because of his divine grace.

A professional juggler was seen one day at the altar of the church juggling a handful of balls.

"Why are you doing this in the church?" the pastor asked.

"This is what I know how to do and I want to dedicate my talent to God."

The juggler went out to give free shows to the sick in the city's hospitals.

It is my choice to make. What will I do with my heart, my most precious gift? Will I give it to the Lord or to the world?

Prayer: In everything we give thanks to thee. May we today give our hearts and lives to thee. For Jesus' sake we pray. Amen.

April 14

"Therefore they gathered them together, and filled twelve baskets with fragments of the five barley loaves, which remained over and above unto them that had eaten." — John 6:13

Jesus saw the multitude of people and knew they were very hungry. His heart was touched in such a way that he performed a miracle. He did not provide just enough bread and fish to give

100

each one a taste. There was enough for all to be filled, and then there were twelve baskets full left over.

God treats us just this way every day. He gives us so many blessings we always have enough and to spare.

Do we show the same mercy to our fellow man as we expect God to show towards us? What if God forgave our sins in the same way we forgive others? What if God provided for us in the same way we provide for those in need? We expect him to be so merciful to us and often forget to show mercy to those about us.

> There's a wideness in God's mercy,
>   Like the wideness of the sea;
> There's a kindness in his justice,
>   Which is more than liberty.
>
> For the love of God is broader
>   Than the measure of man's mind,
> And the heart of the Eternal
>   Is most wonderfully kind.

Prayer: Our heavenly Father, help us today to remember our Saviour Jesus Christ and the great gift he made for us. Cleanse us and make us worthy. We ask in the name of Jesus. Amen.

April 15

". . . she remembereth not her last end; therefore she came down wonderfully: she had no comforter." — Lamentations 1:9

In our Scripture verse the writer was talking about the city of Jerusalem, and the fact that the pleasures of the day had blotted out the thoughts that there would be a time of reckoning in the future.

We should not have as our aim in life only animal indulgence in the day at hand. Neither should we live only for what we hope to gain tomorrow. To be happy we must have a high aim in life, and seek to enjoy each day as we work to accomplish our aim.

An artist painting a picture sees the finished picture in his mind's eye before he puts the first color on the canvas. Yet he enjoys the work of painting and the ultimate finishing of the picture.

Psalm 16:8 reads, "I have set the Lord always before." This verse is the secret of a successful and happy life. It will give us

101

the enthusiasm to enjoy today and the desire to prepare for to-morrow.

Prayer: Clothe us with thy righteousness and give us joy as thy children today. In his name we pray. Amen.

April 16

"And if it seem evil unto you to serve the Lord, choose you this day whom ye will serve . . . but as for me and my house, we will serve the Lord." — Joshua 24:15

Mary was in a large department store when a friend came rushing by. "Hello, Mary, what are you doing?"

"Oh, I am just browsing," was Mary's reply.

I saw Mary in the library and asked the same question. I received the same pat answer: "Oh, I am just browsing."

Some people develop the habit of just browsing through life with no real purpose in mind.

Life spent merely in browsing is wasted. We must choose whom we will serve and then work with a will to accomplish that service.

> Give us great dreams, O God, while Thou art giving,
> And keep the end; it is enough if we
> Live by the hope, nor falter in the living,
> That lures us on from dust to dignity.
>
> Give us the courage of the soul's high vision,
> Though its fulfillment here we never see;
> The heart to make and keep the brave decision,
> And faith to leave the ultimate with Thee.

— Marie Le Nart

Prayer: Lord, help me to make the most of every day. Let me not waste the precious moments of life in wandering like a butter-fly from leaf to leaf. May my purpose be a noble one. Give me grace to accomplish it. Amen.

April 17

"Freely ye have received, freely give." — Matthew 10:8

"Give, and it shall be given unto you; good measure, pressed down, and shaken together, and running over, shall men give into your bosom. For with the same measure that ye mete withal it shall be measured to you again." — Luke 6:38

102

Give plenty of what is given to you,
  Listen to pity's call;
Don't think the little you give is great,
  And the much you get is small.

— Phoebe Cary

Two men gave large gifts to an orphanage in our city. One of the men went to the office of the superintendent and sat for a few moments chatting before he left his check. None of the children saw him or heard of his gift.

The other man filled his pockets with quarters and went to the home when the children were outside playing. He gave each child a piece of money, a kind word and a loving pat or hug. As he was about to leave he dropped by the main office and left a check.

Both men gave liberally but one also gave a little bit of himself to each child.

We too must be sure that as we give to worthy causes in life we do not neglect also to give of ourselves.

Put a song in someone's heart and you will find a song in your own.

Prayer: Father, we are rich in thy mercy. May we today share with someone in need. In the name of Christ we pray. Amen.

April 18

"When I was a child, I spake as a child, I understood as a child, I thought as a child: but when I became a man I put away childish things." — I Corinthians 13:11

"Don't fuss about trifles. Don't permit little things — the mere termites of life — to ruin your happiness" (from the writings of Dale Carnegie).

Joy was a pretty girl with a happy name — but she was not happy. Always she was bothered about the little trifles of life. She could not enjoy a picnic because her hair might blow out of place. She could not relax at school if she failed to get time to refresh her makeup between classes. Her life was just a miserable story of little bothers.

Tom, Joy's brother, was ugly and freckled but he was happy in life. He knew what he hoped to achieve in school and he never worried when some little things went wrong. He just thought about his goal and pressed on.

If a wren can cling
To a spray a-swing
In the mad May wind, and sing and sing,
As if she'd burst for joy;
Why cannot I
Contented lie
In His quiet arms beneath the sky,
Unmoved by earth's annoy?

— F. B. Meyer

Prayer: Help us today to be thoughtful of others. Give us an opportunity to show thy love to someone. We ask in the name of Jesus. Amen.

April 19

"And to love him with all the heart, and with all the understanding, and with all the soul, and with all the strength, and to love his neighbor as himself, is more than all whole burnt offerings and sacrifices." — Mark 12:33

The gospel of love has built hospitals, orphans' homes, schools and many other worthy things too numerous to mention.

Love makes a home happy and lack of love causes homes to break apart. A popular little chorus ran as follows:

It's love, it's love
It's love that makes the world go 'round
It's love, it's love
It's love that makes the world go 'round.

A boy twelve years old saved his allowance and bought a long bicycle seat.

"Why get that type seat when you had a good one?" asked his buddy.

"So I can ride my baby sister in front of me," was his reply.

He loved his little sister so much he wanted her to share his fun.

We enjoy many things because we are Christians. Our nation is better because Christians love and want to share the gospel story.

We've a story to tell to the nations,
That shall turn their hearts to the right,
A story of truth and sweetness,
A story of peace and light,
A story of peace and light.

For the darkness shall turn to dawning,
And the dawning to noon-day bright,
And Christ's great kingdom shall come on earth,
The kingdom of love and light.

— Colin Sterne

Prayer: May we spend this day rejoicing in thy love. In Jesus name we pray. Amen.

April 20

"And the Spirit and the bride say, Come, And let him that heareth say, Come. And let him that is athirst come. And whosoever will, let him take the water of life freely."

— Revelation 22:17

Since its beginning, America has been a land where every poor boy can climb to greater heights if he has the determination and ability to work. Children of immigrants have climbed to honorable places in our government, in our courts and in the business world. Our land has been one which calls out to youth, "Come, run along my highways to honor and position."

There is a highway to mansions in the sky more important than the one to material and earthly success. We are all free to accept the call of our Lord and go along that road.

'Tis not for man to trifle! Life is brief.
  And sin is here.
Our age is but the falling of a leaf,
  A dropping tear.
We have no time to sport away the hours;
All must be earnest in a world like ours.

Not many lives, but only one have we —
  One, only one;
How sacred should that one life ever be —
  That narrow span!
Day after day filled up with blessed toil,
Hour after hour still bringing in new spoil.

— Horatious Bonar

Prayer: O Spirit of the Living God, look down upon us today and send us a shower of blessings. In Jesus name we pray. Amen.

April 21

"Go ye therefore, and teach all nations, baptizing them in the name of the Father, and of the Son, and of the Holy Ghost: Teaching them to observe all things whatsoever I have commanded you: and, lo, I am with you alway, even unto the end of the world." — Matthew 28:19, 20

When Japan attacked our country at the beginning of World War II, many men rushed to the recruiting offices all over our country. Our country was in great danger and they were eager to fight for the cause of freedom. Twenty odd years later we found ourselves in a war for which we had little stomach. Our boys are being sent far from home to fight and die for a cause which is not always clear to us. Men are not rushing to go. Many of the ones who go are bitter.

Christ left us instructions and orders to fight for the supreme cause of winning the lost world to the cause of Christianity. Are we rushing to obey his orders?

Who can surrender to Christ, dividing his best with the stranger,
Giving to each what he asks, braving the uttermost danger
All for the enemy, Man? Who can surrender till death
His words and his works, his house and his lands,
His eyes and his heart and his breath?
Who can surrender to Christ? Where is the man so transcendent,
So heated with love of his kind, so filled with the spirit resplendent
That all of the hours of his day his song is thrilling and tender,
And all of his thoughts to our white cause of peace Surrender, surrender, surrender?

— Vachel Lindsay

Prayer: Father, make us diligent to fight for the cause of Christ, our Lord. Give us courage always to stand for the right. In the name of Jesus we pray. Amen.

April 22

"The grass withereth, the flower fadeth: but the word of our God shall stand forever." — Isaiah 40:8

A thing of beauty is a joy for ever:
Its loveliness increases; it will never
Pass into nothingness.

— John Keats

Little Joe brought a handful of wild flowers to his mother. She tenderly put them in a glass of water. In spite of water and care they were gone in a few days.

"Why do beautiful things have to fade away?" Joe asked his mother.

"They are not entirely gone," answered his mother. "I will always remember how sweet my little boy was to bring me some flowers."

Kind words and deeds keep right on living even when we cannot see their symbols anymore.

Prayer: We give thanks for thy loving care in days past. In the name of Jesus we pray. Amen.

April 23

"A good name is rather to be chosen than great riches, and loving favor rather than silver and gold." — Proverbs 22:1

Who steals my purse steals trash; 'tis something, nothing;
'Twas mine, 'tis his, and has been slave to thousands;
But he that filches from me my good name
Robs me of that which not enriches him,
And makes me poor indeed.

— William Shakespeare

When James was a young boy he often thought his father was old fashioned. At times he resented not being able to live in a more modern manner. One day he left home and went out to make his own way in the world. He tried hard to find a job but times were hard and he had no luck. Almost out of funds, tired and discouraged he came to the home of a man his father had told him about.

"Son, I will help you get a job. I admire your father, and you would have to be a good boy to be his son."

So the two together went to look for a job, and soon the boy was hired because of his father's good name.

I heard of another young man many years later when times were good, who had difficulty getting work in his community because his father was a drunkard. Often the boy was made to

107

suffer because the name he wore was not one of which he could be proud.

We can all work for a good name. What about your name?

Prayer: Help us in times of stress to remember our good name and keep it pure. In Christ's name we pray. Amen.

April 24

"For I know whom I have believed and am persuaded that he is able to keep that which I have committed unto him against that day." — II Timothy 1:12

Most children have faith in their parents. They seem instinctively to feel that father and mother will provide for them. Should we not trust our Heavenly Father?

A ten-year-old boy living far out in the country helped his father cut and load a cord of wood. "I will take the wood to town and sell it. Then I will buy some gifts for the family," the father promised.

The father spent the entire day driving to town and up and down the streets trying to sell the wood. At last when dark had almost settled he was successful in making a sale. All the stores were closed and he made the long drive home without any gifts.

"The children stayed up until they were exhausted waiting for you to return," his wife told him.

"What will I do?" he asked her. "The stores were all closed by the time I sold the wood."

"Give each of them a piece of money and on Saturday we will all go to town and buy something," his wife advised.

How pleased the children were with their coins and the prospect of a trip to town! Going to town seemed much nicer than just a gift brought home.

Sometimes we fear our Heavenly Father has forgotten us, but he always has a better gift in store for us than we expected.

Prayer: May we think today on things that are Christ-like. We pray in the name of Jesus. Amen.

April 25

"The thief cometh not, but for to steal, and to kill, and to destroy: I am come that they might have life, and that they might have it more abundantly." — John 10:10

"Life is made up, not of great sacrifices or duties, but of little things, in which smiles and kindnesses and small obligations, given habitually, are what win and preserve the heart and secure comfort" (Sir Humphry Davy).

Christ wants us to have life more abundantly; yet he did not at any time advise people to seek for glory, fame, or fortune. He wants us to have a more abundant life; yet he did not set an example of extravagant living.

What is an abundant life? It is one filled with serenity and peace. We can have serenity by putting our lives in his care. We can have peace by seeking to follow his will.

The man and woman who close their door on the world at night and enjoy fellowship with their own children are happy indeed. So also is life with Christ.

> Into my heart's treasury
> I slipped a coin
> That time cannot take
> Nor a thief purloin, —
> Oh, better than the minting
> Of a gold-crowned king
> Is the safe-kept memory
> Of a lovely thing.
>
> — Sara Teasdale

Prayer: May we have a larger life by thinking on lovely things. Keep us from being impatient and irritable today. We pray through the name of Jesus. Amen.

April 26

"For whom the Lord loveth he chasteneth, and scourgeth every son whom he receiveth. If ye endure chastening, God dealeth with you as with sons; for what son is he whom the father chasteneth not? — Hebrews 12:6, 7

Is there anyone or anything you despise more than a child or pet that is never restricted in any way? If people are to be agreeable and pleasant, they must live by some restrictions.

Two boys lived on the same block. Tim was required to go to bed at eight-thirty on school nights. Brady was not required to go to bed at all unless he wanted to. Brady's parents often wondered why Tim made such good grades — why he was so good in sports — why he grew up to be so popular. They could not understand why their son did not accomplish as much as Tim and why he never received so much as a kind word from his teachers. Restrictions made the difference!

We must all learn to live by life's restrictions. We cannot say "yes" to every request, every whim.

> All that we say returns,
> The bitter word or sweet;
> Days, weeks, or years may intervene,
> But soon or late
> The spoken word and speaker meet.

> All that we do returns:
> The deed that's true or base
> We may forget, but all unseen
> And parallel
> The doer and the deed keep pace.
> — John Richard Moreland

Prayer: Father, if temptation assails us today, give us strength to resist it. If trouble comes our way give us courage to face it. We pray in the name of one who faced both temptation and trouble. Amen.

April 27

"And I will make them and the places round about my hill a blessing; and I will cause the shower to come down in his season; there shall be showers of blessing." — Ezekiel 34:26

Before the days of air-conditioned cars a family stopped at our house on a hot summer day. They had traveled several hundred miles and were so exhausted from the heat that the mother had to go to bed for a while.

After visiting for an hour our friends felt they must press on toward their destination. How we hated to see them start out in the heat again! As we stood by the car bidding them goodbye a cloud came over the sun. In a few moments they drove away in a shower of rain. We were so glad that they would be cooled and refreshed as they traveled.

When life seems unbearably hard and we think it is impossible to go on, God often sends a refreshing shower. Sometimes it is merely a word of encouragement from a friend.

> Who loves the rain
> And loves his home,
> And looks on life with quiet eyes,
> Him will I follow through the storm;
> And at his hearth-fire keep me warm;
> Nor hell nor heaven shall that soul surprise,

Who loves the rain,
And loves his home,
And looks on life with quiet eyes.
— Frances Shaw

Prayer: Father, we would begin the day aright with worship. We feel refreshed and renewed from our rest of the night. We ask thee to guide us today. In the name of Jesus we pray. Amen.

April 28

"O thou that hearest prayer, unto thee shall all flesh come."
— Psalm 65:2

Oh how I need a friend today,
To help me o'er life's rugged way.
There is a friend who cares, I say,
The one who hears me when I pray,
Who knows each idle word I say.
He climbed a rough high hill one day
That I might have the right to pray.

— Amy Bolding

There comes a time in every life when we have only one source of comfort. We should be very careful to keep the line open at all times to our God, the source of our comfort and strength.

That I may grow a little braver
    To face life's trials and never waver
From high ideals that I have made,
    To face life squarely, unafraid.
That I may yet more patient be
    With those, who faltering lean on me.
To profit by mistakes I've made
    And let them from my memory fade.
That I may always faithful be
    To those who put their trust in me.
For these, dear, heavenly Lord,
    I pray that I may prove worthwhile today!

Prayer: O Lord, help us to be honest in dealing with ourselves, as we expect others to be when they deal with us. May we realize that if we cheat in life, we hurt ourselves most of all. Make us willing to accept thy Lordship over us. Grant us power to live for thee regardless of hardship or trial. We pray for the sake of one who gave all for us, Jesus our Saviour. Amen.

April 29

"So God created man in his own image." — Genesis 1:27

"But Jesus answered them, My Father worketh hitherto, and I work." — John 5:17

Little Johnny was out working on his wagon. He was attempting to change the wheels.

"Why are you tearing up your wagon?" a neighbor asked.

"I am changing my wheels like daddy does on the car," answered Johnny.

Most little boys seek to be like their fathers. Most little girls seek to play house just like mother. We as children of a Heavenly Father should seek to work as he works. The most miserable person in the world is one who has nothing to do, nothing to demand his time and effort — or who simply does not care to work.

We were created in the image of one who worked. We should strive to live up to that image.

> If God measured everybody else by me,
> How near the mark do you s'pose they'd be?
> Would they leave steps as they pass this way,
> Through sands of Time, that men might say,
> "We found the church in their lives revealed"?
> His word of Life in their hearts concealed."
> Oh, a beacon light I'd strive to be
> If God measured everybody else by me.
>
> — W. D. Smith

Prayer: Lead us through the hours of the day that we may walk as we would have our children walk. In the name of one who set a perfect example we pray. Amen.

April 30

"It is good for a man that he bear the yoke in his youth."
— Lamentations 3:27

"Take my yoke upon you, and learn of me; for I am meek and lowly in heart; and ye shall find rest unto your souls. For my yoke is easy, and my burden is light." — Matthew 11:29, 30

Susan owned a small parakeet. Often she hung his cage on the screened back porch and opened the door. The little bird would fly all around and have a wonderful time. If strangers came in and began to talk, the bird would quickly fly to the cage and go inside. Susan would say, "He feels safer in his cage."

There are many kinds of bondage that make people happy. A father is happy to go home at night to his wife and children. They are the reason he is bound to his job and must work hard. Yet he is happy.

Children who are taught to obey their parents are happier than children who have no demands made upon them. They know what to depend upon and feel secure.

Christians who take the yoke of Christ find their life restricted in some ways but they are happy. Like children they know who will take care of them, and on whom they can depend.

> Then hold my hand, most gracious God,
> Guide all my goings still;
> And let it be my life's one aim,
> To know and do thy will.

Prayer: We thank thee for thy care and providence for us. Give us grace to live and serve thee as we should. In the name of Jesus our Lord we pray. Amen.

May:

Thoughts on Christian Homes

May 1

"Ye are the light of the world. A city that is set on an hill cannot be hid. Neither do men light a candle and put it under a bushel, but on a candlestick; and it giveth light unto all that are in the house." — Matthew 5:14, 15

We read in the papers that the great evangelist, Billy Graham, was coming to our town for a one-night service. Most of us had never had an opportunity to see or hear him. People went to the service in great numbers. I do not remember the sermon and I do not remember the songs, but I remember the lights. As we went through the turnstile at the door each person was handed a small candle and a match. At a certain time in the service all were asked to light their candles and hold them up. All other lights were off for the moment. What an impressive sight!

Often when I am tempted to think that my life is of no consequence or worth I remember all the thousands of candles shining that night and how all together they made a beautiful sight.

God has given each person on earth some kind of light to shine, and some purpose for shining that light.

> Trim your feeble lamp, my brother:
> Some poor sailor tempest tossed,
> Trying now to make the harbor,
> In the darkness may be lost.
>
> Let the lower lights be burning!
> Send a gleam across the wave!
> Some poor fainting, struggling sea-man,
> You may rescue, you may save.

Prayer: May the light of Christ's love shine from our lives today. We pray in the name of Jesus our Lord. Amen.

May 2

"Wherefore let him that thinketh he standeth take heed lest he fall." — I Corinthians 10:12

> We are all blind until we see
> That in the human plan
> Nothing is worth the making if
> It does not make the man.
>
> Why build these cities glorious
> If man unbuilded goes?

In vain we build the work, unless
The builder also grows.
— Edwin Markham

We are often tempted to think we are more important or better equipped than the other fellow. Then we make ourselves weak, and fail where we should have succeeded.

Look at Peter in the Bible. He was so proud of himself. He felt he would follow Jesus in spite of all hardship! Yet, when the test came he denied knowing Christ. True, he was broken-hearted afterward, but then it was too late to recall his denial.

Another giant character in the Bible was Samson. He was very strong physically but he gave his strength away carelessly — and suffered the consequences.

When we think we can whip the world alone, we need to take stock and see if we are depending too much on self. The old proverb still holds, "Pride goeth before destruction, and a haughty spirit before a fall."

Prayer: Dwell in our hearts as thou didst dwell with the mighty men of old. We ask in the name of Jesus our Saviour. Amen.

May 3

"My soul cleaveth unto the dust: quicken thou me according to thy word." — Psalm 119:25

Within my earthly temple there's a crowd:
There's one of us that's humble, one that's proud,
There's one that's broken-hearted for his sins,
And one that unrepentant sits and grins,
There's one that cares for nought but fame and self.
From much perplexing care I would be free
If I could once determine which is Me!

As children we used to play a game called "Who Am I?" We would pretend to be someone and the other children would try to guess who we were by asking us questions.

Sometimes we need to stop and ask ourselves the question, "Who am I?"

Are we the person our family sees each day at home — or are we the person our friends meet at social gatherings? Are we the same person wherever we may be?

The books we read, the magazines we look at, the places we go all have a part in making us the person we are. If we want to be a kind person we will think about kind things. If we want to be a good student we will spend time studying. If we want to be looked upon with respect we will make sure we choose people with high ideals for our companions.

Who are you? Who do you want to be? Seek to develop into that person.

Prayer: Father, we may at times grow discouraged and wonder who we are. Help us always to remember we are children of the King of kings. We thank thee for thy love towards us. For Jesus' sake we pray. Amen.

May 4

"In all thy ways acknowledge him, and he shall direct thy paths." — Proverbs 3:6

". . . but wisdom is profitable to direction."

— Ecclesiastes 10:10

We were about to make a turn at a dangerous intersection. The car coming toward us was signaling that he would be turning. This meant that the way would be clear for us. Just as my husband started to accelerate the car and make the turn he followed an urge to wait, and said, "Sometimes people drive along with the turn signal on when they have no plan for turning."

Sure enough, in a flash the car with turn signal still flashing whizzed by, going straight ahead. If we had accepted his signal and turned, a horrible wreck would have resulted.

Christ's directions are sure and safe. We can follow them in perfect assurance. Many young people, and older, follow the signals of false leaders and their lives are hopelessly wasted, if not horribly wrecked.

> To every man there openeth
> A way, and ways, and a way,
> And the high soul climbs the high way,
> And the low soul gropes the low:
> And in between, on the misty flats,
> The rest drift to and fro.
> But to every man there openeth
> A high way and a low,
> And every man decideth
> The way his soul shall go.

— John Oxenham

Prayer: Help us remember today that no one else can do the work thou hast assigned to us. May we place our lives in thy hands and be directed of thee. In Jesus' name we pray. Amen.

119

May 5

"Cast thy bread upon the waters: for thou shalt find it after many days." — Ecclesiastes 11:1

Two little girls were sitting side by side on the doorstep. They were hugging each other and showing their mutual affection. Soon they were up running and playing. Little Lynn accidently hit Janie with a ball. Suddenly Janie said ugly things to Lynn and the child ran home crying.

When they gave love to each other they were happy. When they became angry and gave ugly words they received ugly words in return. So it is throughout life.

> Give to the world the best that you have,
> And its best will come back to you.
> Give love and love to your heart will flow,
> And strength to your inmost needs.
> Have faith and scores of hearts will show
> Their faith in your work and deeds.
> For life is a mirror for king and for slave
> 'Tis just what we are and do.
> So give the world the best that you have
> And its best will come back to you.

Prayer: Dear Lord, help me to give my best each day to all I chance to meet. May I serve and be a blessing without thought of what it will cost or what it will return. Amen.

May 6

"And the Lord said unto Cain, Where is Abel thy brother? And he said, I know not: Am I my brother's keeper?"

— Genesis 4:9

Leaving my car at the entrance to a downtown parking lot I saw a large sign. It read, "We are not responsible for packages left in cars."

The thought came to me, "But I am responsible for the package of life God has given me." So I walked a bit more carefully across the busy intersection. But that did not satisfy me for I remembered the words of Cain, "Am I my brother's keeper?"

It is not enough to be careful for ourselves; we have others to think about, too. If we are Christians we are responsible to God for our brothers.

One of the blind poet's songs reminds us of our duty.

120

Rescue the perishing, Care for the dying,
Snatch them in pity from sin and the grave;
Weep o'er the erring one, Lift up the fallen,
Tell them of Jesus the mighty to save.

Rescue the perishing, Care for the dying;
Jesus is merciful, Jesus will save.

— Fanny J. Crosby

Prayer: Help us Heavenly Father to realize we are our brother's keeper. Amen.

May 7

"Bear ye one another's burdens, and so fulfil the law of Christ."
— Galatians 6:2

The big business man slipped onto a stool and ordered a cup of coffee. The cafe was a small one in a New Mexico village. The owner-operator-cook-waiter was lonely.

"Where are you from?" he asked his customer.

"Lubbock, Texas," was the reply.

"Oh, I knew a man from Lubbock. He owned a ranch near here." The proprietor was all smiles. He mentioned the rancher's name, and asked, "Ever heard of him?"

The business man thought of a beautiful home near his own. He thought of the rancher's widow living there alone. "He and his wife were some of our closest friends. We miss him since he died."

As men in a lonely place will do, they talked about their mutual friend. The one had known him in a social way, the other as a big rancher in a small town.

"Well, I'll tell you one thing. We all thought well of him in this community. He was quick to go where sympathy was needed, and willing to stay and help with the work."

To show sympathy is a most wonderful trait,
And it's one that is too hard to find;
But a better trait still is to never be late
With help that is tender and kind.

— J. T. Bolding

Prayer: Lord, help us to be thoughtful of the needs of others; always ready to be helpful in time of need. In Jesus' name we pray. Amen.

121

May 8

"But, beloved, we are persuaded better things of you, and things that accompany salvation, though we thus speak."

— Hebrews 6:9

Jack was a rowdy in school. All the teachers dreaded him.

One fall a new teacher came to the school. He began to keep Jack so busy doing things the boy simply forgot to be rowdy. One day Jack fell back into his old ways, and knocked one of the other pupils down. The teacher took the fallen boy and comforted him. To Jack he merely said, "Jack, I expect better things from you."

Jack became a great success in life because that teacher in a quiet way brought out the very best by believing it was there — and expecting it.

> There are loyal hearts, there are spirits brave,
> There are souls that are pure and true;
> Then give the world the best you have,
> And the best will come back to you.
>
> Give the truth, and you will be paid in kind,
> And a song with a song will meet;
> The smile which is sweet will surely find
> Other smiles that are just as sweet.
>
> For life is a mirror of king and slave —
> 'Tis just what we are, and do:
> Then give to the world the best that you have,
> And the best will come back to you.
>
> — Madeline S. Bridges

Prayer: Dear Heavenly Father, help us today to be our best. May we be kind to the lonely, and helpful to those in need. Give us the desire to be our best in work and in play. Amen.

May 9

". . . and, lo, I am with you alway, even unto the end of the world." — Matthew 28:20

"Thou shalt increase my greatness, and comfort me on every side." — Psalm 71:21

Did you ever walk around in the midst of thousands of people and feel lonely? That was just how I felt at a convention which I was attending in our town. Then I saw an old friend across the hall and we were soon engaged in conversation.

Life is lonely at times for the person who is a Christian. He often feels that all the world is passing him by. But he need not feel lonely. Jesus has promised always to be with us. He is at our side day and night. When we feel lonely we should just talk to God. He is there close by, ready to hear. And this is interesting. When we have finished talking to God he will often lead us to someone who also needs a friend or to someone to whom we can witness.

One is walking with me over life's uneven way,
Constantly supporting me each moment of the day;
How can I be lonely when such fellowship is mine,
    With my blessed Lord divine!

In life's rosy morning when the skies above are clear,
In its noontide hours with many cares and problems near,
Or when evening shadows fall at closing of my day
    Jesus will be there alway.

— Haldor Lillenas

Prayer: Our heavenly Father, help us today to remember thou wilt never fail nor forget thy children. If trouble should come, help us to know thou art there to comfort and care. We thank thee for thy presence always. Amen.

May 10

"The Lord make his face shine upon thee, and be gracious unto thee: The Lord lift up his countenance upon thee, and give thee peace." — Numbers 6:25, 26

Each day Marilyn ran to meet the postman. There would be letters for Mother or Daddy, but none for her.

"Why don't you bring me a letter?" she asked the postman.

"I see a letter God has written you," the postman replied. "Look at the little green leaves coming up in the flower bed. God is telling you Spring is here."

All day the little girl was happy. God had written her a letter. She saw God in the trees, in the animals running down the walk, and in the refreshing shower of rain that fell in the afternoon.

God writes every person in the world a love letter if he only has eyes to see it and read it. If we see God in the beautiful earth he has created his face will shine upon us and give us peace.

        Alas for him who never sees
        The stars shine through his cypress-trees!

Who, hopeless, lays his dead away,
Nor looks to see the breaking day. . . .

— Whittier

Prayer: Father, help us to see today the beauties in nature. Help us to realize thou hast made the earth for us to enjoy and care for. Give us the realization that as a seed dies it is born again to come forth in new beauty. Amen.

May 11

"The steps of a good man are ordered by the Lord: and he delighteth in his way. Though he fall, he shall not be utterly cast down: for the Lord upholdeth him with his hand."

— Psalm 37:23, 24

Last summer we visited the seashore with our two small grandsons. The boys had so much fun standing on the beach and letting the waves wash over their feet and legs. They laughed and jumped as children do. Then they found an empty can. They would throw the can as far out in the water as possible, and then it would come riding back on a wave. They were really having fun.

Suddenly a larger than usual wave came in and the boys were tossed to the ground and were covered with water. They struggled to their feet and were about to cry when their mother called out, "That was a big one, but you managed fine." They laughed again and went on having fun.

Suddenly they noticed their can had drifted far away and would not come back. They were disappointed, but soon found something else to interest them and went on having a good time.

Life is like that. Sometimes we are cast down by he tides of life. Sometimes we lose something very precious and dear — but always we must go on. And God speaks words of encouragement. God will give us the strength and courage to face it all.

In shady green pastures, so rich and so sweet,
God leads his dear children along;
Where the water's cold flow bathes the weary one's feet,
God leads his dear children along.

Prayer: Dear Father, help us to trust in thy leadership and care, in the valleys as well as on the mountain top. Amen.

124

May 12

"Thou shalt worship the Lord thy God, and him only shalt thou serve." — Matthew 4:10

We start at the bottom on our climb through life. We start as new-born babies and slowly climb to adulthood. And throughout our journey of life there are hills to climb. Sometimes the climb is difficult. But there are things we can take along that will make it easier and happier.

First of all we must carry love for God in our hearts. You will be surprised how much this will help to make the climb easier. Then we must take with us love for our fellow man. We must take along consideration for others. Others also are climbing life's highest hill and they might need a helping hand.

> Many are calling for light from on high,
> Then let us help while we may;
> Will we not answer their pitiful cry?
> Oh, help somebody to-day.
>
> Out on the mountain of folly and sin
> Far from the straight narrow way;
> Who then will help bring the wanderer in?
> Oh, help somebody to-day.
>
> From early morning till cometh the night,
> Patiently labor and pray;
> Turning the lost from the wrong to the right,
> Oh, help somebody to-day.
>
> — W. J. Henry

Prayer: Our Father, help us today to realize the way up is down to service. May we realize true greatness comes from being right in our hearts and may we be like Jesus in heart and action and spirit. Amen.

May 13

"Blessed is the man that endureth temptation: for when he is tried, he shall receive the crown of life, which the Lord hath promised to them that love him." — James 1:12

Many years ago on Lincoln's birthday a cartoon appeared in some of the newspapers. The cartoon pictured a log cabin close to the base of a high mountain. On top of the mountain was pictured the White House. Against the side of the mountain was pictured a ladder. The foot of the ladder touched the cabin, and the top rung reached the mansion on the top of the mountain. The caption read, "The ladder is still there."

Young people need to realize there is a ladder to climb. They may not all reach the top but God promises a reward for those who try to succeed in life. There are still men today who have had to climb a long ladder to success.

> Courage, brother, do not stumble,
>   Though thy path be dark as night;
> There's a star to guide the humble;
>   Trust in God and do the right.

Prayer: Our Father, we thank thee, that thy mercies are still upon us. We thank thee for the love thou dost shed around us. Let thy everlasting arms be underneath us as we seek to climb higher each day. Help us to seek and do thy will always. We ask in the name of Jesus Christ. Amen.

May 14

"Love worketh no ill to his neighbor." — Romans 13:10

We were so surprised one afternoon soon after we moved into a new home to have a large group of neighbors drop in. They brought cold drinks and cookies and made a party out of the visit. Isn't it wonderful to have friends and congenial neighbors!

But ill-tempered or suspicious neighbors can be a source of much unhappiness. One of my friends is constantly having a feud with some of her neighbors. If they happen to let the lawn sprinkler get near her car as it stands in the drive she tries to make them pay for having the car washed. She does not enjoy her neighbors. She is always unhappy.

> If we knew the cares and crosses
> Crowding 'round our neighbor's way
> If we knew of all his losses
> Sorely grievous day by day;
> Would we then so often chide him
> Casting o'er his life a shadow,
> Leaning on his heart a strain?
>
> Let us reach into our bosoms
> For the key to other lives,
> And with love to erring nature,
> Cherish good that still survives;

126

So that when our disrobed spirits
Soar to realms of light again,
We may say, dear Father, judge us
As we judged our fellow men.

Prayer: Holy Father, as we come into thy presence help us to examine our hearts and purge out any evil thoughts toward our neighbors. We ask for the sake of Christ. Amen.

May 15

"And the vessel that we made of clay was marred in the hands of the potter; so he made it again another vessel. . . ."

— Jeremiah 18:4

"We are the clay, and thou our potter; and we all are the work of thy hand." — Isaiah 64:8

Once as we traveled through the state of Alabama we stopped at a charming cottage where clay pots were for sale. The owner was also the potter. For our benefit and interest he put some clay on his potter's wheel and shaped a graceful vase while we watched, fascinated. Around the small shop he had all shapes and sizes of clay products to sell, all made by his hands.

How interesting it is to think of God as the great potter who shapes all kinds of lives and directs them.

When the potter places a piece of clay on the wheel he has in mind exactly what he wants to mold. God has a plan for everyone of us, and only if we submit our lives into his hands will we find happiness and success. We always should be careful to seek to know God's will for our lives. His plan is best.

Thy will, O God, not mine, be done!
  I know thy will is best;
If, sometimes, otherwise it seems,
  I still believe and rest.

Thy will is best, — 'tis there I rest;
  In shadow or in sun,
My prayer to thee shall ever be:
  Thy perfect will be done.

— T. O. Chisholm

Prayer: Dear Heavenly Father, make known to us what thou wouldst have us be. Let all be glorious within our hearts as we submit to thy will. In the name of Christ we pray. Amen.

May 16

"He maketh the barren woman to keep house, and to be a joyful mother of children. Praise ye the Lord." — Psalm 113:9

The rights of women — what are they?
The right to labor and to pray,
The right to watch while others sleep,
The right o'er others' woes to weep,
The right to succor in distress,
The right while others curse to bless,
The right to love while others scorn,
The right to comfort all who mourn,
The right to shed new joy on earth,
The right to feel the soul's high worth,
The right to lead the soul to God
Along the path the Saviour trod.

I know a young mother who was left alone with two small children to rear. She was forced to get a job and work to keep food and clothing for them. Each Sunday found her sitting with them in the sanctuary. She gave to them every spare moment she could take away from her work. Often I thought how fortunate they were to have a mother who loved them so much. Of this world's goods they had barely enough — but of love they had an abundance.

Fortunate indeed is the child who has a good mother.

Prayer: O God, our Holy Father, we thank thee today for giving us gentle mothers, patient mothers, long-suffering and kind mothers. Help us always to appreciate our mothers and their self-sacrifice shown for us. For the sake of Christ we pray. Amen.

May 17

"We must obey God rather than men." — Acts 5:29

Tom was a very young business man, and he was anxious to succeed. He was happy with his work and the future looked bright to him. One day a very prominent man asked him to go to lunch with him. The man tried to find out all he could about Tom's boss. Tom did not say much. Finally the man came to the point and said: "I will make it worth your while if you will get a certain list of names from your boss' files for me."

Tom wanted the man's favor very much, and he knew just where the list was kept. "I will think about it," said Tom.

That night Tom kept repeating the verse, "Thou shalt not steal."

Next morning his wife asked him what had kept him awake so much. "I am facing a decision," said Tim. "I can get a list of names of our customers for another business and make a nice sum of money."

"Why Tom, you should never give such a thing a second thought," exclaimed his wife. "Isn't it better to obey God than please men?"

Tom called the man and refused to do as he wished.

Prayer: Dear Father, fill our hearts with the love that prompts courage in the face of temptation. Help us always to take a stand for the right. For Christ's sake we pray. Amen.

May 18

"Now in the morning as he returned to the city, he hungered. And when he saw a fig tree in the way, he came to it, and found nothing thereon. . . ." — Matthew 21:18-22

Does Christ come to your life seeking fruit and find none? You have some talent; use it to the best of your ability and you will gain more talent. Refuse to use what talent you have and you will soon lose it completely.

Two sisters were gifted singers. One readily and cheerfully agreed to always sing when asked. The other always waited to be begged. As time went on the first sister was increasingly in demand. The other was seldom and finally never asked.

God comes to us with opportunities and as we respond willingly he uses us more and more. If we fail time and time again to respond we are soon left out.

The fig tree was cursed for bearing no fruit.

> A sacred burden in this life ye bear,
> Look on it, bear it solemnly,
> Stand up and walk beneath it steadfastly;
> Fail not for sorrow, falter not for sin,
> But onward, upward, till the goal ye win.
> — Frances Anne Kemble

Prayer: Our Gracious Heavenly Father, the bountiful giver of all good and precious gifts, we thank thee. We thank thee for the talents we have. Help us to use our gifts to bear fruit for thy kingdom. May we dedicate our lives for service to thee each day. Teach us how to bear the most fruit. In the name of Jesus Christ our Saviour we pray. Amen.

May 19

"Wherefore seeing we also are compassed about with so great a cloud of witnesses, let us lay aside every weight, and the sin which doth so easily beset us, and let us run with patience the race that is set before us." — Hebrews 12:1

Some women are just naturally better housekeepers than others. Most of us get by on our housecleaning but what about cleansing our minds!

I read of a convict who resented the world. Each time he was released from prison he tried to get revenge and got into new trouble. At last a kind man won his confidence and showed him he must clean up his own heart and thoughts. The man put aside the thought of getting revenge and spent his time trying to help other ex-convicts find a place in life. In this way he found true usefulness and happiness.

> I have Jesus dwelling with me
>   Every hour of every day,
> So whatever may befall me,
>   "All is well," my heart can say.
>
> In this world of living pleasure
>   "Jesus only" would I know;
> Satisfied His steps to follow,
>   And His great salvation know.
>   — Mrs. C. H. Morris

Prayer: Almighty Father, help us today to cast out of our lives the things which would keep us from serving thee. Help us to remember we are precious in thy sight and seek to serve thee better. In the name of our Lord Jesus we pray. Amen.

May 20

"For unto everyone that hath shall be given, and he shall have abundance: but from him that hath not shall be taken away even that which he hath." — Matthew 25:29

For more than thirty years a man in Boston saved his children's outgrown shoes. Finally three hundred pairs of shoes hung in the attic. They told the story from birth to adulthood of four children. A reporter heard about the shoes and wrote a story. A doctor working for a school for retarded children read the story. He called and asked for the shoes to be used in his

130

school. They were gladly given. That man's thrift helped others who could not help themselves.

We must make what we have count for good. There are many ways to find uses for our material goods as well as our talents.

> Somebody did a golden deed,
>   Proving himself a friend in need;
> Somebody sang a cheerful song,
>   Brightening the sky the whole day long,
>
> Somebody made a loving gift,
>   Cheerfully tried a load to lift;
> Somebody told the love of Christ,
>   Told how His will was sacrificed,
>
> Was that somebody you?
>
> — John R. Clements

Prayer: Dear Father, we thank thee for giving us talents with which to serve thee. Help us to have the attitude of willingness to help others. For the sake of Christ Jesus we pray. Amen.

May 21

"Hosanna to the son of David: Blessed is he that cometh in the name of the Lord: Hosanna in the highest."

— Matthew 21:9

The Scripture above gives us a picture of Jesus when he was being honored and praised. He never once acted proud or haughty. Through all honor or mistreatment he remained meek and lowly.

A boy on the high school football team was always glad when he could make a touchdown. Whenever he could get his hands on the ball he raced for the goal. He liked to hear the fans call his name and praise him! One day the coach suspended him from the team for two weeks. He was shocked.

"I am your best player. Why mistreat me?" he exclaimed.

"Praise has gone to your head," replied the coach. "As a result, you refuse to work with the rest of the team so that you may have all the praise for yourself."

> Is anybody happier
>   Because you passed his way?
> Does anyone remember
>   That you spoke to him today?

131

This day is almost over,
    And its toiling time is through;
Is there anyone to utter now,
    A friendly word for you?

Did you waste the day, or lose it?
    Was it well or poorly spent?
Did you leave a trail of kindness,
    Or a scar of discontent?

Prayer: Our Father, help us when we have been triumphant and successful to remain humble. May we ever give thee the praise and glory for the blessings which come our way. May we never be proud and haughty. For the sake of Jesus Christ our Lord we pray. Amen.

May 22

"And be ye kind one to another, tenderhearted, forgiving one another, even as God for Christ's sake hath forgiven you."

— Ephesians 4:32

There is a destiny that makes us brothers;
    None goes his way alone:
All that we send into the lives of others
    Comes back into our own.

— Edwin Markham

It would take pages and pages to tell all the ways we can be kind to one another. If we look up and see the millions of stars at night we marvel at their number and beauty. Ways of showing kindness are just as numerous and just as beautiful. Our lives can become beautiful if we clothe ourselves with kindness.

Let's resolve to begin or increase our deeds of kindness at once. We can show kindness by forgiving others, and by concern for the feelings of others.

We should be kind to all. Why should we be kind even to those who mistreat us? Because God sent his son to die for us and has forgiven us our sins.

Prayer: Father, as we come before thee may we determine to develop a better attitude in our relationship with others. Help us to be forgiving of those who offend us. Control our tongues as we speak to others. For the sake of one who was never unkind, Jesus Christ, we pray. Amen.

May 23

"Blessed are they that dwell in thy house: they will be still praising thee." — Psalm 84:4

One morning I went to a sidewalk sale. People were milling about examining the merchandise. Two ladies were in front of a table filled with boots. They were attempting to try on the boots standing up. After they had almost fallen several times they found some they thought were suitable and took them to the check out desk.

"You could go inside the store and sit down to try them on," the clerk said.

"We have already decided on these," replied the ladies. And they paid their money and went away.

How often we make things harder by not inquiring which way is best. We stumble and fall and get misfits because it takes more time to go into the house of the Lord and ask his directions for our decisions.

Prayer: Grant to us, most loving Father, the ability to find what is thy purpose for our lives. May we find comfort and guidance in thy house. In the name of Christ our Lord we pray. Amen.

May 24

"Bear ye one another's burdens, and so fulfil the law of Christ."
— Galatians 6:2

Mack and Joe were brothers. Each day they walked to school together. Always Mack carried Joe's books. One day a lady was sitting on her porch and she called to the boys, "Why doesn't the little boy carry the books sometimes?"

"Because I like to carry them," Mack replied. Had the woman looked closer, she would have noticed that because Joe had deformed hands and arms he could only carry something very light.

When Joe and Mack were adults there came a time in Mack's life when he needed to borrow some money. Joe had become a successful business man. He was glad to let Mack have the money. Said Joe, "This is to help pay you for all the times when you carried my books and helped me get back and forth to school."

> I need the lives of others
>   To make my life complete;
> I need your recognition
>   To light my humble street.

Some friends are rich, some are poor,
And some have moderate fee —
I treasure every one of them,
They mean so much to me.

— Walter Werner

Prayer: Father, help us to be worthy of those friends who help us bear our burdens each day. In the name of Christ we pray. Amen.

May 25

"And whosoever will be great among you, let him be your servant: Even as the Son of man came not to be ministered unto, but to minister, and to give his life a ransom for many."

— Matthew 20:27, 28

Leta was a small girl but she liked to help her mother with the housework. Often she waited to run and play until the work was finished. One summer the neighbors invited her to go on a vacation trip with them.

"Why did you ask Leta and not me?" her brother asked.

"We have noticed how much Leta works around the house and we thought she deserved a trip," the neighbor replied.

Jesus lived a life of service. He would have enjoyed just staying in his wonderful home in heaven, but because we needed salvation he came to earth to make a way for us to share that home.

No service in itself is small,
None great, though earth it fill;
But that is small that seeks its own
And great that seeks God's will.
Then hold my hand, most gracious God,
Guide all my goings still;
And let it be my life's one aim
To know and do thy will.

Prayer: We thank thee, our Father, for places to serve in this great world. Help us to share our faith with others and keep our doubts to ourselves. We thank thee for those who have unselfishly served to spread thy kingdom. Accept our prayer for Jesus' sake. Amen.

May 26

"We look for new heavens and a new earth wherein dwelleth righteousness." — II Peter 3:13

Have you ever been seeking a lost key or some other important item? You became so fascinated with the search that all else was forgotten until you were successful in finding what you looked for. We look for a home in heaven and we should be so fascinated with our preparation and search for that home that all else takes second place.

We must invite others to search with us also. There will never be too many seeking that heavenly home.

As you try to ascend the steep mountains of life
  Which seem always to stand in your way,
And you try to supply someone's need in the strife,
  You'll find out you need help every day.
For your needs, on your climb, to the Saviour then look.
  Says his word, his supply is complete.
With his presence assured, as he says in his book,
  Every day in his way is so sweet!

— J. T. Bolding

Prayer: O God, indwell in our hearts today. Give us love and patience to face the problems of the day. May we recognize the saving power of hope in Christ our Lord. May we feel the wonderful fascination of life as we prepare and look for our eternal home. In the name of one who died for our sins we pray. Amen.

May 27

"He that loveth his brother abideth in the light, and there is none occasion of stumbling in him. But he that hateth his brother is in darkness, and walketh in darkness, and knoweth not whither he goeth, because that darkness hath blinded his eyes."

— I John 2:10, 11

I have a friend who is a very successful lawyer. I often wondered why his brothers were just plain business men and seemed not to have gone to school past high school. When their mother died I attended the funeral. The minister told how the father had died when the children were small, leaving the mother without funds. The older boys had left school and worked to support the family. They had sacrificed to send their younger brother

135

and sister to college. The lawyer had told the minister of his brothers' unselfishness and wanted them recognized that day.

> Give us, Lord, a chance to be
> Our goodly best, brave, wise and free,
> Our goodly best for ourself, and others,
> Till all men learn to live as brothers."
>
> — English Prayer

Prayer: Dear Lord, help us to love our brothers as we love ourselves. Help us to follow the teaching of Jesus Christ, thy son. Pardon us when we are selfish and forget others. May we learn to be merciful to all men and treat them as brothers. We ask in the name of Jesus Christ. Amen.

May 28

"We have thought of thy lovingkindness, O God, in the midst of thy temple." — Psalm 48:9

"To get peace, if you do want it, make for yourselves nests of pleasant thoughts. None of us yet knows, for none of us has been taught in early youth, what fairy palaces we may build of beautiful thoughts — proof against all adversity. Bright fancies, satisfied memories, noble histories, faithful sayings, treasure-houses of precious and restful thoughts, which cannot disturb, nor pain, make gloomy, nor poverty take away from us — houses built without hands for our souls to live in." — Ruskin.

> Let us, then, labor for an inward stillness —
> An inward stillness and an inward healing;
> That perfect silence where the lips and heart
> Are still, and we no longer entertain
> Our own imperfect thoughts and vain opinions,
> But God alone speaks in us, and we wait
> In singleness of heart, that we may know
> His will, and in the silence of our spirits,
> That we may do His will, and do that only.
>
> — Longfellow

Prayer: Our Father in heaven, help us today to develop kind thoughts. Give us quiet and meditation that we may correct our mistaken thoughts and formulate wise plans. Give us inward silence and stillness as we wait to know the will of our God. We pray in the name of Jesus, thy son. Amen.

May 29

"Lay not up for yourselves treasures upon earth, where moth and rust doth corrupt, and where thieves break through and steal: But lay up for yourselves treasures in heaven, where neither moth nor rust down corrupt, and where thieves do not break through nor steal: For where your treasure is, there will your heart be also." — Matthew 6:19-21

Our Lord teaches that spiritual treasure is permanently superior to material treasure. We cannot serve two masters. We must choose where our main treasure will be stored. How can we lay up treasures in heaven?

We can share our material wealth to help carry on the work of the church. We can give the personal touch of help to those in need. God looks at how much we keep for ourselves as well as what we give.

> Let me go where saints are going,
> To the mansions of the blest;
> Let me go where my Redeemer
> Has prepared His people's rest.
> I would gain the realms of brightness,
> Where they dwell for evermore;
> I would join the friends that wait me,
> Over on the other shore.
> Let me go; 'tis Jesus calls me;
> Let me gain the realms of day;
> Bear me over, angel pinions;
> Longs my soul to be away.

> — L. Hartsough

Prayer: Our Father, make us grateful for thy blessings as we lay up our treasure in heaven. For Jesus sake we pray. Amen.

May 30

"Verily I say unto you, Wheresoever this gospel shall be preached in the whole world, there shall also this, that this woman hath done, be told for a memorial of her."

> — Matthew 26:13

> How fair the roses are today
> Upon each soldier's grave!
> How proudly in the breeze of May
> We see Old Glory wave!
> Drop fragrant, smiling blossoms where

This honored dust has come
And for one of those who were not there
The day the boys came home.
— Clarence Flynn

Time has dimmed the memories of World War I and of World War II. Science has developed new weapons, new wonders and new problems. Ideals sometimes grow dim. We cannot go back. We only remember and honor those who made today possible for us.

Julia Ward Howe wrote the poem, "Battle-Hymn of the Republic." Once at a Memorial Day service in Boston she was to be honored for her contribution. A fine singer arose to sing the song. By the time he reached the words, "In the glory of the lillies Christ was born across the sea," the whole audience was standing and singing with him.

There will come a day when the redeemed will be gathered in heaven. All will join in the song of praise to him who died to make their salvation possible. What a glorious Memorial Day that will be!

Prayer: Our God and Father, may we in fellowship with thee allow our minds to dwell upon the sacrifices made by the young men who left homes and loved ones to fight for the freedom of our country. In Jesus' name. Amen.

May 31

"A merry heart maketh a cheerful countenance: but by sorrow of the heart the spirit is broken." — Proverbs 15:13

People are born with an instinct for happiness. We wish to be happy. How can we be happy and have a merry heart?

James was walking to school. He felt just plain mad. Breakfast had not been to his liking. Sister Jane had hurried off to walk with her chum. James trudged along cross and angry. Just then Mrs. Royace came out of her door.

"James, would you walk along with me and hold my dog's leash?" she called.

James took the leash. He liked Mrs. Royace's dog.

"Why don't you sit on the porch while I take your dog for a walk?" asked James. And he hurried off with the dog. After a few moments James came back, happy and whistling. He had forgotten his troubles.

If you and I, just you and I
Should laugh instead of worry;
If we should grow — just you and I
Kinder and sweeter hearted,
Perhaps in some near by and by
A good time might get started;
Then what a happy world 'twould be
For you and me — for you and me.

Prayer: Dear Father, help us to find our lost laughter and happiness by helping others. We wish to be excited and happy with life. Give us today the ability to help others and in helping to find true peace and happiness. For the sake of Christ we pray. Amen.

June:

Timely Thoughts

June 1

"To everything there is a season, and a time to every purpose under the heaven: A time to be born, and a time to die; a time to pluck up that which is planted." — Ecclesiastes 3:1, 2

This is the time of year when we hate to stay inside. There is so much new life all about us in the great out-of-doors. We have such big plans for what we will plant, and what we will see as our plants grow.

Families are like the springtime. When children are little we plan carefully how we will train and teach them. We want for them the best schools and advantages. We must not forget that what we plant in the child's heart at home will bear fruit throughout his life. We must plant love for others, pluck out ugly habits and ways. God has a purpose for all his children. We must see that they are properly nourished and trained to fulfill that purpose.

> The year's at the spring,
> And day's at the morn;
> Morning's at seven;
> The hillside's dew-pearled;
> The lark's on the wing;
> The snail's on the thorn;
> God's in His heaven, —
> All's right with the world.
>
> — Browning

Prayer: Our dear Father, who loved us and planned for us the seasons of life, help us to enjoy to the fullest each one. Help us to find something good and pleasant about each age through which we pass. May we give thee the praise for life. In the name of Christ our Lord we pray. Amen.

June 2

"I will praise thee: O Lord my God, with all my heart: and I will glorify thy name for evermore." — Psalm 86:12

If we would spend our time praising God instead of grumbling we would find joy in our hearts.

When Dick was a teen-ager he had a paper route. When he was older he worked after school in a grocery store. Everybody liked Dick. He was always so polite and cheerful.

One summer Dick was made manager of the produce department in the store. One of the other boys in the store went to the head manager, and asked, "Why did Dick get the job? I have worked here a long time — much longer than he has."

"Because Dick always praises the other workers," said the manager. "He is happy and often whistles as he works. A happy leader gets more work from the other boys."

> Then hide it not, the music of thy soul,
> Dear sympathy expressed with kindly voice,
> But let it like a shining river roll
> To deserts dry — to hearts that would rejoice.
>
> Oh, let the symphony of kindly words
> Sound for the poor, the friendless, and the weak,
> And He will bless you, He who struck the chords
> Will strike another when in turn you seek.

Prayer: Our Father who art in heaven, may we today praise thy name. May we see the good in those about us and seek to help them on their way. Help us to forget unpleasant things and remember the pearls of character that are good. In the name of Jesus Christ our Lord we pray. Amen.

June 3

"A friend loveth at all times. . . ." — Proverbs 17:17

Mrs. Lowery and Mrs. Box had been friends since they were girls in school. They visited often, kept each other's children and were just good friends.

Mrs. Lowery's husband was a good business man and so they were soon quite well off. They moved across town to a new home. At first the women called each other and talked on the phone each day. Then they began to see less and less of each other. Then one day Mrs. Lowery heard that her friend's husband had been killed in an accident and her friend was badly hurt. She rushed to the hospital. She took the children to her own home and cared for them many weeks until their mother was released from the hospital.

"You didn't have to go to all that trouble for me," said Mrs. Box.

"You are my friend, and I wanted to help," was Mrs. Lowery's reply.

> There is no friend like an old friend
> Who has shared our morning days,
> No greeting like his welcome,
> No homage like his praise.

144

Fame is the scentless sunflower,
With gaudy crown of gold;
But friendship is the breathing rose,
With sweets in every fold.

— Oliver Wendell Holmes

Prayer: Our Father, make us worthy of our friends. Make us like the friend who gave his life to redeem our souls. For it is in his name we pray. Amen.

June 4

"For his anger endureth but a moment; in his favor is life: weeping may endure for a night, but joy cometh in the morning."

— Psalm 30:5

"Wherefore comfort one another with these words."

— I Thessalonians 4:18

Troubles and trials come and go, but our God always remains the same. "He shall gather the lambs with his arms and carry them in his bosom" (Isaiah 40:11).

We are frail and often in need of comfort and strength. God stands ever ready to give us the strength and comfort we need. God's providence never places you where his grace cannot keep you.

Is your heart o'er burdened with its grief and care?
Are you fainting now beneath the cross you bear?
Tell it to Jesus at the place of prayer,
    Carry all your sorrows to Him.

Do you long for comfort in your sore distress?
Come to Christ your Saviour and your sins confess;
Tell it all to Jesus, He will heal and bless,
    Carry all your sorrows to Him.

Are you sad and lonely? Is the pathway drear?
Tarry then no longer in your doubt and fear;
Tell it all to Jesus, He is always near,
    Carry all your sorrows to Him.

Prayer: Dear Father, guide us along the way. Help us not to stray from the homeward pathway. Roll away our heavy burdens. Give us the comfort of faith. In the name of our Saviour Jesus Christ we pray. Amen.

June 5

"Ye are the salt of the earth: but if the salt have lost his savor, wherewith shall it be salted? it is thenceforth good for nothing, but to be cast out, and trodden under foot." — Matthew 5:13

One time I became ill and had to go on a diet with very little salt. The food tasted so flat and I found I just didn't want to eat much. We bought salt substitutes but they were not much help. How glad I was when I could again use some salt on my food. Everything seemed so good.

Jesus wants us to be the kind of people who make our community a better place to live. He said that even a few good people can leaven the whole lump. When we are tempted to choose the wrong side of a question for our own gain, we should ask ourselves, "Am I being the salt of the earth?"

> Once I tossed a twig
>   Into a surging spring,
> And watched it quickly ebb
>   Like some unshackled thing.
> Drifting in the current,
>   Independently and free,
> Bobbing with a rhythm,
>   It bounced buoyantly.
>
> Once a word I uttered,
>   And it echoed through the place
> Like a solitary urchin
>   With a tired, and worried face;
> And it struck a note of gladness,
>   And a hope was lifted high;
> It was just an idle gesture,
>   But it turned away a sigh.
>   — Laurence Estes

Prayer: Help us to strive always to be a blessing to those about us. For Jesus sake we pray. Amen.

June 6

"For I reckon that the sufferings of this present time are not worthy to be compared with the glory which shall be revealed in us." — Romans 8:18

In recent months and years we have had an outbreak of young people who seem to have no goals in life. They live in filth, and they waste their time telling us what is wrong with the world. If

146

the improvement of the world were really their goal, they would go out and work for it.

Our real goals are the ones for which we work and toil. People who have no goals get into all kinds of trouble. They either rust out, take drugs to make them forget reality, or they get bored and frustrated with the world.

> I know a man whose name is "New" —
> God said, "I have a task for you."
> New answered with a life of shame,
> He cast reproach on Jesus' name,
> And Satan now his life doth claim!
>
> I know a man whose name is "Mead" —
> God said, "You're chosen: you're to lead."
> Mead answered with a life of prayer
> And cast on God his every care.
> O, Lord, may I be so aware!
>
> — Jewel Alice McLeod

Prayer: We thank thee, Father, for giving us the desire to make our lives count for thee. Help us reach the high goals set for those who love the Lord. Help us to prepare for things eternal. We ask in Christ's name. Amen.

June 7

"But the path of the just is as the shining light, that shineth more and more unto the perfect day." — Proverbs 4:18

Very often we hear someone say, "I must stop and catch up." Sometimes they are talking about finances. Sometimes they are talking about physical strength. The housewife is often talking about catching up on her cleaning.

In Africa when the natives have been walking or running a long way, they never say they must stop and rest. They say, "We must stop and give our soul time to catch up."

In this hurried world we desperately need to let our souls have time to catch up. We need to stop and take time to think on beautiful and holy things.

> Stay, stay at home, my heart, and rest;
> Home-keeping hearts are happiest,
> For those that wander they know not where
> Are full of trouble and full of care;
> To stay at home is best.
>
> — Longfellow

Prayer: O God, our Almighty Father, help us to calm our restless hearts. Forgive our wrong and foolish quests. Guide us in the way of inward peace. In the name of one who said, "My peace I leave with you," we pray. Amen.

June 8

"Above all, taking the shield of faith, wherewith ye shall be able to quench all the fiery darts of the wicked. And take the helmet of salvation, and the sword of the Spirit, which is the word of God." — Ephesians 6:16, 17

Little Jody Alexander loves to play war. He often rushes at his playmates with the lid to the garbage can held in front of him and a long stick for a sword. He feels entirely safe with such fine armor.

How often we go out to meet the world in a warfare with sin with just such flimsy armor! Ephesians 6:11 says: "Put on the whole armor of God, that ye may be able to stand against the wiles of the devil."

A little time in reading
God's word shows me the way
That I should walk and worship
My Lord throughout each day.

A little time in praying
Keeps me within His will,
And brings my heart much gladness
To know He loves me still.

— Jewel Alice McLeod

Prayer: Dear Father, we are a land of many faiths and creeds. Help us never to forget that there is only one God — the God who created us, the God who can keep and sustain us in a world of trouble and chaos. Help us to preserve our faith in thee. Help us to show others the way of salvation. In the name of Jesus we pray. Amen.

June 9

"Be strong and quit yourselves like men, O ye Philistines, that ye be not servants unto the Hebrews, as they have been to you: quit yourselves like men, and fight." — I Samuel 4:9

During the depression of the early 1930's, I was a young married woman. Soon I was a young mother with three children.

148

We could have given up the struggle for a livelihood and gone on relief. We chose rather to heed the battle cry, "Conserve every bit of food you can."

Never have I worked so hard and had so many cans of food in my pantry. If some friend had extra beans in the garden we gathered beans. If we had extra milk or butter we helped someone who had none. We are proud of the heritage of thrift and industry we have left our children. We have tried to teach them to be good stewards of what God gives them and to help those in need.

> If any little love of mine
>   May make a life the sweeter,
> If any little care of mine
>   May make a friend's the fleeter,
> If any lift of mine may ease
>   The burden of another,
> God give me love and care and strength
>   To help my toiling brother.

Prayer: Our Father, we thank thee for giving us enough sunshine to make our pathways gay and happy. We thank thee for enough rain to make us appreciate the good days. May we fight the battle of life like brave men. In Jesus name we pray. Amen.

June 10

"A man that hath friends must show himself friendly; and there is a friend that sticketh closer than a brother."

— Proverbs 18:24

The Dinwoody family joined the church on Sunday evening. Mr. and Mrs. Lively had never seen them before but they invited them to go home with them for a period of fellowship. That was friendship in action.

A church in the far West where most of the people were far from relatives planned a church-wide Thanksgiving dinner. They became friends in action. We will find life sweeter if we seek ways to show friendship to others.

> This is no time for fear, for doubts of good,
> For broodings on the tragedies of fate.
> It is a time for songs of brotherhood,
> For hymns of joy, of man's divine estate.
> Though echoes of old wars depress the heart,
> Though greed and hate still curse men's nobler ways,

149

Though foul suspicion blasts our life apart,
It is a time for confidence and praise.
Let prophets prophecy, let poets sing,
Our dreams are not in vain. The night is past.
Together, as new hopes are wakening,
Let us proclaim, The Kingdom Comes at last!
Our Babels crash. Let selfish flags be furled.
As brothers all, we build a Friendly World.
— Thomas Curtis Clark

Prayer: Dear Father, master of all the universe, help us to show ourselves more friendly to those about us, to those who need to see religion in action. Help us ever to rely on the one friend who sticketh closer than a brother. For in the name of that wonderful friend, Jesus, we pray. Amen.

June 11

"And he saith unto them, Follow me, and I will make you fishers of men." — Matthew 4:19

A young pastor had eaten lunch with some church members. All they talked about was a fishing trip they had enjoyed lately and another they planned to take in the near future. The young preacher felt a little sorry for himself.

"I am so busy that I have not been able to go fishing in several years," he thought. "Why do I have to work so hard and they have life so easy?"

That night at the church services the minister was dressing for a baptismal service. He wore boots under his robe, to protect his clothes. Suddenly it seemed God spoke to him — "You are a fisher of men. Follow me and I will make your harvest of souls great."

With a light heart he entered the service. From then on when people talked of fishing, he thought and talked of winning the lost.

So I'll win the one next to me,
And you'll win the one next to you;
In all kinds of weather
We'll all work together,
And see what can be done.
So I'll win the one next to me,
And you'll win the one next to you;
In no time at all,
We'll win them all,
Win them, win them, one by one.

150

Prayer: Dear Father, give us power to become fishers of men. Give us courage to seek the lost. In Christ's dear name we pray. Amen.

June 12

"Whereas ye know not what shall be on the morrow. For what is life? It is even a vapor, that appeareth for a little time, and then vanisheth away." — James 4:14

The above Scripture tells us how brief life is. I John 2:17 tells us how to live forever, "And the world passeth away, and the lust thereof: but he that doeth the will of God abideth for ever."

In John 3:16 we read, "For God so loved the world that he gave his only begotten son that whosoever believeth on him might not perish but have everlasting life."

In Psalm 16:11 we find that joy in Christ is everlasting, ". . . at thy right hand there are pleasures forevermore."

What though my dreams break on some rock-bound shore
And leave but fragments scattered on the sands!
Shall I be grieving for them evermore,
Or shall I bind them up with eager hands,
And laugh again, and prance again . . . and keep
As souvenirs their broken wings, nor hide
Their scars, nor be afraid Fate yet may sweep
Them back to sea on some outgoing tide?

Why should one fear the vague, oncoming years
If courage speak the final, dauntless word
That puts the seal of silence on our fears?
For I can tell you this: that I have heard
A wondrous melody on Hope's last string,
Seen Winter's icy grip give way to Spring.

Prayer: Dear Lord in Heaven, make us ever mindful that thou holdest the keys to life and death. Help us to serve thee in such a way that whether we are on this earth a brief or a long time we will be prepared for the joy eternal, prepared for thy children. In the name of Christ who gave himself for us, we pray. Amen.

June 13

"And now abideth faith, hope, and love, these three; but the greatest of these is love." — I Corinthians 13:13

A woman went to a diamond mine to search for diamonds. She found a large stone. After it was polished and cut she had something very valuable.

If the woman had not gone and searched for the diamond she would never have found it. If she had not shared her profits with the owners of the mine she could not have taken the stone away.

Love is like the diamonds in the mine. Love must be searched for. Love must be earned. Love must be polished and kept pure and shining. Love must be shared.

> Love thyself last. Look near, behold thy duty
>> To those who walk beside thee down life's road;
> Make glad their days by little acts of beauty,
>> And help them bear the burden of earth's load.
>
> Love thyself last, and thou shalt grow in spirit
>> To see, to hear, to know, and understand.
> The message of the stars, lo, thou shalt hear it,
>> And all God's joys shall be at thy command.
>
> — Ella Wheeler Wilcox

Prayer: O God, today help us to go forth to share love and kindness with those about us. Kindle high and holy purposes in our hearts. Teach us to love those about us. We ask in the name of one who loved more than any other, Christ our Saviour. Amen.

June 14

"For as the body without the spirit is dead, so faith without works is dead also." — James 2:26

My friend down the street called me on a very cold day: "Could you possibly come and stay with my children for about thirty minutes? I have to run to the school and pick up the older ones."

I was very busy but I loved my friend. And I knew the sudden Norther made it dangerous for little folks to walk far.

The baby was asleep but the four-year-old was very much awake. He brought some of his story books for me to read. We had a lovely time reading, and soon his mother returned.

> He stopped to pat a small dog's head,
> A little thing to do;
> And yet, the dog, remembering,
> Was glad the whole day through.

152

He gave a rose into the hand
Of one who loved it much;
'Twas just a rose — but, oh, the joy
That lay in its soft touch.

He spoke a word so tenderly —
A word's a wee small thing;
And yet, it stirred a weary heart
To hope again, and sing.

— Louis Snelling

Prayer: Our Father, the one to whom we turn in all our trials and problems, we ask thee to make us more aware of the ones around us who are in need of little acts of kindness. For the sake of Christ we pray. Amen.

June 15

"And they said one to another, Behold, this dreamer cometh."
— Genesis 37:19

". . . and your young men shall see visions, and your old men shall dream dreams." — Acts 2:17b

Joseph is the dreamer mentioned in the first verse. Joseph kept himself pure in order to serve God and he lived in hope that some day his dreams would come true. All young people should keep their hearts and bodies pure so that when the time comes for their dreams to come true, they will be worthy and prepared.

My home must have a high tree
Above its open gate,
My home must have a garden
Where little dreamings wait,
My home must have a wide view
Of field and meadow fair,
Of distant hill, of open sky,
With sunlight everywhere.

My home must have a friendship
With every happy thing,
My home must offer comfort
For any sorrowing,
And every heart that enters
Shall hear its music there,
And find some simple beauty,
That every life may share.

153

My home must have its mother,
May I grow sweet and wise.
My home must have its father
With honor in his eyes.
My home must have its children;
God grant the parents grace,
To keep our home through all the years,
A kindly, happy place.

Prayer: God, give us Christian homes. May we be willing to dedicate them to thee. In the name of Christ. Amen.

June 16

"Behold, the Lord's hand is not shortened, that it cannot save."
— Isaiah 59:1

"And the hand of the Lord was with them: and a great number believed, and turned unto the Lord." — Acts 11:21

'Twas battered, scarred, and the auctioneer
Thought it scarcely worth his while
To waste his time on the old violin;
But he held it up with a smile:
"What am I bidden, good people," he cried,
"Who'll start the bidding for me?"

A dollar, a dollar, now two. Only two?
Two dollars, and who'll make it three?
Three dollars once, three dollars twice — going for three?"
But no! from the room far back a grey-haired man
Came forward and picked up the bow.
Then wiping the dust from the old violin
And tightening up the strings,
He played a melody pure and sweet —
As sweet as an angel sings.
The music ceased; and the auctioneer,
With a voice that was quiet and low,
Said, "What am I bid for the old violin?"

And he held it up with the bow.
"A thousand dollars? And who'll make it two?
Two thousand! And who'll make it three?
Three thousand once, three thousand twice,
And going — and gone," said he.
The people cheered, but some of them cried,

154

"We don't quite understand — what changed its worth?"
Swift came the reply: "The touch of a master's hand."
And many a man with life out of tune
And battered and torn with sin,
Is auctioned cheap to a thoughtless crowd,
Much like the old violin.
A mess of pottage, a glass of wine,
A game, and he travels on —
He is going once, and going twice, he's going,and almost gone.
But the Master comes, and the foolish crowd
Never can quite understand
The worth of a soul, and the change that's wrought
By the touch of the Master's hand.

Prayer: Touch our lives with thy healing hand. Amen.

June 17

"They that seek the Lord shall not want any good thing."

— Psalm 34:10

Christian fathers want good things for their families. Since goodness comes from God, fathers must first seek God if they are to obtain true goodness for their families.

There is an appointed way to reach the Lord. Jesus said, "I am the way, the truth and the light."

When a man seeks to live in God's will, all the blessings he needs will be poured out upon him and his children.

God give us men! A time like this demands
Strong minds, great hearts, true faith, and ready hands;
Men whom the lust of office does not kill;
Men whom the spoils of office cannot buy;
Men who possess opinions and a will;
Men who have honor; men who will not lie;
Men who can stand before a demagogue
And damn his treacherous flatteries without winking;
Tall men, sun-crowned, who live above the fog
In public duty and in private thinking;
For while the rabble with their thumb-worn creeds,
Their large profession and their little deeds,
Mingle in selfish strife, Lo! Freedom weeps,
Wrong rules the land, and waiting justice sleeps.

— J. G. Holland

155

Prayer: Grant the fathers of our day the feel of thy guiding hand upon their lives. May they hear thy voice even amid the tumult of daily work and care. Help the fathers of our land to awake to their sense of responsibility. In the name of Jesus our Saviour we pray. Amen.

June 18

"Having your conversation honest among the Gentiles: that, whereas they speak against you as evildoers, they may by your good works, which they shall behold, glorify God in the day of visitation." — I Peter 2:12

Carrol called her friend on the phone and said some ugly things to her because she had the mistaken idea her friend had talked about her. So their friendship came to an end.

> If you were busy being kind
> Before you knew it you would find
> You'd soon forget to think 'twas true
> That someone was unkind to you.
>
> If you were busy being glad
> And cheering people who are sad,
> Although your heart might ache a bit,
> You'd soon forget to notice it.
>
> If you were busy being good
> And doing just the best you could
> You'd not have time to blame some man
> Who's doing just the best he can.
>
> If you were busy being true
> To what you know you ought to do,
> You'd be so busy you'd forget
> The blunders of the folks you've met.
>
> If you were busy being right
> You'd find yourslf too busy quite
> To criticise your neighbor long
> Because he's busy doing wrong.

Prayer: Our Father, as we come before thee, help us to put aside the tendency to criticize others. Let the sunshine of thy love and kindness be reflected in our dealings with others. For the sake of Jesus Christ we pray. Amen.

156

June 19

"That he would grant you, according to the riches of his glory, to be strengthened with might by his Spirit in the inner man; That Christ may dwell in your hearts by faith.

— Ephesians 3:16, 17

A wise man said, "Personality has the power to open many doors — but only character can keep them open."

I once knew a man who had a great talent for speaking in public. But — within he was like a raging torrent. If the speaker before him ran as much as a minute over his allotted time, he began to fume. If someone failed to bow and scrape to him as he walked to the platform he would become very angry. In no way did he show the inner peace that God expects Christians to have.

> A man's a man who, knowing life is meant
> For work, for work's own sake works on, content.
> His head and hands, his heart's behest obey,
> True as the sun and faithful as the day.
> His task engages all he is or can,
> And in its joy he feels himself — a man!
> What'er his work, it is his only pride
> To scant no measure and no weakness hide.
> He hails as "Master"! Him and Him alone.
> By whose achievements better grow his own.
> A man's a man, and may, by self-control
> And by his worth to Man, become — a useful soul.

Prayer: Father of all mankind, make us realize we need the inner peace given only by thee. Help us to serve others and in so doing to serve thee. In the name of one who gave his life for us, Jesus Christ, we pray. Amen.

June 20

"So teach us to number our days, that we may apply our hearts unto wisdom." — Psalm 90:12

One time we were all packed and ready to leave for our vacation.

"Just a few more moments while I run out to the hospital and make a last visit to one of our members," said my husband.

A boy driving too fast ran into our car at an intersection. The car was almost a total wreck but my husband was not seriously hurt.

This experience made us stop and think. This might have been my husband's last hour on earth. Any hour, any minute, may be our last hour or minute.

So — let us number our days, and apply our hearts to wisdom.
'Tis not for man to trifle! Life is brief,
    And sin is here.
Our age is but the falling of a leaf,
    A dropping tear.
We have no time to sport away the hours,
All must be earnest in a world like ours.

Not many lives, but only one have we —
    One, only one;
How sacred should that one life ever be —
    That narrow span!
Day after day filled up with blessed toil,
Hour after hour still bringing in new spoil.

                    — Horatius Bonar

Prayer: Dear Father, bless us when we have periods of waiting Illumine the spirits of thy people with thy love. Help us always to know thy will is best. In the name of Christ. Amen.

June 21

"And he said unto them, How is it that ye sought me? wist ye not that I must be about my Father's business?" — Luke 2:49
"Not slothful in business; fervent in spirit; serving the Lord." — Romans 12:11

Men dream about the time when their sons will enter the business world. God's son also had a business to enter. It was the business of establishing the kingdom of heaven on earth.

If you would be happy in the business world there are a few basic rules to follow. Jesus followed all of them.

Forget yourself and put your best into the job.
Keep an open-mind and be tolerant of others.
Serve others sincerely.
Learn to be practical.
Love your work and think of it as important.
Be true to lofty ideals.
Learn something daily.
Be enthusiastic.

Never forget that you are a child of the King and give your allegiance to Him first.

158

Prayer: Our Father, who guides our steps each day, as we go about our daily work help us to say as David of old: "I will lift up mine eyes unto the hills, from whence cometh my help." In the name of the giver of all help. Amen.

June 22

"For man also knoweth not his time: as the fishes that are taken in an evil net, and as the birds that are caught in the snare; so are the sons of men snared in an evil time, when it falleth suddenly upon them." — Ecclesiastes 9:12

This is the longest day in the year. All the days before are a fraction or more shorter and all the days after will be a fraction or more shorter. We should make every day count for good. There is a time in all our lives when we realize that with the passing of each day our life is growing shorter.

Some people fall into the evil net of saying, "It is too late for me to accomplish anything in life." It will be too late only if we let it be. We should keep trying.

I wrote my first book after I was fifty years old. Often I made mistakes typing by the hunt and pound method. Often I would have liked just to lie down and read a good story. Accomplishments are never gained if we get caught in the net of laziness. Today may be the longest day of your life. Seek to use it well.

> Let us then be up and doing,
> With a heart for any fate;
> Still achieving, still pursuing,
> Learn to labor and to wait.
>
> — Longfellow

Prayer: Give us this day, dear Father, the courage to do our best, whatever the task may be. Give us a vision of the lost, needy world and a desire to tell them of Christ. For it is in his name we pray. Amen.

June 23

"Thou art my rock and my fortress; therefore for thy name's sake lead me, and guide me." — Psalm 31:3

There are all kinds of pebbles in the world. There are smooth round ones, and jagged sharp ones broken from larger rocks. They may be found almost any place. Some pebbles may be rubbed and polished; some make nice walks to keep our feet dry. Some are used to mix with cement and make buildings and foundations.

For the Christian there is The Rock, Christ Jesus. What a blessing! What a comfort!

> O sometimes the shadows are deep,
>   And rough seems the path to the goal,
> And sorrows, sometimes how they sweep
>   Like tempests down over the soul!
>
> O sometimes how long seems the day,
>   And sometimes how weary my feet;
> But toiling in life's dusty way,
>   The Rock's blessed shadow, how sweet!
>
> O near to the Rock let me keep,
>   If blessings or sorrows prevail;
> Or climbing the mountain way steep,
>   Or walking the shadowy vale.
>
> Oh then to the Rock let me fly,
>   To the Rock that is higher than I;
>
> — E. Johnson

Prayer: Father, Rock of our salvation, guide and lead us in the paths of right. For Christ's sake we pray. Amen.

June 24

"But God said unto him, Thou fool, this night thy soul shall be required of thee: then whose shall those things be, which thou hast provided?"

"So is he that layeth up treasures for himself, and is not rich toward God." — Luke 12:20, 21

We see the truth of the above text illustrated in our country today. America is a rich nation. More people have comfortable homes and plenty of food and luxuries than ever before. Yet our people are unhappy, restless and dissatisfied. As a result our nation is filled with crime. People are afraid to walk on the streets alone at night. Even in the daytime some heinous crimes are committed. What has gone wrong? We have forgotten God and turned to self-indulgence. Those who seek to lay up treasures for themselves are losing their souls. How tragic!

Here lies a miser
Who lived for himself,
    Winter and Summer, gathering pelf;
Now where he is and how he fares,
    Nobody knows and nobody cares.
                    — Found on a tombstone

Prayer: Help us, O God, to put away any sin or possession that would keep us from serving thee. For Christ's sake we pray. Amen.

June 25

"For he saith, At an acceptable time I hearkened unto thee, and in a day of salvation did I succor thee: behold, now is the acceptable time; behold, now is the day of salvation."
                    — II Corinthians 6:1, 2

When my husband was a boy living on a farm, one of his chores was to get in wood and kindling at night. One morning when his father arose to make the fire, there was no wood and no kindling. The tired boy had forgotten. His father crawled back into his warm bed and called to the son to get up. How cold and dark it was trying to find the wood and kindling in the morning!

"Daddy I didn't mean to forget."

"You didn't mean not to forget either," his father replied.

Many are putting off salvation until a better time. Many will let the time pass and be too late.

    There is a tide in the affairs of men,
        Which, taken at the flood, leads on to fortune;
    Omitted, all the voyage of their life
        Is bound in shallows and in miseries.
                    — Shakespeare

Prayer: Lord of all mankind, ruler of our universe, we ask thee today to give us an urgency in the affairs of the heart. May we trust thee and prepare for the tomorrow of eternity. For the sake of Jesus Christ we pray. Amen.

June 26

"And the Spirit and the bride say, Come. And let him that heareth say, Come. And let him that is athirst come. And whosoever will, let him take the water of life freely."
                    — Revelation 22:17

161

One summer I picked cotton on a farm in Texas. I weighed less than a hundred pounds and I hated the sun. But I needed the clothes I could buy with the money. Those were the longest rows in the world! I would get so thirsty during the long afternoon. One day when we were just about to finish a bale, the farmer's wife came to the field, and brought some cold lemonade. How refreshing it was!

We are often thirsty and tired in this life. Christ offers us the refreshing water of life, freely.

> High in the Father's house above
> My mansion is prepared;
> There is the home, the rest I love.
> And there my bright reward.
>
> With Him I live, in spotless white,
> In glory I shall shine;
> His blissful presence my delight,
> His love and glory mine.
>
> All taint of sin shall be removed,
> All evil done away;
> And I shall dwell with God's Beloved
> Through God's eternal day.

Prayer: Our Father, who sits upon the throne, help us to be prepared for the day when thou shalt come to make all things new. In the name of Christ we pray. Amen.

June 27

"And above all things have fervent charity among yourselves; for charity shall cover the multitude of sins." — I Peter 4:8

In my Mission Society meeting an appeal was read from a college student for help. He wanted empty cartons, pretty bottles, crayons. He was working in the very poorest part of town and he wanted to help the children make Christmas gifts out of our discarded things. At the very bottom of his letter he stated, "It would be so nice if we could have enough money to buy each child an apple."

Almost everyone in the meeting put in a generous offering toward purchase of the apples. We could enjoy our own feast if we had helped those children have a little treat.

I gave my life for thee, My precious blood I shed,
That thou might'st ransomed be. And quickened from the dead;
I gave my life for thee, what hast thou given for me?

162

My Father's house of light, My glory circled throne,
I left for earthly night, For wanderings sad and lone;
I left it all for thee, Hast thou left aught for me?

I suffered much for thee, more than thy tongue can tell,
Of bitterest agony, To rescue thee from hell;
I've borne it all for thee, What hast thou born for me?

And I have brought to thee, Down from my home above,
Salvation full and free, My pardon and my love;
I bring rich gifts to thee, What hast thou brought to me?

— Frances Havergal

Prayer: O God, the Father of lights, from whom cometh every good and perfect gift, help us to be generous to those less fortunate than ourselves. For the sake of Christ our Saviour we pray. Amen.

June 28

"Their heart is divided; now shall they be found faulty."

— Hosea 10:2

When someone is having serious physical trouble we rush him to the doctor or give first aid ourselves, if possible.

What can we do when someone has a divided heart? If we say we trust Christ, yet are trying to rely on ourselves for salvation, we have a divided heart. If we are trying to serve God and mammon, we have a divided heart.

We can render first aid to our hearts by depending on Christ solely for our redemption, by serving him with our whole heart.

The dark stream of evil is flowing apace;
Awake, and be doing, ye children of grace,
Let's seek with compassion the souls that are lost,
Well knowing the price their redemption has cost.
While singing with rapture the Saviour's great love,
And waiting for Him to translate us above —
"It may be tomorrow, or even tonight" —
Let our loins be well girded, and lamps burning bright.

Prayer: Help us O God, to give thee our whole heart. To serve thee in such a way that others will see our example and follow. Let us shake off the sloth of worldly ease and self-indulgence. We pray for the sake of Jesus Christ. Amen.

June 29

"My grace is sufficient for thee; for my strength is made perfect in weakness." — II Corinthians 12:9

We heard a child scream and rushed out of the house. A strange dog had wandered into the yard and was tumbling our two-year-old daughter on the ground. We did not think of ourselves for a single moment. We rushed to the child and rescued her. We had the strength of ten as we pushed that dog away.

Our Heavenly Father hears when his children call and is quick to answer and protect us from evil.

> If grace were bought, I could not buy;
> If grace were coined, no wealth have I;
> By grace alone I draw my breath,
> Held up from everlasting death;
> Yet, since I know His grace is free,
> I know the Saviour died for me.
>
> — George W. Bethune

Prayer: Dear Father, help us to remember today that God never forgets his children. No matter how rough the road, help us to remember to trust in the dark hour. We are grateful for thy grace and strength. In the name of Christ we pray. Amen.

June 30

"Go ye therefore, and teach all nations, baptizing them in the name of the Father, and of the Son, and of the Holy Ghost."

> — Matthew 28:19

The world grows smaller each year. With jet airliners we can travel farther in a day than most of our parents traveled in a lifetime. Yet Christ's great commission is still in effect today. We are still obligated to go and tell the story.

> If ever Jesus has need of me,
>   Somewhere in the fields of sin,
> I'll go where the darkest places be,
>   And let the sunshine in;
>
> I'll be content with the lowliest place,
>   To earth's remotest rim,
> I know I'll see his smiling face,
>   If it's done with a thought of Him.

The lowliest deed will be reckoned great
  In the book that the angels keep,
If it helps another along the road
  That is often rough and steep.

A kindly word may let sunshine in,
  Where life's rays are sadly dim;
And love can win a soul for God
  If it's done with a thought of Him.

— Chas. H. Gabriel

Prayer: Dear Father, give us more zeal to labor in thy vineyard. Give us more strength in daily prayer to go out seeking the lost in this world. May we make an earnest effort today to witness for thee. For we ask in the name of our Lord and Saviour Jesus Christ. Amen.

July:

Our Country So Dear

July 1

"But they that wait upon the Lord shall renew their strength; they shall mount up with wings as eagles; they shall run and not be weary; and they shall walk, and not faint." — Isaiah 40:31

How we look forward to our vacation time in the summer! We need a time away from our daily work — a time of getting a new perspective on life. When we have been away from work a few days we usually go back with renewed zeal and energy.

We should never take a vacation from God. We just should look for him in different places. He is always there to renew and strengthen us.

> July is a grand old month:
> The time to go a-fishing,
> Time to lazy in the shade
> And spend much thought in wishing!
> It is the time to day-dream
> For you simply cannot work
> When all your thoughts are on the
> Spot where bass or crappie lurk!
>
> But when the month is over,
> And vacation-time is through,
> You find this trip of make-believe
> Has renewed youth in you,
> For if you'd really left your
> Work, and gone to catch that fish
> The chiggers and mosquitoes
> Would have made you their main dish!
> — Jewel Alice McLeod

Prayer: Our Father, help us to use our vacation time well. May we ever be mindful that there is no vacation from sin in the world. May we remember we are thy representatives wherever we may be and may we always act as Christians should. We ask in the name of Christ our Saviour. Amen.

July 2

"Thy word have I hid in my heart, that I might not sin against thee." — Psalm 119:11

A wise sage has said: "If we would have the Bible in the heart we must first put it in the head."

Not long ago a four-year-old girl came to visit me. She asked me to be quiet so she could say the "Lord's Prayer." She had a queer way of pronouncing some of the longer words but she could repeat all the verses. Her baby sitter had taught her the words each afternoon when she put her to bed for her nap.

Another home I know well practices repeating verses of Scripture before the evening meal. The children are proud of the passages they have learned in this way.

In a Sunday School class we sing the following verse.

> I am so glad that our Father in heaven
> Tells of His love in the Book He has giv'n,
> Wonderful things in the Bible I see;
> This is the dearest, that Jesus loves me.

> I am so glad that Jesus loves me,
> Jesus loves me, Jesus loves me;
> I am so glad that Jesus loves me,
> Jesus loves even me.

Prayer: Help us this day, O God, to determine to hide thy words in our hearts — to make plans to share thy word with others — to live by the teachings found in thy Holy Book. We thank thee for the comfort and peace we find in reading the Bible. We pray in Jesus' name. Amen.

July 3

"Preaching the kingdom of God, and teaching those things which concern the Lord Jesus Christ, with all confidence, no man forbidding him." — Acts 28:31

Paul had so much concern for the spread of the gospel that he suffered many things in order to spread the word. My favorite missionary is Adoniram Judson, an early-day missionary in Burma. Hardships seemed to be the only lot of the poor man, yet he would not give up. He was possessed with a burning desire to translate some of the New Testament into the language of the Burmese — a desire which almost caused him to lose his life. He had to spend many days in prison. In spite of all Adoniram's hardships, other young men in America, seeing his example, went to become missionaries also. They did not look at the hardships but rather kept their eyes on the goal to be reached.

> All ye saints of light proclaim,
> Jesus the light of the world;
> Life and mercy in His name,
> Jesus the light of the world.

170

Hear the Saviour's earnest call,
    Jesus the light of the world.
Send the gospel truth to all,
    Jesus the light of the world.

We'll walk in the light, beautiful light,
    Come where the dew drops of mercy are bright;
Shine all around us by day and by night,
    Jesus the light of the world.

Prayer: Father in Heaven, help us to double our efforts to win unresponsive people to thy kingdom cause. Challenge us to spend our time showing a divine concern for the lost. In the name of Christ we pray. Amen.

July 4

"Sing unto God, sing praises to his name: extol him that rideth upon the heavens by his name JAH, and rejoice before him." —Psalm 68:4

Over a century and a half ago some men met in Philadelphia. They declared the independence of our nation. The day was tense. Some of the brave statesmen made a few jests to try to ease the tension. Franklin said: "We must all hang together or we will all hang separately."

It is a time for great rejoicing and thanksgiving when a nation is free. But, there is no power to keep us free except the power of God. We may have the greatest number of weapons, and be the smartest people in the world, but we must have God on our side.

Did they finish the fight that day
    When the Liberty Bell was rung?
Did they silence the noise of war
    When Liberty's triumph was sung?
Was Freedom made sovereign indeed
    When the old bell pealed to the world
That the reign of oppression has ceased
    And the banner of freedom unfurled?
A battle has waged since the world was new;
    The battle is on, God calleth for you.

Prayer: O, Father, may we go forth to the fight in majesty today. Give us high-hearted fortitude and patience. Make us her-

171

alds of God's love. May we as Americans strive to be worthy of the fair name of our country. We pray in the name of the Prince of Peace, Jesus Christ. Amen.

July 5

"But let him that glorieth glory in this, that he understandeth and knoweth me, that I am the Lord which exercise lovingkindness, judgment, and righteousness, in the earth: for in these things I delight, saith the Lord." — Jeremiah 9:24

We had been traveling since early morning. Then we came to the Sunset Crater in Arizona. The road leading to the parking area is very restful and relaxing. When we were parked it seemed so good to get out and walk. We noticed a path leading up the side of the crater. Being in need of exercise we started walking, and the higher we went the more exciting the view became. We turned back before we reached the top. When we were back at the car we took stock. Our feet and legs were black from the dust of the burned lava which made up the path we had climbed. In our excitement we had not noticed what was happening to us.

Often in the excitement of some worldly pleasure we fail to notice its effect upon us until we are hopelessly soiled and defiled.

> O work thy works in God.
> He can rejoice in naught
> Save only in himself
> And what himself hath wrought.

Prayer: Dear Lord, our Master, we love thee and long to serve thee in the very best way. Draw us unto thyself. Take away from our lives the filth and grime of the sins of this world. Just for Jesus' sake we pray. Amen.

July 6

"Come unto me, all ye that labor and are heavy laden, and I will give you rest." — Matthew 11:28

"But no one has asked me," we hear sometimes. Do we always have to be asked? Can't we volunteer? So many church members grow dull and cross complaining that they are not asked to do things. They should find a need and volunteer.

Sally was very angry with her best friend. She felt left out

172

of a project on which her class was working. Sally felt her friend should have insisted that she help.

Mother was ashamed of Sally. That night she put a large platter of fried chicken right in front of Sally's plate. As soon as the blessing had been asked, Sally took her favorite piece off the top of the platter.

"Why Sally, you didn't wait for me to beg you to take some chicken," said Mother.

"Mommie, you know I don't have to be asked to take fried chicken," Sally laughed.

"You shouldn't have to be asked to help your class either," said Mother.

Sally got the point. Did you?

Prayer: Our Father, help us as thy children to volunteer to serve in places of need. May we not neglect the gift that is within us. This life is ours; help us to use it aright. We ask this in the name of the giver of life, Christ our Lord. Amen.

July 7

"Finally, brethren, whatsoever things are true, whatsoever things are honest, whatsoever things are just, whatsoever things are pure, whatsoever things are of good report; if there be any virtue, and if there be any praise, think on these things."
— Philippians 4:8

We must control our time, our activities, our thoughts.

"Why do you always keep your little dog on a leash?" I asked a neighbor child.

"Oh, if I didn't he would run away."

God knows our human weakness. So he warns us to keep our thoughts on the best things. God knows we would stray away from him if he gave us perfect freedom.

> Keep to the right, within and without,
>   With stranger and pilgrim and friend;
> Keep to the right and you need have no doubt
>   That all will be well in the end.
>
> Keep to the right in whatever you do,
>   Nor claim but your own on the way;
> Keep to the right, and hold on to the true,
>   From the morn to the close of life's day!

Prayer: Heavenly Father, grant us power to look upon the world and see anew the things that are holy. We have so little

173

time to spend on earth, help us make secure foundations for the life to come. Grant us the ability to see the best in our fellow man and praise him for that best. May our thoughts ever be directed toward things which will make the world a better place. We pray in the name of one who was always pure and perfect, Jesus Christ. Amen.

July 8

"Ye are the salt of the earth: but if the salt have lost his savor, wherewith shall it be salted? it is thenceforth good for nothing, but to be cast out, and to be trodden under foot of men."

— Matthew 5:13

Jesus gave us a task to perform, the task of spreading the gospel. He described Christians as salt and as light to spread the gospel and make the earth a better place.

Tell it out among the nations that the Lord is King;
Tell it out! Tell it out!
Tell it out among the nations, bid them shout and sing;
Tell it out! Tell it out!
Tell it out with adoration that He shall increase,
That the mighty King of glory is the King of Peace;
Tell it out with jubilation, let the song ne'er cease;
Tell it out! Tell it out!

— Frances R. Havergal

Prayer: Help us Lord to bring the good news of salvation to those who do not know thee. Grant that we may truly be as lights in this sin-darkened world. In the name of Christ we pray. Amen.

July 9

"Forasmuch as ye know that ye were not redeemed with corruptible things, as silver and gold, from your vain conversation received by tradition from your fathers; But with the precious blood of Christ, as of a lamb without blemish and without spot."

— I Peter 1:18, 19

In the Mountain Lake Sanctuary at Lake Wales, Florida, stands the beautiful Singing Tower. The tower was erected by Edward Bok. Edward came to America as an immigrant boy from Holland. For some reason the family had lost all they possessed and were very poor. Edward determined to win back for them a place in life of which they could be proud. He worked very hard writing books, editing a paper, and making himself a useful citizen during World War I.

When people go to the lovely Bok tower to rest and meditate, they cannot help remembering the little boy who fought such a hard life of poverty and hardship, to become famous and useful.

As Americans we have many wonderful traditions handed down to us from our forefathers. We must never take them as a matter of course but ever strive to be worthy of our heritage.

Prayer: Our Father, as we think of the great men who have made our nation a wonderful place in which to live, make us grateful. Help us always to seek to uphold the traditions of fair play and honesty. Just for the sake of Jesus. Amen.

July 10

"If the Son therefore shall make you free, ye shall be free indeed." — John 8:36

As Americans we have a multitude of freedoms that many people in the world do not enjoy. We have freedom to think and say what we please. We have freedom to worship in the church of our choice. We have freedom to move about from place to place as we please. We have freedom to try new ventures — and if we fail, to get up and try again. We were given these freedoms by those who went before us.

There is no freedom quite so wonderful as the freedom we received from Christ our Saviour — freedom from the yoke of sin.

> Looking upward every day,
>   Sunshine on our faces,
> Pressing onward every day
>   Toward the heavenly places.
> Growing every day in awe,
>   For thy name is holy;
> Learning every day to love
>   With a love more lowly.

Prayer: Dear Lord, as we think so often this month of the great freedoms we enjoy, make us truly grateful for the freedom given us by the Holy Son. Help us to hold up before our family high ideals. May we fight against the evil one who would conquer our hearts. May we ever draw nearer to thee. Have compassion, O God, on our human frailties. We ask in thy holy name. Amen.

175

July 11

"For what shall it profit a man, if he shall gain the whole world, and lose his own soul?" — Mark 8:36

Often I remember a time when I was twenty-four. My husband was pastor of a very small church and he often makes more in a day now than he made in two weeks then. We were so poor that I think even the poor folks could call us poor. When I was the most discouraged I secured *The Life of Helen Keller* from the school library.

I think the babies were neglected a little while I devoured that book. When I had finished I faced the world with new courage. If one so handicapped could inspire and help others, why shouldn't I?

> They took away what should have been my eyes,
> (But I remembered Milton's Paradise)
> They took away what should have been my ears,
> (Beethoven came and wiped away my tears)
> They took away what should have been my tongue,
> (But I had talked with God when I was young).
> He would not let them take away my soul,
> Possessing that, I still possess the whole.
>
> — Helen Keller

Prayer: Dear Father, ruler of our destinies, give us always hope and courage. Help us always to remember our Bible, the symbol of hope, the direct word from thee. May we ever be mindful that the hope offered in the Holy Word transcends all human affliction with an overwhelming glory. We pray in the name of one who was all-glorious. Amen.

July 12

"These things I have spoken unto you, that in me ye might have peace. In the world ye shall have tribulation: but be of good cheer; I have overcome the world." — John 16:33

Many years ago in England, Dr. Thomas Withering watched an old gypsy woman gather some leaves from the garden and make a brew. She gave the mixture to people with swollen ankles and legs. From watching and experimenting, the medicine called digitalis was discovered. Many people with heart trouble have benefited from it.

A number of our most useful medicines and vaccines have been found by happy accidents. Penicillin was one of the greatest of these happy accidents.

We should never be too young or too old to keep alert for new discoveries and new thoughts.

> In every seed to see the flower,
> In every drop of dew
> To reverence a cloistered star
> Within the distant blue;
> To wait the promise of the bow,
> Despite the cloud between,
> Is Faith — the fervid evidence
> Of loveliness unseen.
>
> — John Banister Tabb

Prayer: Dear Father, as we bring ourselves before thee today, may we ever be ready to grow and develop into better people. May we seek the good of others and set forward thy kingdom. Inspire us with grace and truth. Help us to take advantage of every opportunity to show the fruits of the Spirit. For the sake of Jesus we ask. Amen.

July 13

"Come ye children, hearken unto me: I will teach you the fear of the Lord. What man is he that desireth life, and loveth many days, that he may see good? Keep thy tongue from evil, and thy lips from speaking guile. Depart from evil, and do good; seek peace and pursue it." — Psalm 34:11-14

The beautiful Callaway Gardens at Pine Mountain, Georgia, is a nice place to go for quiet and meditation. At first people just walked about and enjoyed the lovely flowers and shrubs. Now there is a beautiful little chapel where one can go for a quiet moment of prayer and thought.

How very many hasty words and deeds would be left unsaid and undone if people took time for meditation before speaking or acting! Find a time and place for your own private talk with God each day.

> In this hour of worship
>   Grant thy presence, Lord!
> Here, the world forgotten,
>   Feed us on thy word.
> From our sins and sorrows
>   Here we seek release;
> Of thy love persuaded
>   Find the path of peace.

177

Prayer: Let the meditations of our hearts and the words of our mouths be acceptable in thy sight, O Lord, we pray. With reverent hopeful hearts help us to seek to know more of thy will in our lives. We ask these favors in the name of Christ our Redeemer. Amen.

July 14

"Bless the Lord God of Israel from everlasting to everlasting; and let all the people say, Amen, Praise ye the Lord."
— Psalm 106:48

It was Tom's first week at college and he was anxious to make friends. As he met new boys and girls he tried to remember the advice of his parents: "If you meet young people who are proud of their home town, church and family, they are usually worthy of friendship."

Tom was shocked at how many of his new acquaintances made fun of their home towns and wanted to be big shots.

One day as Tom walked across the campus he was homesick. Another boy fell in step beside him, "I wish you could see the trees in my home town this time of year."

"Are they large?" Tom asked.

"No," replied the boy. "The trees in our town do not grow too large because of the scaricty of rainfall. But I like them and miss them."

The two boys were soon fast friends and each told the other good points about their homes.

> Since we deserve the name of friends,
> And thine effect so lives in me,
> A part of mine may live in thee
> And move thee on to nobler ends.

> — Tennyson

Prayer: Teach us, dear Father, the responsibility of being good citizens of our communities. Cause us to remember that others worked and toiled that we might have the blessings we now enjoy. Make us grateful. In the name of one whose presence will bless, Jesus Christ. Amen.

July 15

"Thou, which hast showed me great and sore troubles, shalt quicken me again, and shalt bring me up again from the depths of the earth." — Psalm 71:20

178

There are so many wonderful things in life that we must focus on a few and make the most of them. To make sure that we focus on the right things for our lives we must first seek the leadership of the Lord. Then we must read and study about the opportunities that the world affords. Twenty-five years ago we would have laughed anyone out of the room if they had said they wanted to fly around in space. We now have many more ways of finding the things on which people can focus their lives.

We should never think we are too smart to use the example of other people's past experience.

> I would be true, for there are those who trust me;
> I would be pure, for there are those who care;
> I would be strong, for there is much to suffer;
> I would be brave for there is much to dare.
>
> I would be friends of all — the foe, the friendless;
> I would be giving and forget the gift;
> I would be humble, for I know my weakness;
> I would look up — and laugh — and love — and lift.

Prayer: Our Father, help us to have a spirit of trust and love as we choose a focus for our lives. Help us to be teachable. We thank you for parents, teachers, friends and pastors who through our life have helped us to know right from wrong. We ask in Christ's name. Amen.

July 16

"And he said unto them, Whose is this image and superscription? They say unto him, Caesar's. Then saith he unto them, Render therefore unto Caesar the things which are Caesar's and unto God the things that are God's." — Matthew 22:20, 21

As Christians we are citizens of two worlds. We are indeed citizens of the present world. We usually live in a specific town, county, state, and nation. We owe to the government our loyalty and taxes.

But we are also citizens of the Kingdom of God. We are God's representatives here on earth. Often we have to stand against the crowd to uphold our beliefs for both our nation and our Heavenly Kingdom. As we spread the Kingdom of God we also help make our earthly world a better place in which to live.

> God only is the creature's home,
>   Though rough and straight the road:
> Yet nothing less can satisfy
>   The love that longs for God.

179

How little of that road, my soul,
  How little hast thou gone!
Take heart, and let the thought of God
  Allure thee further on.

— F. W. Faber

Prayer: Father of all nations, help us to be good citizens of both our worlds. We would work to make our nation strong. Help us always to seek to bring in thy Kingdom. May we realize we are an example to others and be just the kind of example you would have us to be. We ask in the name of Jesus Christ. Amen.

July 17

"He saved others; himself he cannot save. If he be the King of Israel, let him now come down from the cross, and we will believe him." — Matthew 27:42

"And when he had thus spoken, he showed them his hands and his feet." — Luke 24:40

Sitting next to a friend in church I noticed that even through her gloves large mishapen knots showed on her hands. The ugly mishaped hands did not look bad to me because I knew my friend was the cook for a large hospital. She cooked and also supervised the kitchen by day; at night she cared for an invalid mother. Her hands were hands dedicated to love.

Christ could have remained in heaven, but he chose to come to earth. He accepted the horror and shame of the cross for others — for us who are so unworthy.

Have you failed in your plan of your storm-tossed life?
Place your hand in the nail-scarred hand;
Are you weary and worn from its toil and strife?
Place your hand in the nail-scarred hand.

Are you walking alone through the shadows dim?
Place your hand in the nail-scarred hand;
Christ will comfort your heart, put your trust in Him,
Place your hand in the nail-scarred hand.

Is your soul burdened down with its load of sin?
Place your hand in the nail-scarred hand;
Throw your heart open wide, let the Savior in,
Place your hand in the nail-scarred hand.

180

Prayer: Dear Lord, help us ever to be aware that if we want to be happy we must place our hands in the hands of Christ. Make us willing to use our own hands to help others. We pray in the name of Jesus our Lord. Amen.

July 18

"The fear of the Lord is clean, enduring forever: the judgments of the Lord are true, and righteous altogether. More to be desired are they than gold, yea, than much fine gold: sweeter also than honey and the honeycomb." — Psalm 19:9, 10

Alfred was a big, strong boy and people often imposed on him. All year he had arrived at school early and helped the teacher get ready for the day. At the close of the school year the teacher gave out some small prizes to different pupils. She forgot to give one to Alfred. He felt discouraged, and decided he would just sleep later next year and not help.

When all the pupils assembled for the final chapel, the principal presented some awards. He called Alfred's name.

"For being the most co-operative and helpful boy."

Alfred was glad that even if the teacher hadn't noticed his helpfulness, the principal had.

> If thou hast thrown a glorious thought
> Upon life's common ways,
> Should other men the gain have caught,
> Fret not to lose the praise.
>
> Accept the lesson — look not for
> Reward. From out thee chase
> All selfish ends — and ask no more
> Than to fulfil thy place.

Prayer: Our Father, may we be ever mindful that we work on earth for the good of mankind. If we feel left out and forgotten, help us always to remember that thou art the one who judges our actions, our deeds and our works. Help us to be unselfish. We ask for the sake of Christ. Amen.

July 19

"Do all things without murmurings and disputings: That ye may be blameless and harmless, the sons of God, without rebuke, in the midst of a crooked and perverse nation, among whom ye shine as lights in the world." — Philippians 2:14, 15

How we love to see a child who will go and perform his assigned tasks without murmuring or disputing. We say to ourselves, "What a nice child that is!"

Our Heavenly Father likes to see his children obey without complaint also.

> Some murmur when their sky is clear
>   And wholly brought to view,
> If one small speck of dark appear
>   In their great heaven of blue;
> And some with thankful love are filled
>   If but one streak of light,
> One ray of God's good mercy, gild
>   The darkness of their night.
>
> In palaces are hearts that ask,
>   In discontent and pride,
> Why life is such a dreary task,
>   And all good things denied.
> And hearts in poorest huts admire
>   How love has in their aid
> (Love that never seems to tire)
>   Such rich provision made.

Prayer: Our Father, who art so good to us, who each day gives us life and love and happiness, help us to banish discontent from our lives. May we ever sing a song of praise to thee. May we shine as the light of the world when we seek to tell others of thy great love. We ask in the name of Christ. Amen.

July 20

"Favor is deceitful, and beauty is vain: but a woman that feareth the Lord, she shall be praised." — Proverbs 31:30

When I was a little girl I liked to go to my grandmother's farm. My favorite pastime there was taking a pan of corn and coaxing the chickens to follow me. I would throw out just enough corn to make them follow me to a pen. Then I would put some corn in the pen and shut the door as quickly as I could. The chicken who was caught in the pen sometimes ended up in the frying pan. Sometimes I would enjoy the chicken as a pet for a while.

Sin allures us in just such deceitful ways. We are sure we are to get a nice reward, and suddenly we are caught in a net that does us harm — and sometimes destroys us.

182

Lead us, O Father, in the paths of right;
Blindly we stumble when we walk alone,
Involved in shadows of a darksome night,
Only with Thee we journey safely on.

Lead us, O Father, to Thy heavenly rest,
However rough and steep the path may be,
Through joy or sorrow, as Thou deemest best,
Until our lives are perfected in Thee.

— W. H. Burleigh

Prayer: Our Father, the origin of all truth and reason, make our lives with thee like songs sung in gladness and joy. Use us as instruments to allure people to follow thee. We ask in the name of Jesus Christ our Lord. Amen.

July 21

"He that goeth about as a talebearer revealeth secrets: therefore meddle not with him that flattereth with his lips."

— Proverbs 20:19

Susie was talking to her close friend. The friend, burdened with worry, revealed to her that she was about to secure a certain position. In a few hours Susie was with another companion and revealed her friend's hope of securing the position. But she had revealed the fact to a false friend! In a few hours word had gone all around the little town. The man who had been about to hire Susie's friend decided something must be wrong, or so many people would not be talking about it.

Susie lost a friend, for never again would her friend speak to her. The friend lost the position and had to move to another city to find work. All this happened because someone was a tale-bearer.

He that shall rail against his absent friends,
Or hears them scandalized, and not defends,
Sports with their fame, and speaks what'er he can,
And only to be thought a witty man.
Tells tales, and brings his friends in disesteem,
That man's a knave, — be sure beware of him.

— Horace

Prayer: Father, make us aware of people with flattering lips. Help us to speak the truth and seek to build up all we know by kind words and loving deeds. We ask in the name of Christ. Amen.

183

July 22

"Look down from heaven, and behold from the habitation of thy holiness and of thy glory: where is thy zeal and thy strength, the sounding of thy bowels and of thy mercies toward me? are they restrained?" — Isaiah 63:15

A minister who was growing old was admonished by his children to stop preaching so hard. His reply to them was, "I cannot rest while souls are lost in sin. I will have all eternity to rest in."

We should have zeal for our daily living. We should have zeal for winning the lost. We too can rest in eternity, and think of the reward for winning a soul to Christ.

> Lead me to some soul today,
> Oh, teach me, Lord, just what to say;
> Friends of mine are lost in sin,
> And cannot find their way.
>
> Few there are who seem to care,
> And few there are who pray;
> Melt my heart and fill my life,
> Give me one soul today.
>
> — Will H. Houghton

Prayer: Almighty Father, keep us true to our best selves. Protect those we love today. Make us considerate of those about us and give us courage to witness to others of thy saving grace. We ask in the name of Jesus our Saviour. Amen.

July 23

"Let us not be weary in well doing: for in due season we shall reap, if we faint not." — Galatians 6:9

When her mother left to run some errands, Evelyn enthusiastically started to clean her room and get ready for company the next day. In about an hour she became tired and a little lonely. It would be nice just to telephone her friend Betty and chat for a few minutes.

When mother returned at noon Evelyn and Betty were still talking and laughing on the phone.

"But Evelyn, I depended on you to get the work done before our company came," exclaimed Mother.

Sometimes when we grow weary and think we are the only ones working for God we are tempted to stop and just waste a few days.

184

I am only one,
But still I am one.
I cannot do everything,
But still I can do something;
And because I can not do everything,
I will not refuse to do the something
that I can do.

— Edward Everett Hale

Prayer: O God, our Father, search our hearts today. Fill us with a desire to be sincere and truthful. May we worship thee with our whole heart. Give us a spirit of patience. May we ever be loyal in our service for thee. We ask in the name of our Saviour, Jesus Christ. Amen.

July 24

"For as the body is one, and hath many members, and all the members of that one body, being many, are one body: so also is Christ." — I Corinthians 12:12

Leroy, an only child, was a member of the band. He played the clarinet very well. His mother thought him superior to all the other band members; so she was constantly going to the director and asking for Leroy to be given a solo part. The band director became very annoyed with the mother. He could not think of a way to show her that the band must work as a group, not as individuals.

Finally there came a day when the town was having a celebration and the band was going to march. The director talked with Leroy and they formed a plan.

As the fond mother stood on the curb watching for the band to come by she was amazed to see no sign of her darling child. Then after all the others had gone by, Leroy walked down the street all alone, blowing a sad little tune on his horn. The mother was so angry she rushed to the band director and was about to tear him apart.

"Isn't that what you wanted?" he asked her, "your child carrying on alone?"

Prayer: O Lord, may we be willing to be a part of thy kingdom. May we work with others to make the whole more perfect. We pray for Christ's sake. Amen.

July 25

"I beseech you therefore, brethren, by the mercies of God, that ye present your bodies a living sacrifice, holy, acceptable unto God, which is your reasonable service." — Romans 12:1

It may not be our lot to wield
The sickle in the ripened field;
Nor ours to hear, on summer eves,
The reapers song among the sheaves;

Yet where our duty's task is wrought
In unison with God's great thought,
The near and future blend in one,
And whatsoe'er is willed is done!

And ours the grateful service whence
Comes, day by day, the recompense;
The hope, the trust, the purpose stayed,
The fountain and the noonday shade.

— Whittier

Isn't it wonderful that God asks that we present ourselves to him as we are? God does not say we must present our bodies *if* they are beautiful and agile, *if* our minds are well educated. If we give God the best we have he will, in time, make our best better. We will grow in grace and knowledge as our Lord wills us to do.

Prayer: Lord, may we today commit our lives to thee, and wilt thou make them count in thy service. May we find the best way to worship thee and the best way to serve. Give us fresh determination to be wholly thine. We ask in the name of Christ. Amen.

July 26

"I will behave myself wisely in a perfect way. O when wilt thou come unto me? I will walk within my house with a perfect heart." — Psalm 101:2

When George Washington was a young boy he wrote some rules of behavior. In all his life, even after he had become president, he tried to follow these rules. Some of them are as follows:

"Every action in company ought to be with some sign of respect to those present."

"Sleep not when others speak; sit not when others stand;

speak not when you should hold your peace; walk not when others stop."

"Be no flatterer; neither play with any one that delights not to be played with."

"Do not give your opinion unasked."

"Let your countenance be pleasant."

"Use no reproachful language against any one, neither curse, nor revile."

"Be not hasty to believe flying reports to the disparagement of any."

"Associate yourself with men of good quality."

Prayer: Dear Father, help us to grow in wisdom and dignity. May we make our character one of uprightness and model living. We ask in the name of the one perfect man, Jesus. Amen.

July 27

"Silver and gold have I none; but what I have that I give thee. In the name of Jesus Christ of Nazareth, walk. And he took him by the hand, and raised him up." — Acts 3:6, 7

Few of us have a great amount of money to give to those about us in need; but there are other gifts.

A young boy had run away from home because his father was a drunkard and often beat him. He came to a bridge and under it sought shelter from the cold. A small boy chasing his dog ran under the bridge and saw the older boy.

"Why are you here?" he asked.

"I have no place else to go and I am hungry and cold," the poor boy replied.

"Come to my house. My mother loves boys, and she will feed you."

So the two boys went to the humble farm home. True to her son's prediction the mother took in the runaway lad. She kept him for several years and he learned to work, and to love and be loved.

Prayer: Father, help us to look about and see those in need of love, of knowledge of thee, of comfort and strength. May we ever be willing to give of what we have to others. We ask in the name of Jesus. Amen.

July 28

"But be ye doers of the word, and not hearers only, deceiving your own selves." — James 1:22

As children of God one business should be predominant in our life. It is the soul-winning business. It is wonderful to go to church and hear a good message. It is still more important to go out and put that message into action. There is no Christian so weak or incapacitated that he cannot pray for the lost.

> Did Christ o'er sinners weep,
> And shall our tears be dry?
>
> Give me a faithful heart,
> Likeness to thee,
> That each departing day
> Henceforth may see
> Some work of love begun,
> Some wanderer sought and won,
> Some deed of kindness done,
> Something for thee.

Prayer: Our Father, make us mindful of the lost world about us. May we always remember thy great commission and seek to carry out thy commandments. May our business in life be first of all to serve thee. We ask in the name of one who lived only to serve, Jesus Christ. Amen.

July 29

"Remember the sabbath day, to keep it holy. . . . But the seventh day is the sabbath of the Lord thy God: in it thou shall not do any work, thou, nor thy son, nor thy daughter, thy manservant, nor thy maidservant, nor thy cattle, nor thy stranger that is within thy gates." — Exodus 20:8, 10

How rested and happy we feel when we spend Sunday in a quiet way — worshiping God and being grateful for home and family!

> Hail to the day which He, who made the heaven,
> Earth, and their armies, sanctified and blest,
> Perpetual memory of the Maker's rest!
> Hail to the day when He, by whom was given
> New life to man, the tomb asunder riven,
> Arose! That day His church doth still confess,
> At once Creation's and Redemption's feast,

Sign of a world called forth, a world forgiven.
Welcome that day, the day of holy peace,
The Lord's own day! to man's creator owed,
And man's Redeemer; for the soul's increase
In sanctity, and sweet repose bestowed;
Type of the rest when sin and care shall cease,
The rest remaining for the loved of God!

Prayer: Father, help us to honor the Sabbath on earth. We want to share the joys of heaven when this life is o'er. May we be careful to obey thy commandments here and now. Give us the realization that in all thy commandments thou didst plan what was best for thy children. Give us ability and courage to stand for the right when so much of the world wants only the wrong. We ask in the name of Jesus Christ. Amen.

July 30

"For the Lord is good; his mercy is everlasting; and his truth endureth to all generations." — Psalm 100:5

One time we had some very dear friends. They would look after our place while we were on vacation and we would do anything we could for them. Suddenly they changed. They did not want to visit with us anymore and refused our friendship. We were deeply hurt because we did not know the reason why they treated us so strangely. We did not know why they ceased to be our friends.

God is a friend who never changes. Always he wants what is best for us; always he loves us and seeks to lead us aright.

I have a friend indeed,
A friend I often need,
And when I need him he is always near,
To chide me when I'm wrong,
To fill my heart with song,
Or make the hidden way seem clear.

Now Jesus is his name,
His love is e'er the same;
And tho' my love for him may feeble grow,
Still thro' my tears I see
My friend awaiting me,
And hand in hand we onward go,

189

It is enough for me
To know that he will be
A friend when all the rest forget my name;
When thro' the gates of gold
My chariot wheels have roll'd,
He'll be my loving friend the same.

— C. Austin Miles

Prayer: Father make us mindful of the one true friend, we ask in his name. Amen.

July 31

"The love of Christ constraineth us." — II Corinthians 5:14

One time in Virginia I heard a young lady play the piano in a concert. "How God has blessed her," I thought.

Later I made her acquaintance. To my amazement I found she practiced five hours each day. No wonder she could play; she cared enough about it to pay the price in practice.

A football player, injured in the game, begged the coach to let him go back and try again. Most great things in the world have been accomplished because someone cared enough to pay the price.

Our only purpose, as we live,
    Is something of ourselves to give
To others as they pass nearby —
    But what give I?

The painter paints for all to see,
    The singer gives a melody,
The rich upon cash gifts rely —
    But what give I?

I have no talents, large or small,
    Nor have I wealth; it seems that all
I have is love that cannot die —
    And this give I.

— Dorothy Lee

Prayer: Our Father, help us to care about a lost world — a world in need of love. May we realize that poems die and music fades away but the soul lives on forever. May we care enough to win the lost. In his name we pray. Amen.

August:

Vacation Thoughts

August 1

"But ye shall receive power, after that the Holy Ghost is come upon you: and ye shall be witnesses unto me both in Jerusalem, and in all Judaea, and in Samaria, and unto the uttermost part of the earth." — Acts 1:8

During the days when the dread disease polio stalked our land many people had to live in iron lungs. The iron lung was powered by electricity. In the hospitals there were battery powered units to be used in case the electricity went off for a few moments. In the homes where iron lung victims lived the family would have to work hand pumps to keep the patients breathing if the electric power failed.

As Christians we often feel that our power as God's children is very weak; but he has promised us "standby power" in the form of the Holy Spirit. we can call for help any time, day or night, and be assured that our prayer will be answered.

> God dropped a spark into everyone,
> And if we find and fan it to a blaze
> It'll spring up and glow like — like the sun,
> And light the wandering out of stony ways.
>
> — John Mansfield

Prayer: Dear Father, giver of all power on earth and in heaven, help us always to call upon thy name in time of need. Give us the power we need to make our lives count in service for thee. We ask in the name of Jesus. Amen.

August 2

"Oh, that men would praise the Lord for his goodness, and for his wonderful works to the children of men!" — Psalm 107:8

To the artist He is the One Altogether Lovely.
To the architect He is the Chief Corner Stone.
To the baker He is the Living Bread.
To the banker He is the Hidden Treasure.
To the biologist He is the Life.
To the builder He is the Sure Foundation.
To the educator He is the Great Teacher.
To the farmer He is the Lord of the Harvest.
To the geologist He is the Rock of Ages.
To the jurist He is the Righteous Judge, the Judge of all men.

193

To the florist He is the Rose of Sharon and the Lily of the valley.

To the jeweler He is the Pearl of Great Price.

To the lawyer He is the Counselor, the Lawgiver, the Advocate.

To the horticulturist He is the True Vine.

To the newspaper man He is the Good Tidings of Great Joy.

To the oculist He is the Light of The World.

To the philanthropist He is the Unspeakable Gift.

To the philosopher He is the Wisdom of God.

To the preacher He is the Word of God.

To the sculptor He is the Living Stone.

To the servant He is the Good Master.

To the statesman He is the Desire of All Nations.

To the student He is the Incarnate Truth.

To the theologian He is the Author and Finisher of Our Faith.

To the traveler He is the New and Living Way.

To the toiler He is the Giver of Rest.

To the sinner He is the Lamb of God that taketh away the sin of the world.

To the Christian He is the Son of the Living God, the Saviour, the Redeemer and the Lord.

Prayer: Dear Father, help us to know in our own hearts what Christ means to us. Help us ever to trust in his salvation for our souls. We ask in his name. Amen.

August 3

"For there is no distinction between Jew and Greek: for the same Lord is Lord of all, and is rich unto all that call upon him: for, Whosoever shall call upon the name of the Lord shall be saved." — Romans 10:12, 13

In a small town in a Western state there was discovered a man who had escaped from a prison in the East over twenty years before. He was arrested and carried back to the scene of his original crime. The people in the little western town were shocked; his wife and children were heartbroken. Then someone said: "Let's get up a petition. Let's show the governor back there what a good citizen our friend has been these twenty years." Name after name went on the petition. Then a friend made a trip to the East to take the petition to the governor personally, and to plead for mercy.

The governor was so touched by the loyalty of the man's friends that he did grant him a pardon and the man returned home.

> The wounds I might have healed,
>   The human sorrow and smart!
> And yet it never was in my soul
>   To play so ill a part.
> But evil is wrought by want of thought
>   As well as want of heart.

— Thomas Hood

Prayer: Father of all mercies, we ask thee to make us merciful to those in need. Make us kind to the friendless and ever grateful for the mercy thou hast showered upon us. For the sake of Christ we ask. Amen.

August 4

"But seek ye first his kingdom, and his righteousness; and all these things shall be added unto you." — Matthew 6:33

> A hand in the dark clutched tight to my heart,
> A voice sounded close to my ear.
> A tear from his face dropped hot on my cheek;
> He breathed with the quickness of fear.
>
> The message he brought was a heart-rendering one
> Of darkness and pain, even death.
> And then with a hope he dared not express
> He waited with bated breath.
>
> "But why should I go? There are others to send
> And I have too much here to do."
> "O yes," he replied, "there are others I know,
> But they are exactly like you."
>
> "But why should I go? You are nothing to me;
> My friends and my family are here."
> "O yes," he replied, "Then you'll understand
> What it cost to lose those who are dear."
>
> "But why should I go? I have God for myself;
> I'll pray and I'll give when I please."
> "O yes, that is true." And he sighed in despair,
> "I had hoped to find one among these."

As he turned from my side he let my heart go
And it turned cold, even as stone.
My ears heard the silence, the tear burned my face
And I felt so terribly alone.

My call broke the silence. He quickly turned
To hear me say, "God I am Thine."
Together we went, and no loneliness felt
For His tears were mingled with mine.

Prayer: Our Father, make us mindful of thy call today. May we be watchful for those in need of the gospel story. We ask in the name of the living Christ. Amen.

August 5

"The Son of Man came not to be served but to serve, and to give his life a ransom for many." — Matthew 20:28

Every day God is seeking laborers for his vineyard. He calls young and old, and he offers all the same reward.

Churchill said to the British people during the World War II, "I can promise you nothing but blood, sweat and tears."

It is only human to ask, "What will I have for this task?"

In Matthew 19:27, the disciples asked, "Lo, we have left everything and followed thee. What then shall we have?"

Many refuse the call to work in the Master's vineyard. Many do not want to serve unless they are sure of a great reward. We must examine our motives and be sure we have the right spirit as we serve.

A few can touch the magic string,
And noisy Fame is proud to win them —
Alas for those who never sing,
But die with all their music in them.

Nay, grieve not for the dead alone
Whose song has told their heart's sad story —
Weep for the voiceless who have known
The cross without the crown of glory.

— Oliver Wendell Holmes

Prayer: God, give us the will to obey thy call. Help us to realize there is a task just for each of us. Make us willing to serve in the lowliest place as well as the highest. We ask in the name of him who served all. Amen.

August 6

"Let us then pursue what makes for peace and for mutual upbuilding." — Romans 14:19

Tom was a teen-ager and he wanted very much to stay home on Sunday and read the paper, look at television and just loaf. "Why can't I worship here?" he asked.

It was Saturday night and the family had been enjoying a nice fire in the fireplace. Tom's father went to the fireplace and pushed the logs apart, and turned off the gas feeder.

"Why do that? We will be up another hour," Tom complained.

"Well, son, you see if the logs are separate and the power of the gas is turned off the fire soon dies out."

"I know, but why do it?"

"You are like the logs. If you go to services and stay close to the power of God and to the fellowship of other Christians, you keep burning bright for God."

Once to every man and nation comes the moment to decide,
In the strife of Truth with Falsehood, for the good or evil side;
Some great cause, God's new Messiah, offering each the bloom or blight,
Parts the goats upon the left hand, and the sheep upon the right,
And the choice goes on forever 'twixt that darkness and that light.

— James Russell Lowell

Prayer: Our Father, help us choose the right. Amen.

August 7

"In him we have redemption through his blood, the forgiveness of our trespasses, according to the riches of his grace which he lavished upon us." — Ephesians 1:7, 8

Men may and do attend church in many different attitudes. Some have an attitude of reverence and worship. Others seem filled with an attitude of criticism; they see nothing beautiful or good about the services or the people present.

Some come seeking forgiveness for mistakes made. We should all do so. We should all lay aside the attitudes of arrogant self-sufficient pride and respond in reverence to Christ.

God gives his child upon his slate a sum —
To find eternity in hours and years;

197

With both sides covered, back the child doth come,
His dim eyes swollen with shed and unshed tears;
God smiles, wipes clean the upper side and nether,
And says, "Now, dear, we'll do the sum together!

Prayer: Dear Father, fill our souls with the forgiveness and love that overcomes all things bad and evil. In our own strength we can do nothing but we ask for thy strength and help today. In Christ's name we pray. Amen.

August 8

"And the Lord make you to increase and abound in love one toward another, and toward all men, even as we do toward you."

— I Thessalonians 3:12

God has a plan for every life. God plans all things. He even has a perfect plan for the stars and planets. How do we find the perfect plan God has for us?

We need to read and study God's plan book, the Bible. We must make the right choices; the right companions will help us make these choices. We should never seek revenge when we feel we have been wronged. God will punish the wrong doer. We must learn to work as best we can and trust God for our provisions.

Lord, help me have that perfect day,
    That I may do your will, your way.
Lord, help me do that perfect work,
    And never the burdens of service shirk.
Lord, help me have that perfect light.
    And know your presence in darkest night.
Lord, help me be a perfect friend
    So that I might lift lives to begin again.
Lord, help me have that perfect heart,
    That Jesus' love it will impart.
Lord, help me have that perfect love
    That my work here might count above.
Lord, help me have that perfect day
    That I might walk the Jesus way.

Prayer: Father, help us to know that we will be judged by one who sees and knows all things. May we strive to have more love for our fellow man. Make us more obedient, willing servants. We ask in the name of Christ. Amen.

198

August 9

"In the day of prosperity be joyful, but in the day of adversity consider: God hath set the one over against the other to the end that man should find nothing after him." — Ecclesiastes 7:14

Sally awoke to see sunbeams shining across the floor of her room. But her face was not bright and sunny.

"What can I do in this dull place to have a good time?"

She started the day with the wrong question. Had she asked, "What useful work can I do today?" she would have been happier.

Each day God gives us something to do for his glory and the improvement of the world. It may be a small task; but if we are on the lookout for someone to help, someone to cheer — the hand of someone down and out, to grasp and lift up — then we will have joyful days and unknown strength.

> My heart leaps up when I behold
> A rainbow in the sky:
> So was it when my life began;
> So is it now I am a man;
> So be it when I shall grow old,
> Or let me die!
> The child is father of the man;
> And I could wish my days to be
> Bound each to each by natural piety.
>
> — William Wordsworth

Prayer: Father of all the earth, make our hearts to leap with joy as we behold the wonders of thy world. We ask in the name of one who was the wonder of wonders, Jesus. Amen.

August 10

"When it is evening, ye say, It will be fair weather: for the sky is red. And in the morning, It will be foul weather today: for the sky is red and lowering. O ye hypocrites, ye can discern the face of the sky; but can ye not discern the signs of the times?" — Matthew 16:2b, 3

Sometimes we grow so busy that we forget that time marches on and opportunities are lost. I heard the story of a small child who fretted because his father never attended Sunday School and church with him. His excuse was that he could not leave the small grocery store he owned.

199

"Mother, do you think daddy is a Christian?" asked the youngster.

"Yes, I hope so," the mother replied. "Why?"

"How will he get away from the store long enough to go to heaven?"

All the long August afternoon,
    The little drowsy stream
Whispers a melancholy tune,
As if it dreamed of June
    And whispered in its dream.

The silent orchard aisles are sweet
Through the sere grass, in shy retreat,
Flutter, at coming feet.
    With smell of ripening fruit.
    The robins strange and mute.

There is no wind to stir the leaves,
    The harsh leaves overhead;
Only the querulous cricket grieves,
And shrilling locust weaves
    A song of summer dead.

— William Dean Howells

Prayer: Father, we thank thee for the seasons of the year. We find something beautiful in each one. May we always find beauty in the seasons of our lives. In the name of Christ we pray. Amen.

August 11

"The meek will he guide in judgment: and the meek will he teach his way. All the paths of the Lord are mercy and truth unto such as keep his covenant and his testimonies."

— Psalm 25:9, 10

The longer I live the stronger I believe that God goes before us and makes a way for us. Just today I heard of a young lady who was standing in a crowd waiting to board an airplane. As she stood there someone ran by and snatched her purse. She had only a few dollars in it but she left her place in line and went to the information office to report the theft. She came back to find the plane had gone without her. She was cross, and disgusted with her misfortune. Just a few hours later the word came: the plane had gone down in a ball of fire and sixty-three

200

people had lost their lives. For some reason God kept her from getting on that plane.

Would you live for Jesus and be always pure and good?
Would you walk with Him within the narrow road?
Would you have Him bear your burden, carry all your load?
Let Him have His way with thee.

— Cyrus S. Nusbaum

Prayer: Our Father, we belong to thee body and soul. Make us willing to follow in the path thou hast planned for us. We do not know the future but we trust our lives to thee. We pray in the name of Christ. Amen.

August 12

"If any one has the world's goods and sees his brother in need, yet closes his heart against him, how does God's love abide in him?" — I John 3:17

How can we compare spiritual feeding and physical feeding? Yet both are mentioned in the Bible. We show how much we care for men's souls by the way we care for their bodies.

How can we show we care?

We can have compassion for the oppressed, visit the sick, show kindness to strangers. All the kind deeds in the world will not take the place of the blood of Jesus in the day of judgment if we have not believed on him.

I dare not slight the stranger at my door,
Threadbare of garb and sorrowful of lot,
Lest it be Christ that stands; and goes His way
Because I, all unworthy, knew Him not.

I dare not miss one flash of kindling cheer
From alien souls, in challenge glad and high.
Ah, what if God be moving very near
And I, so blind, so deaf, had passed Him by?

Prayer: Our Father, as we prepare for that great day of judgment when Jesus shall come in glory with a sceptre of righteousness, may it be with humble and grateful hearts. May we prepare for the receiving of heavenly rewards by serving thee on earth. We ask for the sake of Jesus our Saviour. Amen.

August 13

"That the trial of your faith, being much more precious than gold that perisheth, though it be tried with fire, might be found unto praise and honor and glory at the appearing of Jesus Christ." — I Peter 1:7

George Muller was a famous English Christian. He felt led of the Lord to establish an Orphan-House. He had no money and planned to run the home on faith alone. In the year 1836 he started his venture. Many times God opened the way for food and clothing just at the right moment. I like to remember the time when Mr. Muller and the matrons had prayed until one o'clock in the night because there was not even a piece of bread for the children's breakfast. Finally, he started for home, tired and discouraged. For some reason he did not walk the path he usually took going home. As he walked along he met a man also walking.

Mr. Muller introduced himself and they walked along together. When they came to the place to part the new friend took out his purse and gave Mr. Muller ten pounds for the orphans. Can't you just see him getting up early the next morning to buy food for the orphans! But — can't you also see George Muller on his knees giving thanks to God!

Prayer: Dear Father, strengthen our faith. Help us to know thou art never asleep but always ready to answer our pleas. We ask in the name of Jesus Christ. Amen.

August 14

"Humble yourselves therefore under the mighty hand of God, that he may exalt you in due time." — I Peter 5:6

As we read and study the Bible we sometimes want to surrender our lives to God — but not quite our whole lives. We want to retain our favorite sin, our favorite sport, or even just some time we can spend without any instructions from God.

If God has wrought a transforming experience of grace in our hearts, we will show evidence of surrender to him.

When we cease to struggle against God's will for us, then we know a real, glorious victory.

> All to Jesus I surrender,
> All to Him I freely give;
> I will ever love and trust Him,
> In His presence daily live.

All to Jesus I surrender,
Make me, Saviour, wholly thine;
Let me feel the Holy Spirit —
Truly know that Thou art mine.

All to Jesus I surrender,
Lord, I give myself to Thee;
Fill me with Thy love and power,
Let Thy blessing fall on me.
> — Judson W. Van De Venter

Prayer: Father in heaven, give us a changed heart that will be surrendered to thy will. Fill us with thy transforming power. May we ever respond to thy call and be truly surrendered Christians. We pray for Christ's sake. Amen.

August 15

"By faith Abraham obeyed when he was called to go out to a place which he was to receive as an inheritance; and he went out not knowing where he was to go." — Hebrews 11:8

Every person wants to have a good name. Some want a great name enough to sacrifice and work for it. A name seldom comes by accident — usually by study, talent and work.

For Christian people their call usually comes from God. God has a purpose for our lives and he calls us for the fulfillment of that purpose. Like Abraham we must obey the call. We are not told how Abraham was called and we know all calls for service are not alike. Sometimes our service is just to witness to those about us in our home town. Sometimes it is to go far from home and serve in strange places.

One of the most attractive girls in our church felt called to go to Africa as a Journeyman Missionary. It almost broke her parents' hearts to see her go, but they prayed for God's will to be done. Her mother said, "We know she is safer in Africa if it is God's call than she would be in Texas against his will."

It may not be on the mountain height,
Or over the stormy sea;
It may not be at the battle front
My Lord will have need of me;
But if by a still small voice He calls
To paths I do not know,

I'll answer, "Dear Lord, with my hand in Thine,
I'll go where you want me to go."

— Mary Brown

Prayer: Father, make us willing to follow thy call and go out not knowing where, but to serve. For Jesus' sake. Amen.

August 16

"He watereth the hills from his chambers: the earth is satisfied with the fruit of thy works." — Psalm 104:13

David and Danny had some small chickens and a mother hen. They were supposed to close the door to the pen securely each night to keep out harmful enemies of the chickens. Early each morning the chickens could be heard scratching and pecking at the door, wanting out. If the dew was heavy they were often kept in until the middle of the morning. If the day was nice they were out early to catch bugs and eat tender grass.

God knows when we need freedom, and when we need to be watched over closely. Often we peck away at some restraint and feel resentful; but God knows what is best for us.

I know not where his islands lift
Their fronded palms in air;
I only know I cannot drift
Beyond his loving care.

— Whittier

Prayer: Father of all mankind, help us to know that thy dealings with thy children are always best. Oft we feel shut in and the way seems dark. Give us faith to know that when the time is right thou wilt open the door to better things. For the sake of Christ we pray. Amen.

August 17

"I know whom I have believed, and am persuaded that he is able to keep that which I have committed unto him against that day." — II Timothy 1:12

A passenger on a river boat was watching the pilot.

"How long have you been a pilot?" the passenger asked.

"I have been a pilot on these very waters for over thirty years," the man replied.

"Then by now you must know every rock and sand bar along the shores."

"Oh, no," the pilot replied. "I do not know anything like all the dangerous places along the shores."

"But how do you pilot the boat safely?"

"I know where the deep water runs and I pilot the boat in the deep water."

We may not know all the dangers along the shores of life, but we will be safe if we keep in the deep waters of God's will and love.

> Though I were hung on the highest hill,
> I know whose love would follow me still.
>
> Though I were drowned in the deepest sea,
> I know whose love would come down to me.
>
> — Old Ballad

Prayer: Lord our God, who searches our hearts for love and leads us in the way we should go, establish in us the desire to live ever close to thee. We ask in the name of Christ. Amen.

August 18

"Say not ye, There are yet four months, and then cometh harvest? behold, I say unto you, Lift up your eyes, and look on the fields; for they are white already to harvest." — John 4:35

We planted just a few tomato vines, but they grew so profusely that our back yard was overrun with tomatoes. We were kept busy giving away tomatoes to our friends and neighbors. When they were ripe they had to be harvested quickly or they would be ruined. At times I suspected that there were field mice nibbling off the ripe ones.

Jesus was talking about a harvest of lost souls. They, too, are everywhere. They, too, must be harvested at the proper time or it may be too late. Even like the mouse nibbling at the tomatoes, Satan is ever ready to devour souls.

> Why do you wait, dear brother,
>   Oh, why do you tarry so long?
> Your Savior is waiting to give you
>   A place in His sanctified throng.
>
> What do you hope, dear brother,
>   To gain by a further delay?
> There's no one to save you but Jesus,
>   There's no other way but His way.
>
> — George F. Root

Prayer: Our Father, Lord of the harvest, help us today to look on the fields and go forth to reap. Show us the paths you would have us take to serve thee best. We pray in the name of Christ our Saviour. Amen.

August 19

"For God so loved the world, that he gave his only begotten Son, that whosoever believeth in him should not perish, but have everlasting life." — John 3:16

We have all heard the story of the little girl who came home from Sunday School and told her mother, "We studied about God's only forgotten son today."

God still loves us and longs for us to come to his only begotten son. He could have asked us to perform all kinds of rituals in order to be saved, but he only asks us to believe. He could have said "only the people of one nation, or one race"; but he said, "Whosoever." This means that all who believe — regardless of nation, or race, or social status — will be saved.

And his gift of love is the same for all who believe, "everlasting life."

> Love sent my Savior to die in my stead,
> Why should he love me so?
> Meekly to Calvary's cross He was led,
> Why should He love me so?
>
> Nails pierced His hands and his feet for my sin,
> Why should He love me so?
> He suffered sore my salvation to win,
> Why should He love me so?
>
> Oh how He agonized there in my place,
> Why should He love me so?
> Nothing witholding my sin to efface,
> Why should He love me so?
>
> — Robert Harkness

Prayer: Father in Heaven, we are silent before thy great love. We are so unworthy of such sacrifice. Enable us to worship thee in spirit and in truth. We ask in the name of Christ. Amen.

August 20

"Whereby are given unto us exceeding great and precious promises." — II Peter 1:4

As believers we have a peculiar treasure in God's promises.

206

We are very wealthy if we believe and carry out the conditions of God's promises.

There is a story told about when Abraham Lincoln was entertaining a friend in the White House. The friend coaxed one of the children to come and sit on his lap saying, "I will give you this watch fob if you will."

The child went to the man and sat quietly on his lap. When the friend was ready to leave President Lincoln reminded him he had not given the child the watch fob.

"Oh, I could not do that," replied the friend. "This is an old family heirloom."

"Then never come to my home again. I do not wish my children to know I entertain liars." The President sent the man away.

> Yet in the maddening maze of things,
>   And tossed by storm and flood,
> To one fixed trust my spirit clings:
>   I know that God is good!

> — Whittier

Prayer: Our Father, we thank thee that thy promises are true. We thank thee most for the coming of the promised Saviour of the world. For it is in his name we pray. Amen.

August 21

"Worthy is the Lamb who was slain, to receive power and wealth and wisdom and might and honor and glory and blessing!"
> — Revelation 5:12 (RSV)

When we read that the Lamb was slain, we know his mission on earth has been finished. Christ has been appointed the heir of all things. So we know he is reigning in heaven. Hebrews 1:3 reads: "He reflects the glory of God and bears the stamp of his nature, upholding the universe by his word of power. When he had made purification for sins, he sat down at the right hand of the Majesty on high."

> I serve a risen Saviour, He's in the world today;
> I know that He is living, whatever men may say;
> I see His hand of mercy, I hear His voice of cheer,
> And just the time I need Him He's always near.

> Rejoice, rejoice, O Christian, lift up your voice and sing
> Eternal hallelujahs to Jesus Christ the King!

The hope of all who seek Him, the help of all who find,
None other is so loving, so good and kind.

He lives, He lives, Christ Jesus lives today!
He walks with me and talks with me along life's narrow way.
He lives, He lives, salvation to impart!
You ask me how I know He lives:
He lives within my heart.

— Alfred Ackley

Prayer: Father in heaven, help us today to see all things through the eyes of faith and tell others of the reigning Christ. We pray in the name of Jesus. Amen.

August 22

"Truly, truly, I say unto you, he who believes in me will also do the works that I do; and greater works than these will he do, because I go to the Father." — John 14:12

A young man who had recently surrendered to become a minister, went to his pastor and said: "How can I serve Jesus. I just must find a way to start my service."

"Look all around you and find some place where he is not. Go there and take him with you," the pastor replied.

Before we can work great works for Christ we must get our eyes off our selves. Then we must recognize that we have a responsibility and the world has a need.

No one else can witness for you,
   Nor can others flash your smile;
None can do what you're supposed to
   As you tread life's blessed mile.

For your deeds you have to answer
   For each neglect you give account.
You're the one whom God has chosen
   That assignment to fulfil.

With habits still unfrozen
   Follow now his blessed will.

— J. T. Bolding

Prayer: Father, give us the courage to be free from doubt. Help us to seek thy will in our lives and go forward with a vision to accomplish thy purpose. We ask in the name of Jesus. Amen.

August 23

"God is a spirit, and they who worship him must worship in spirit and in truth." — John 4:24

In Dallas, Texas, a few years ago a father, mother and four children attended Sunday School and church regularly. Then the father obtained a better job and they bought a new car. Each Sunday it seemed more convenient to get into the new car and go visit friends or relatives than to attend church.

One Sunday they passed the church as the people were gathering for services. The little five-year-old in the back seat leaned out the window and called, "Good-bye, God. We have a new car and don't need you any more."

The father and mother were convicted of their neglect and the following Sunday found them back in their old places in God's house.

> Faithfully faithful to every trust,
>   Honestly honest in every deed,
> Righteously righteous and justly just;
>   This is the whole of the good man's creed.

Prayer: Help us, our dear Lord, ever in word and deed to own thee as our Lord and Saviour. Amen.

August 24

"As it is written in the prophets, Behold, I send my messenger before thy face, which shall prepare thy way before thee."

— Mark 1:2

> Around the corner I have a friend
> In this great city that has no end,
> And he is lost — a fine strong man,
> But he is lost! And I always plan
> To speak to him about God's love,
> Of Christ who came down from above —
> And of how he died on the cross to pay
> The sinner's debt. I think each day
> "Somehow I must speak my heart to Jim:
> Tomorrow I'll have a talk with him."
>
> Tomorrow comes, and crowding cares
> Clutter my day with busy affairs.
> The day is done and again I vow
> Tomorrow I'll speak to Jim somehow.

For my friend is lost: he does not know
The peril he risks; he must not go
Year after year like this and die
Before I tell him how truly I
Desire to see him give his heart to Christ,
Repent, believe, and make a new start.
But tomorrow comes and tomorrow goes
And the distance between us grows and grows.
Around the corner! Yet miles away —
     "Here's a telegram, sir. . . .
     Jim died today."
While I delayed, thus came the end:
Jim lost a soul; Christ lost a friend!

— C. T. Towne

Prayer: O Thou who art the Saviour of all who trust in thee, forgive us for our neglect in telling the story of thy love. Make our witness acceptable unto thee. We ask in the name of our precious Saviour. Amen.

August 25

"I said, I will take heed to my ways, that I sin not with my tongue: I will keep my mouth with a bridle, while the wicked is before me." — Psalm 39:1

Two friends were whispering in church. They could not understand each other correctly. They should have been worshiping. One went away and told what she thought she had heard. The other friend heard what she told and became very angry. They had such an ugly quarrel that one changed her church membership to avoid seeing her one-time-friend again. All because they gossiped in church!

Alas! they had been friends of youth:
But whispering tongues can poison truth;
And constancy lives in realms above;
     And life is thorny; and youth is vain;
And to be wroth with one we love
     Doth work like madness in the brain.
And thus it chanced as I divine,
With Roland and Sir Leoline!
Each spoke words of high disdain
     And insult to his heart's best brother;
They parted — ne'er to meet again!
     But never either found another

To free the hollow heart from paining.
They stood aloof, the scars remaining.
Like cliffs which had been rent asunder;
    A dreary sea now flows between,
But neither heat, nor frost, nor thunder
    Shall wholly do away, I ween,
    The marks of that which once hath been.

                  — S. T. Coleridge

Prayer: O almighty and everlasting God, be merciful to us. We are so hasty in our speech; we make so many mistakes. Turn us from our careless ways and strengthen us as Christians. Make us joyful in well doing. We pray in the name of Jesus Christ. Amen.

August 26

"Honor your father and your mother." — Exodus 20:12

Home life in America today is too often like that described in the poem Longfellow wrote.

Ships that pass in the night, and speak each other in passing,
Only a signal shown and a distant voice in the darkness;
So on the ocean of life we pass and speak one another,
Only a look and a voice, then darkness again and a silence.

More and more parents spend less and less time with their children. We think of the commandment as being given to children, but parents also have an obligation. Parents must deserve honor.

We are given the promise of long days upon the earth if we honor our parents. When I was a very young girl I met a woman who seemed old to me then. She was always telling what wonderful people her parents had been and her grandparents before them. I often thought, "This woman will certainly live a long time; she honors her parents so much."

Sure enough, after I felt myself old, she was still living. She was very near ninety — and still bragging about her people.

Jesus set an example of honor by asking someone to care for his mother when he was dying.

Prayer: Father, as parents make us worthy of honor; as children make us glad to honor our parents. For Christ's sake. Amen.

August 27

"Jesus therefore, knowing all things that should come upon him, went forth, and said unto them, Whom seek ye?"
— John 18:4

When I was a girl just eighteen years old standing before the minister to be married, I did not know all the problems marriage carried with it — the mountains of dishes to be washed, all the floors to be swept, the babies to be cared for. Yet I doubt if I would have turned away had I known.

Christ knew he was soon to go to the cross, and he knew the suffering he would be forced to go through before he could cry, "It is finished." Yet knowing all this he went on, for our sake.

>   Among the things that this day brings
>   Will come to you a call,
>   The which, unless you're listening,
>   You may not hear at all.
>   Lest it be very soft and low,
>   What'er you do, where'er you go,
>   Be listening!
>   Then whatsoe'er the call may be,
>   To service small or great,
>   To cross the seas and speak God's love,
>   To smile, to rule a state —
>   When God shall come and say to you,
>   "Here is the thing that you must do,"
>   Be listening!

Prayer: Father, today let nothing keep us from listening for thy call. Knowing life will not always be easy; grant us the will to go on in service and love. We pray in the name of Jesus Christ. Amen.

August 28

"How sweet are thy words unto my taste! yea, sweeter than honey to my mouth!" — Psalm 119:103

Isn't it wonderful for a friend to say, "I have been thinking of you?"

A man lived next door to an unsaved man. Mr. King often prayed for his neighbor. One day he was earnestly praying, "God, lay a hand on my friend. Save his soul."

Suddenly a voice just seemed to say, "You are the hand. You are the hand; go and touch him."

Mr. King immediately went next door and began to pour out his heart — pleading with his friend to trust Christ.

After he was gloriously saved, the friend said, "I often wondered why you didn't ask me to go to your church."

'Tis the human touch in the world that counts,
    The touch of your hand and mine,
Which means far more to the fainting heart
    Than shelter and bread and wine;
For shelter is gone when the night is o'er,
    And bread lasts only a day,
But the touch of the hand and the sound of the voice
    Sing on in the soul alway.

— Spencer Free

Prayer: Our Father, help us ever to have the sweet taste of thy love in our hearts. Make us realize there are lonely people who need thy love. Make us the hands to lead them to thee. We pray through Jesus our Lord. Amen.

August 29

"And about the eleventh hour he went out, and found others standing idle, and saith unto them, Why stand ye here all the day idle?" — Matthew 20:6

A lazy man was begging help for his family, saying he could not find food and clothing for his family.

"Nor can I," replied an industrious mechanic. "I have to work for it."

Too many people in our world today are standing idle. It seems easier to hold out a hand and be fed by others than to work for food and clothing.

Christians also sometimes grow lazy and merely want to sit in services and be fed, rather than getting out and working to bring new souls into the Kingdom of God.

The heights of great men reached and kept
Were not attained by sudden flight;
But they, while their companions slept,
Were toiling upward in the night;

So in the matter of working he will succeed best who takes most pains, who has no time for idleness.

Prayer: Our Father, give us the courage to work — for our families, for our church and most of all for thee. We ask in the name of thy dear Son. Amen.

August 30

"And he said unto me, My grace is sufficient for thee: for my strength is made perfect in weakness. Most gladly therefore will I rather glory in my infirmities, that the power of Christ may rest upon me." — II Corinthians 12:9

It is not the comforts of life that make us strong, but the trials. How we overcome the trials and handicaps tells the story of how we meet life.

It is said that the engineer who planned the great Brooklyn Bridge in New York, became a bedfast invalid before the bridge could be finished. He did not give up. He had a powerful telescope brought in and from his bed he kept close watch on the progress of the bridge. His body was weak but his mind remained sharp and active.

> It may be I shall never rise
> To place or fame beneath the skies —
> But walk in straitened ways till death,
> The narrow streets of Nazareth.

> But if through honor's arch I tread
> And there forget to bend my head,
> Ah! let me hear the voice which saith,
> "Mine were the streets of Nazareth."

> When I am tempted to repine
> That such a lowly lot is mine,
> There comes to me a voice which saith,
> "Mine were the streets of Nazareth."

Prayer: O thou who art the Saviour of those who trust in thee, make us strong in thy strength. Help us overcome weakness and fear. We ask in thy holy name. Amen.

August 31

"Cause me to hear thy lovingkindness in the morning; for in thee do I trust: cause me to know the way wherein I should walk; for I lift up my soul to thee." — Psalm 143:8

Each day of our lives we are faced with decisions. The question is, Which way will we take? God will direct our paths if we ask him.

I went to the home of a young woman whose husband had been killed just a few hours earlier. She was in a state of shock. He had been a student at an Air Base. His plane had caught

214

fire just a short way from the landing field. He had bailed out too late for his parachute to open.

"If he had just ejected sooner," she sobbed.

How often when it is too late we cry, "If we had just known sooner."

> Guide me, O Thou great Jehovah,
> Pilgrim through this barren land;
> I am weak, but Thou art mighty;
> Hold me with Thy powerful hand;
>
> — Peter Williams

Prayer: Father, we come to thee in prayer because we need thy guidance and help in choosing life's way. We hunger for thy presence and blessings. Thou art the source of the blessings we receive each day. Make us worthy of them. We pray in the name of Jesus. Amen.

September:

Back to School and Work

September 1

"Behold, I stand at the door, and knock: if any man hear my voice, and open the door I will come in to him, and will sup with him, and he with me." — Revelation 3:20

September is a month of many doors opening. There is a change in the home life as children scurry off to school. Then comes the excitement of new grades and new teachers.

Vacations are over and we face our tasks anew.

Opportunity knocks on everyone's door in September. We feel fresh and anxious to make new marks with our time and talents.

> Upon first glance, all seems about the same
> As yesterday or so, when summer still
> Had charge, except a sudden path of flame
> From sumac polka-dotting that green hill.
> My maples haven't yielded yet to yellow,
> Although the goldenrod is speaking loud
> And katydid is playing on his cello;
> Yet summer's hide-and-seeking with a cloud.
>
> On second look, there is a different flair,
> As to a custom-tailored suit; in fact,
> A cricket told me, "Watch, and be aware
> Of stirring wonders gentle summer lacked."
> The theme is change — in earth and air and tree;
> This month is full of personality!

Prayer: O Lord, may we yield to the Master of all times and seasons. Use us in thy service. May we never be proud and haughty, but ever keep an open door for thy entrance. We ask in the name of Jesus. Amen.

September 2

"Man goeth forth unto his work and to his labor until the evening." — Psalm 104:23

"Thou hast blessed the work of his hands, and his substance is increased in the land." — Job 1:10b

A boy I knew some years ago went out to find a job. He had been a paperboy and had done his work well — and had enjoyed it. But now he wanted something more important. Soon he secured a job for after school and for the summer. He was very happy and came rushing home to tell his mother. After that he had increasingly larger and better jobs — but he appreciated each one. He always counted it a privilege to have a place to work.

The world is made up of people who do just common ordinary tasks and who are proud to be working.

> My Master was a worker
> With daily work to do,
> And he who would be like Him
> Must be a worker too;
> Then welcome honest labor
> And honest labor's fare,
> For where there is a worker
> The Master's man is there.
> —W. C. Tarrent

Prayer: Our Father, make us proud of being able to engage in honest labor. May we never sell principle for popularity in our work. We thank thee for the ability to toil, and ask thee to bless those who are ill or unable to find places to labor. We pray in the name of one who toiled each day to bring the Kingdom of Heaven to earth. Amen.

September 3

"Nay, in all these things we are more than conquerors through him that loved us." — Romans 8:37

Jill wanted to be popular on her college campus. She was a Freshman and as yet had not met many of the students. Then she heard there was to be a contest for a Freshman Queen. She decided that she would enter the contest.

"You are not from a rich family," her roommate objected. "You do not go out for some of the social affairs on campus. I would say you are too religious to win a contest."

"I intend to try for it," Jill replied. "People will know me as I am when the contest is over."

When Jill was through making her own posters and going all over campus with them, she had made many friends. They respected and liked her exactly as she was. When the final day arrived she was in the top ten and ended the contest by being next to the queen.

It is not always what we hit, but what we aim at, that helps us grow as people.

Jill thought she could be a queen and she became a princess.

Prayer: Father, we all have unfulfilled dreams and desires. Help us to know we can find completeness and happiness in thee.

In our own strength we often are failures but with thy strength we can reach the unattainable. For Christ's sake we pray. Amen.

September 4

"Then saith Jesus unto him, Get thee hence, Satan: for it is written, Thou shalt worship the Lord thy God, and him only shalt thou serve." — Matthew 4:10

Jesus knew when he was being tempted. He knew when he was in the wrong company and asked that company to leave.

Often the best way to get away from temptation is to run from it.

A little girl was picking and eating ripe strawberries. Her mother had forbidden her to eat the strawberries because she was allergic to them. She thought no one would know. As she was about to leave the strawberry bed she tripped on a vine and fell. When she got up a large stain was on the front of her dress.

> What matter if I stand alone?
>   I wait with joy the coming years;
> My heart shall reap where it hath sown,
>   And garner up its fruits of tears.
> The waters know their own, and draw
>   The brook that springs in yonder heights;
> So flows the good with equal law
>   Unto the soul of pure delights.

Prayer: O God, forgive us when we are weak and descend to temptation. Help us to walk in the way of Jesus Christ, and follow his example of putting aside temptation. We ask in the name of Jesus. Amen.

September 5

"O Lord, how manifold are thy works! in wisdom hast thou made them all: the earth is full of thy riches." — Psalm 104:24

Teddy was watching an ant bed. Sometimes he would take a piece of straw and push an ant away from the opening to the ant hill.

"Mother, do I seem as small to God as the ants do to me?"

"I am sure you probably are much smaller," his mother told him. "But you are better off because God wants everything good for you and sometimes I see you kill the ants."

221

Alas, my God, that we should be
  Such strangers to each other!
O that as friends we might agree,
  And walk and talk together!

May I taste that communion, Lord,
  Thy people have with Thee?
Thy Spirit daily talks with them,
  O let It talk with me!

Like Enoch, let me walk with God,
  And thus walk out my day,
Attended with the heavenly Guards,
  Upon the King's highway.

When wilt Thou come unto me, Lord?
  For till Thou dost appear,
I count each moment for a day,
  Each minute for a year.

— Shepherd

Prayer: O Lord, we humbly beseech thee, open our eyes to behold thee in all thy love and glory. Open our lips that we may magnify thy name. We pray in the name of Jesus. Amen.

September 6

"And as thy servant was busy here and there he was gone."
— I Kings 20:40

All American parents and children seem to be busy here and there. Do we ever stop to see what is going from our lives while we are so busy? A young mother told me her children had so many extra-curricular activities she was never home nights. She was always busy taking them places. She belonged to that growing group of families where the mother as well as the father has a car. Sometimes she said the children were so busy she took one in one direction and the father took another some place else. People that busy are losing all the sacred fellowship God meant for homes to have.

We school our manners, act our parts,
  But He who sees us through and through
Knows that the bent of both our hearts
  Was to be gentle, tranquil, true.

— Matthew Arnold

Prayer: Our Father, help us today to hunger and thirst after righteousness. May we seek to be more like the Master. Help us not to be so busy about worldly affairs that we lose sight of thee. We ask in Jesus' name. Amen.

September 7

"The fear of the Lord is the beginning of wisdom: a good understanding have all they that do his commandments: his praise endureth forever." — Psalm 111:10

One Sunday morning I had been given a message for our pastor's wife. Nothing else seemed to be on my mind except that I give her the message after services. Hurrying down to where she stood I passed two people I should have spoken to, but ignored completely. After I had delivered my message I thought how rude I had been. Hurrying back to find them I apologized but I could tell they were hurt. We certainly need to develop wisdom in the way we speak and act with our friends.

> Loving words will cost but little,
>   Journeying up the hill of life;
> But they make the weak and weary
>   Stronger, braver, for the strife.
> Do you count them only trifles?
>   What to earth are sun and rain?
> Never was a kind word wasted;
>   Never was one said in vain.

Prayer: Our Father, may the testimony of our lips and the testimony of our lives be acceptable in thy sight. Help us today to say something that will lead someone to a closer walk with thee. We ask in the name of Jesus Christ. Amen.

September 8

"The eyes of the Lord are in every place, beholding the evil and the good." — Proverbs 15:3

Pansy had big brown eyes and black hair. She had worked very hard making a little garden in a flower bed. She had some onions and some carrots almost ready to eat. She thought about how proud of her the family would be when she served them. Then one day when she came home from school a dog had dug up almost all her carrots and scattered them about.

Pansy's mother found her sitting on the back step weeping. After they talked about the dog and how he destroyed her garden mother brought up another subject.

223

"Pansy, did you know your heart is God's garden. He wants only good thoughts and deeds to grow there." She put her arm tight around Pansy, "Sometimes the devil comes and tries to destroy God's garden by pulling up the good thoughts and planting bad ones. We are the ones who must be very careful that no one destroys the good in the garden of our hearts."

> The fear of God and sweet content
> Yield riches that will ne'er be spent.

Prayer: Dear God, help us to keep our hearts pure and holy for thy service. Make us strong against the wiles of the devil. We ask for Christ's sake. Amen.

September 9

"Blessed are ye, when men shall revile you, and persecute you, and shall say all manner of evil against you falsely, for my sake." — Matthew 5:11

Most people want to achieve success in life; only a few are willing to pay the price. There are always fences to climb over on the road to success. There are sacrifices of time and effort to be made. There are those who would hold others back because they are too lazy to seek success. A successful person is one who has overlooked the locked gates and the hands trying to hold him back. He has climbed over the fences with hard work and faith in his ability.

> Take a dash of water cold
>   And a little leaven of prayer,
> A little bit of sunshine gold
>   Dissolved in the morning air;
> Add to your meal some merriment
>   And a thought for kith and kin;
> And then, as a prime ingredient
>   A plenty of work thrown in:
> But spice it all with the essence of love
>   And a little whiff of play:
> Let a wise old book and a glance above
>   Complete a well spent day.

Prayer: Our Heavenly Father give us today the perseverance in prayer and work to make our lives successful for thee. In James we are promised, "the effectual fervent prayer of a righteous man availeth much." Make us worthy to claim that promise. We ask in Jesus' name. Amen.

224

September 10

"Take us the foxes, the little foxes, that spoil the vines: for our vines have tender grapes." — Solomon's Song 2:15

We had a lovely tree growing on the back of our lot. I have often thought, "What a fine, strong tree."

Then one day my small son came hurrying in the house, "Mother, the tree on the back fence has fallen over."

Heartbroken we went out to see our lovely tree broken off almost even with the ground. Some kind of a bug or worm had eaten the heart out and just a little gust of wind had blown it over.

So often lives are harmed and ruined, not by big sins but by little ones that eat and gnaw until all the heart is infested and ruined. Just a small wind of adversity can then destroy us.

> And when he fell in whirlwind, he went down
> As when a lordly cedar, green with boughs,
> Goes down with a great shout upon the hills,
> And leaves a lonesome place against the sky.

> — Edwin Markham

Prayer: Father, may we today realize life is not made up of great deeds of valor, but of little duties faithfully carried out day by day. May we make the world a better place by showing little kindnesses to those about us, giving smiles and comfort to those who are lonely. We pray in the name of Jesus. Amen.

September 11

"Open thou mine eyes that I may behold wondrous things out of thy law." — Psalm 119:18

When Gordon's father was reading the Bible at the breakfast table he talked about all the wonderful things in the world today. He could hear the washing machine running in the utility room and so he mentioned how nice that Mother did not have to draw water and heat it in a pot and rub clothes on a rub board.

"Daddy, is there anything that has not been invented new in this great age?" Gordon asked.

"Yes, there are many things man has not improved upon," Father told him. "We cannot change the moon, the stars, or the sun. We cannot find a book better able to guide us than the Bible."

> We search the world for truth, we cull
> The good, the pure, the beautiful,

225

From graven stone and written scroll,
From the old flower-fields of the soul,
And, weary seekers for the best,
We come back laden from our quest,
To find that all the sages said
Is in the Book our mothers read.

— John Greenleaf Whittier

Prayer: Our Father, today open our minds to the Spirit of God that he may reveal to us the wonders of our world. May he reveal the glory of thy love and the truth that is everlasting. We ask in the name of Jesus. Amen.

September 12

"Thy statutes have been my songs in the house of my pilgrimage." — Psalm 119:54

Some sailors were deserting their wrecked ship. They were all in the lifeboats and pushing away from the ship when one of them thought of something.

"Did anyone get the compass?" he called. The word went from lifeboat to lifeboat.

"No. No compass!"

What could they do on these little traveled waters without a compass?

"I will swim back and try to get it before the ship goes down," a brave man called.

So, at much risk to his own life he went back to the ship and sought the compass. When at last he returned with it safely to his companions there was much rejoicing.

"We will all be saved if we stay close together and are guided by the compass."

If we carry the Bible as our companion and guide we will be safe from the winds and storms of this world.

"Run, run, and work," the law commands,
But gives me neither feet nor hands;
But sweeter sounds the gospel brings,
It bids me fly, and gives me wings.

Prayer: Our Father, we thank thee for the privilege of walking with thee. May we ever take thee as our traveling companion. We ask in Jesus' name. Amen.

226

September 13

"He shall cover thee with his feathers, and under his wings shalt thou trust: his truth shall be thy shield and buckler. Thou shalt not be afraid for the terror by night; nor for the arrow that flieth by day." — Psalm 91:4, 5

Little Mellie was the baby of a large family. She often tried to imitate her older sisters. One day she watched as they took hot bread out of the oven. When their backs were turned she tried to open the oven door and was badly burned on her arm.

The sisters and brothers all felt bad because of her pain. Every day until she was better they doctored and petted her. Seeing their concern one day she said, "You hurt because I hurt."

When we are hurt we need only call upon our Father in heaven to heal and restore us.

> We never know another's pain
> We only feel our own.
> We never know real loneliness
> Until we're left alone.
>
> Too oft, it seems, our real concern
> Is just our selfish gain,
> And so we often shut our eyes
> To someone else's pain.
>
> — E. Jay Ritter

Prayer: Father, help us to follow Christ's example and be aware of the pain and need of those about us. We ask in the name of our Lord Jesus Christ. Amen.

September 14

"Keep your heart with all vigilance; for from it flow the springs of life." — Proverbs 4:23

Jesus faced an impure world and yet he lived a perfect life. We are not divine so we cannot be perfect, yet we can take some of the same precautions Jesus took and make our lives purer.

One of the first rules for a pure life is to flee from temptation. Do not go where temptation is and say, "I will resist it." No, run away from it. Look up II Timothy 2:22 and see what Paul told young Timothy to do.

Talk about good things: the laws in the Bible, the love of God for sinners, memorize Bible verses. Jesus quoted some verses when he was tempted.

Avoid bad companions and do not read trashy literature.

Then last, but most important, if you would have a clean life, love God supremely and determine to serve him.

> Not bubbling waters to the thirsty swain,
> Not rest to weary laborers, faint with pain,
> Not showers to larks, not sunshine to the bee,
> Are half so precious as thy love to me —
> My Saviour.

Prayer: O Lord Jesus Christ, we humbly beseech thee, open our eyes to evil about us and help us with thy power to lead clean, pure lives. We pray in the name of Jesus our Lord. Amen.

September 15

"And Jesus stood still, and commanded him to be called. And they called the blind man, saying unto him, be of good comfort, rise; he calleth thee." — Mark 10:49

One of the greatest things about America is that people may seek for better ways of life and find them.

Joseph Pulitzer left his home in Hungary and crossed to the United States when he was a boy of seventeen. He joined the cavalry of the North during the war between the states.

For a number of years Joseph did well just to have food to eat and a place to sleep. But he never minded hard work, and after he was released from the army he started to write and work as a reporter. He had as his motto, Accuracy and Service. He became very wealthy and though he has been dead many years his money still is serving others by way of the Pulitzer Prizes. What did he seek? To help others!

Almost any person can be judged by what they seek in life.

> Sad one in secret bending low,
> A dart in thy breast that the world may not know,
> Striving the favor of God to win,
> Asking his pardon for days of sin;
> Press on, press on, with thy earnest cry,
> "Jesus of Nazareth passeth by."

> — Mrs. Sigourney

Prayer: Great God, our Father, who hast taught us that they who mourn shall be comforted; may we turn to thee in our sin and sorrow. We ask for Jesus name. Amen.

September 16

The Lord is my shepherd;
  I shall not want.
He maketh me to lie down in green pastures:
  He leadeth me beside the still waters.
He restoreth my soul:
  He leadeth me in the paths of righteousness
For His name's sake.

Yea though I walk through the valley
Of the shadow of death,
  I will fear no evil:
For thou art with me;
  Thy rod and thy staff they comfort me.

Thou preparest a table before me
  In the presence of mine enemies:
Thou anointest my head with oil;
  My cup runneth over.

Surely goodness and mercy shall
  Follow me all the days of my life:
And I will dwell in the house
  Of the Lord forever.

— Psalm 23:1-6

"This peaceful idyl (the twenty-third psalm) is a voice out of the maturer life of the psalmist, out of memories of care and battle and treachery; a voice that tells that peace and rest of heart depend not upon the absence of life's burdens, nor on the presence of nature's tranquilizing scenes, but solely upon the shepherding of God." (Marvin R. Vincent)

Prayer: Dear Father, shepherd of all mankind, help us to trust in thee. Give us courage and strength for the dangers of the world. We pray in the name of Jesus. Amen.

September 17

"Come unto me, all ye that labor and are heavy laden, and I will give you rest. Take my yoke upon you, and learn of me; for I am meek and lowly in heart: and ye shall find rest unto your souls. For my yoke is easy and my burden is light."
— Matthew 11:28, 29, 30

A family went out in a boat for a summer outing. Soon a strong wind came up. They all became frightened, except the baby. The baby slept through all the frightening hour they were trying to get back to shore. The baby was clasped tight to her mother's breast and she knew no fear.

As Christians we should trust in our Saviour and know no fear when the storms of life assail us.

> As those that watch for the day,
>   Through the restless night of pain,
> When the first faint streaks of gray
>   Bring rest and ease again —
> As they turn their sleepless eyes
>   The Eastern sky to see,
> Long hours before sunrise —
>   So waiteth my soul for Thee!

Prayer: Our Father, may we ever know that thou art the protector of all who put their trust in thee. May we praise thy Holy name and honor thee with our lives. We ask in the name of Jesus. Amen.

September 18

"And now abideth faith, hope, love, these three; but the greatest of these is love." — I Corinthians 13:13

> If I knew the box where the smiles are kept,
>   No matter how large the key
> Or strong the bolt, I would try so hard
>   'Twould open, I know for me.
>
> Then over the land and sea broadcast
>   I'd scatter the smiles to play,
> That the children's faces might hold them fast
>   For many and many a day.
>
> If I knew a box that was large enough
>   To hold all the frowns I meet,
> I would try to gather them, every one,
>   From nursery school and street,
>
> Then, folding and holding, I'd pack them in
>   And turn the monster key;
> I'd hire a giant to drop the box
>   To the depths of the deep, deep sea.

What is the source of joy for people? Is it love for family, work, home, pleasure, travel? We could write pages and not name all the things people seek after as a source of joy. Yet without the love of Jesus all joy is at best very fleeting. On the other hand if we have the love of Christ in our hearts it helps us to find joy in all other things. Christ's love makes us content with our family, our work and our friends.

Prayer: Our Father, we long for a closer walk with thee. We know if we have thy love in our hearts we will understand each other better. We will seek to bear one another's burdens. Grant us this love in the name of Jesus. Amen.

September 19

"What man of you, having an hundred sheep, if he lose one of them, does not leave the ninety and nine in the wilderness, and go after that which is lost, until he find it? And when he cometh home, he calleth together his friends and neighbors, saying unto them, Rejoice with me; for I have found my sheep which was lost." — Luke 15:4, 6

In this story Jesus showed how active and energetic his love for his children is. His was not a religion of mere talk and sentiment, it was a religion of action.

He went in search of the lost sheep — not for just a little while but until it was found.

When Jesus found the lost sheep he brought it home. We have but to look in almost any direction to find people who are lost from God and need to be brought home. Are we seeking to bring them into the fold?

When the sheep was safely back in the fold there was great rejoicing!

> Hark 'tis the Shepherd's voice I hear,
> Out in the desert dark and drear,
> Calling the sheep who've gone astray
> Far from the Shepherd's fold away.
>
> — Alex Thomas

Prayer: Father, put it in our hearts to go out and seek for the lost around us. We pray in the name of the great Shepherd. Amen.

September 20

"But they constrained him, saying, Abide with us: for it is toward evening, and the day is far spent. And he went in to tarry with them." — Luke 24:29

Suppose they had not asked him in,
Inviting him to share
The comfort of their fireside and
Their simple evening fare.

That intimate companionship
Enabled them to find
A wonder and divinity
To which they had been blind.

For as he blessed and broke the bread
They saw the commonplace
Akin, somehow, to holiness
And touched by heavenly grace.

So it has always been that hearts
Have learned to know Christ best,
When he has been invited in —
A loved and honored guest.

As we travel life's pathway how often do we invite Jesus in to sup with us?

Prayer: Dear Lord, bless us with thy presence at our table. May our ears be open to hear thy word. For Jesus' sake. Amen.

September 21

"Whom have I in heaven but thee? and there is none upon earth that I desire beside thee." — Psalm 73:25

Carelessness and lack of proper consideration are responsible for a large part of the sorrow in the world. Sometimes we are caught in a current and are swept along without giving proper consideration to our deeds. We could stop much of the rough grinding of the cogs of life if we just used oil of consideration for those about us.

A door can be a boon, for it can keep intruders out,
And it can be a comfort when bad weather is about;
But let us not forget that it can also bar the way
To kindly folk who'd drop in, just to pass the time of day.

If we are too much sheltered by the heavy lock and key,
Then we are apt to find out just how lonely we can be;
For heartaches soon vanish, and new happiness begins,
Through the open door that's waiting for a friend to enter in.

— Anne Hayward

232

Prayer: Our Father, give us considerate hearts for those about us. Give us eyes of love to see those in need of extra kindness and consideration. We ask in Jesus' name. Amen.

September 22

"Behold, for peace I had great bitterness: but thou hast in love to my soul delivered it from the pit of corruption: for thou hast cast all my sins behind thy back." — Isaiah 38:17

Are we ever bitter over our sins? We should be. We should never be satisfied with our sinful condition.

God loves us no matter how deep in the pit of sin we sink, if we only seek his help and show that we want to repent.

Two singers were very jealous of each other. Only hate seemed to live in them. Then one grew very ill and could not work. Soon she had no money for doctors and medicine. Her rival decided to help. He announced a benefit concert for the stricken one. The concert was a great success and he brought the money to her. The hate within her heart melted away. She had seen a glimpse of true Christian character.

> Lord, give me eyes that I may see
> The glance of those who look to me
> To help them in their time of need.
> Lord, give me eyes that I may heed.
> Lord give me ears that I may hear
> The voice of service calling clear —
> Service to those not blest as I;
> Lord, give me ears to hear their cry.
>
> — Warren M. Baker

Prayer: Our Father, take all bitterness away from our hearts. Cast our sins behind thy back and make us worthy of thy love. We ask in Jesus' name. Amen.

September 23

"Therefore all things whatsoever ye would that men should do to you, do ye even so to them: for this is the law and the prophets." — Matthew 7:12

Do not expect from others more than you are willing to do for them. Be willing to do for others all you would like from them under the same circumstances. The golden rule is a reasonable and wholesome principle.

Little Billy had a bad habit, biting other children in the nursery school. His teachers tried several forms of punishment but Billy kept on biting the other children.

One day little Mary's mother said to her, "If Billy starts to bite you, you bite him good and hard."

Sure enough in a day or two Billy grabbed Mary's hand and started to bite. Mary gave him such a hard bite on his arm he was never known to bite again.

> I think that good must come of good,
>   And ill of evil — surely unto all
> In every place of time, seeing sweet fruit
> Groweth from wholesome roots or bitter things
> From poison stocks; yea, seeing, too, how spite
> Breeds hate — and kindness friends — or patience
> Peace.

> — Edwin Arnold

Prayer: Father let thy spirit come upon us in such a way that we will always seek to live by the Golden Rule. Help our deeds to be acceptable in thy sight. We ask for Jesus' sake. Amen.

September 24

"Humble yourselves in the sight of the Lord, and he shall lift you up." — James 4:10

Pride in a job well done is fine. But we should remember that without God's blessing it would be for naught. Everything man is and does is from God. The glory and honor should be his and his alone.

> Before Elisha's gate
> The Syrian leper stood
> But could not brook to wait,
> He deemed himself too good:
> He thought the prophet would attend
> And not to *him* a message send.

> Have I this journey come,
> And will he not be seen?
> I were as well at home,
> Would washing make me clean;
> Why must I wash in Jordan's flood?
> Damascus rivers are as good.

> Thus by his foolish pride
> He almost missed a cure;

Howe'er at length he tried,
And found the method sure:
Soon as the pride was brought to yield,
The leprosy was quickly healed.

— John Newton

Prayer: Heavenly Father, may we always do our work well, never forgetting to give thee the glory. In Jesus' name we pray. Amen.

September 25

"Then Paul stood in the midst of Mars' hill, and said, Ye men of Athens, I perceive that in all things ye are too superstitious."
— Acts 17:22

Paul was preaching to the most superstitious people in his day. Today the word superstitious describes people who will not walk under a ladder or who will not sleep in room 13, or many others.

I remember well one day I was going to town in a hurry and a black cat crossed my path. In spite of myself, just for a moment, an old, childish whim came to me and I thought, "You will have bad luck if you don't turn around."

How foolish for Christian people to think that anyone save God can control our fate.

All is of God! If He but wave His hand,
The mists collect, the rain falls thick and loud,
Till, with a smile of light on sea and land,
Lo! He looks back from the departing cloud.
Angels of life and death alike are His;
Without His leave they pass no threshold o'er;
Who then would wish or dare, believing this,
Against His messengers to shut the door?

— J. R. Lowell

Prayer: Our most gracious Father help us to always trust in thee only. Make us good servants of thine. We pray in the name of Jesus. Amen.

September 26

"For if ye forgive men their trespasses, your heavenly Father will also forgive you." — Matthew 6:14

Asking forgiveness is hard for most of us. Sometimes forgiving

235

is even harder. The wrong spirit about little things can hurt us, and often hurt the other fellow.

When we think about how much God has to forgive us for we certainly should be willing to forgive others.

> Oh, it's just the little homely things,
> The unobtrusive, friendly things,
> The "won't-you-let-me-help-you" things
>   That make our pathway light.
> And it's just the jolly joking things,
> The "never-mind-the-trouble" things,
> The "laugh-with-me-it's-funny" things,
>   That make the world seem bright.
> For all the countless famous things,
> The wondrous record-breaking things
> Those never-can-be-equalled things,
>   That all the papers cite,
> Are not like little human things,
> The every-day-encounter things,
> The "just-because-I-like-you" things,
>   That make us happy quite.
> So here's to all the little things,
> The done-and-then-forgotten things,
> The "oh, it's — simply-nothing" things,
>   That make life worth the fight.

Prayer: Father, today give us a forgiving heart. Give us the heart to help others by doing the little things that make life sweeter. We pray in the name of Jesus. Amen.

September 27

"By your words you will be justified, and by your words you will be condemned." — Matthew 12:37

In the ninth commandment (Exodus 20:16) we read, "You shall not bear false witness against your neighbor."

The problems caused by people bearing false witness are many and very harmful. The problems hurt three persons: the one bearing false witness, the one to whom he speaks, and the one about whom he speaks. The verse in Matthew tells us we will be justified or condemned by our words; so we should be extra careful what we say.

If we think someone is telling a story about a friend or acquaintance we should walk away and not listen.

So many kinds of lies there be,
So many ways to lie,
So many tongues hung loose and free
To twist the truth awry.

Despised as liars always are,
God rates as worst the kind
Whose lies are half-truth, stretched so far
All truth is left behind.

Prayer: Dear Father may we resolve today to be truthful in all things. Help us to be wise and considerate of other people and never say unkind things about others. We ask in the name of one who was always kind and pure, Jesus our Saviour. Amen.

September 28

"But as for you, man of God, shun all this; aim at righteousness, godliness, faith, love, steadfastness, gentleness."

— I Timothy 6:11

When you read the words, *Christian Graces,* do they paint a picture of the best Christian you know? Do you picture someone like the person described in the verse above? I do.

A mother I knew thought her daughter must take dancing lessons. "Why?" I asked her.

"Oh, so she will grow up to be more graceful."

That same mother who was so eager for her daughter to have a graceful body, never once took time to see that she was brought up to know the Christian Graces and practice them. Many daughters in Christian homes may not be so graceful, I suppose, but most of them grow up to be good Christian women and work for their churches and communities. God's promise still holds, "Train up a child in the way he should go, and when he is old he will not depart therefrom" (Proverbs 22:6).

God might have used His sunset gold so sparingly
He might have doled His blossoms out quite grudgingly;
He might have put one wee star in the sky
But since He gave so lavishly,
Why should not I?

Prayer: Father, in these days of stress may we ever put Christ as the center of our lives, for in his name we pray. Amen.

September 29

"I was glad when they said unto me, let us go into the house of the Lord." — Psalm 122:1

> God bless all those whose membership is here,
> Thy people, Lord, who love Thy house and Thee.
> God bless the strangers gathered in our midst;
> Lonely, perhaps, and far from home they need
> The blessed comfort of their Father's house,
> The proffered bread of life on which to feed.
> God bless the one who here propounds Thy truths,
> Be in his heart, speak through the words he speaks
> That every listening, eager one may find
> The wisdom and the comfort that he seeks.
> > And when at last, the benediction said.
> > May we go, strengthened for the days ahead.

In the church I attend the children are kept in the nursery until they are four years old. All through the last year, before they promote from the nursery, they are told about the "big church." They are taken on walking tours of the sanctuary and told about the organ and the choir and other things. When they are old enough to attend "big church" they are well prepared for it. They look forward to their first Sunday there. They learn to love the services.

All true Christians like to attend the services in their church. If they do not, they should examine their hearts and see what is wrong.

Prayer: Father, make us appreciate the privilege of attending services in thy visible church. We pray in Jesus name. Amen.

September 30

"They sow the wind, and they shall reap the whirlwind."

— Hosea 8:7

We should stop periodically and look at our sowing. Are we sowing the whirlwind? What are we sowing in the lives of our children, our pupils, or our friends? Remember we will reap what we sow.

Children imitate their elders. So much of their learning comes from watching someone else and doing likewise. Are we sowing good seeds in the things we say and do?

As for friends, are we "sowing seeds of kindness"?

238

Are we sowing seeds of goodness?
　　They shall blossom bright ere long.
Are we sowing seeds of discord?
　　They shall ripen into wrong.
Are we sowing seeds of honor?
　　They shall bring forth golden grain.
Are we sowing seeds of falsehood?
　　We shall yet reap bitter pain.
　　　Whatsoe'er our sowing be,
　　　Reaping, we its fruit must see.

We can never be too careful
　　What the seed our hands shall sow;
Love from love is sure to ripen,
　　Hate from hate is sure to grow.
Seeds of good or ill we scatter
　　Heedlessly along our way;
But a glad or grievous fruitage
　　Waits us at the harvest day.

Prayer: Dear Lord, may we be ever watchful of the words we speak and the things we do. May our influence be for good and not for evil. In Jesus' name we pray. Amen.

October:

God's Care for Us

October 1

"But as many as received him, to them gave he power to become the sons of God, even to them that believe on his name."

— John 1:12

Many people have failed to achieve the best they could in life because they were too full of false pride. They wanted, as the old saying goes, "to rule or ruin."

Nancy was just such a girl. She was pretty and popular. A new girl moved to town who was prettier, and quickly became more popular. From that time forward life in that small town seemed to be a tug-of-war between the two girls for power. Whatever one wanted the other was sure to want it more and try to get it. So both became less and less popular and spent the remainder of their lives trying to out-do each other.

> The haughty feet of power shall fail
> Where meekness surely goes;
> No cunning finds the key of heaven,
> No strength its gates unclose.
> Alone to guilelessness and love
> Those gates shall open fall:
> The mind of pride is nothingness,
> The childlike heart is all.

Prayer: Most loving, heavenly Father, help us today to be sweet and gentle. May we be humble servants, willing to serve thee in this world. We pray in the name of one who had all power on earth and in heaven. Amen.

October 2

"But Jesus said, Forbid him not: for there is no man which shall do a miracle in my name, that can lightly speak evil of me."

— Mark 9:39

Many years ago our phone rang in the early morning hours. Answering I heard my father's voice, "Baby sister is dying; hurry home if you want to see her." Gathering up a few clothes for our own small daughter we hastily set out on a sad journey.

My sister was dying from a disease the doctors called colitis. Five of the doctors in the small town where my parents lived had told them, "No hope."

After we arrived and looked at the wasted, little body, we had no hope either. A nurse, a friend of my mother, came and she and mother started feeding the baby spoonfuls of beaten egg-

243

white. All day long they fed her all she would take. Next day she was much better. The doctors all said, "It is a miracle."

The nurse said "It is the egg-white."

We knew it was the hand of God.

Months later after the child was able to run and play again, my parents heard of a few friends who had met and prayed until far into the night for her, the night she was supposed to die. It was, indeed, an answer to prayer.

Prayer: Help us to pray in faith relying on thy promises. For Christ's sake. Amen.

October 3

"I will smite them with the pestilence, and disinherit them, and will make of thee a greater nation and mightier than they."
— Numbers 14:12

God took the Israelites from Egypt as poor, ignorant slaves. They had not traveled beyond the villages where they had been forced to labor each day; they had not been to schools and learned of the things of the world; yet he made of them a great nation.

"Unexplained as it was in the world, and without parallel in any other nation, it shows that there was some peculiar power at work in the Jewish dispensation, and that the people had been under a special, educating Providence."

Even today God looks after those who believe and trust in him. He still leads and directs his followers.

An infidel, Dryden, says of the Bible:

Whence but from heaven, could men unskilled in arts,
In several ages born, in several parts,
Weave such agreeing truths? or how or why,
Should all conspire to cheat us with a lie?
Unasked their pains, ungrateful their advice,
Starving their gain and martyrdom their price.

Prayer: Our most powerful and mighty God, help us as a nation to trust in thee. Help us as individuals to know there is no power greater than thine. Make us true servants of thine. We pray in Jesus' name. Amen.

October 4

"And we have borne the image of the earthy, we shall also bear the image of the heavenly." — I Corinthians 15:49

When we hear people talking about going to the moon, many of us often say, "One world is enough for me."

If we read the Easter story closely we see that there are people living in two worlds — the world of heavenly things and the world of earthly things. The heavenly will eventually be victorious over death and trouble.

Everyone has some interest in immortality. Christians feel secure in their belief; unbelievers feel a sense of frustration and often defeat.

'Tis Revelation satisfies all doubts,
Explains all mysteries except her own,
And so illumines the path of life,
That fools discover it and stray no more.

What glory gilds the sacred page!
Majestic! Like the sun,
It gives a light to every age;
It gives, but borrows none.

Most wondrous book! bright candle of the Lord!
Star of eternity! the only star
By which the bark of man could navigate
The sea of life, and gain the coast of bliss securely.

Prayer: Father, help us to know we are only here to salute the world as we pass by. We are going in the direction of a different world; a world where there is no sorrow or crying. We ask in the name of Jesus. Amen.

October 5

"Sayest thou this thing of thyself or did others tell it thee?"
— John 18:34

Jesus was speaking to Pilate. Pilate had to answer that he had heard what he had spoken from the Jews.

How many times we hurt others and ourselves by repeating what we have merely heard. Did you ever play gossip? Someone starts a sentence at the beginning of the circle and it is whispered all around. When it comes back to the original person it sounds quite different.

If we knew the cares and crosses
Crowding 'round our neighbor's way.
If we knew of all his losses
Sorely grievous day by day;
Would we then so often chide him

Casting o'er his life a shadow
Leaving on his heart a stain?
Let us reach into our bosoms
For the key to other lives,
And with love to erring nature,
Cherish good that still survives;
So that when our disrobed spirits
Soar to realms of light again,
We may say, dear Father, judge us
As we judged our fellow men.

Prayer: O Lord, make us to walk with thee here in such a way that we will not speak ill of our friends and neighbors. We ask in Jesus name. Amen.

October 6

"*. . . in everything by prayer and supplication, let your requests be made known unto God.*" — Philippians 4:6

We all have heard of people who say they are too busy to pray. Recently I heard of a woman who said she was too busy not to pray. I believe she had a point.

Prayer does not interrupt your time, activities, or life; it is the business of talking things over as we go along with a companion. In life we face questions each day. What? How? When? Where? Only God can answer all of these.

Go when the morning shineth,
  Go when the noon is bright
Go when the eve declineth,
  Go in the hush of night:
Go with pure mind and feeling,
  Fling every fear away,
And in thy chamber kneeling,
  Do thou in secret pray.

Or if 'tis e'er denied thee
  In solitude to pray,
Should holy thoughts come o'er thee
  When friends are round thy way,
E'en then the silent breathing
  Of thy spirit raised above,
May reach His throne of glory,
  Who is mercy, truth, and love.
                        — John Cress Bell

246

Prayer: O Lord, gather thy sheep and lambs and carry them in thy bosom. Feed thy sheep for thou art the great shepherd. We ask in Christ's name. Amen.

October 7

"You are no longer strangers and sojourners, but you are fellow citizens with the saints and members of the household of God." — Ephesians 2:19

We all like to be with the majority when we can do so in good conscience. Do you ever feel that you are the only Christian? You are not. There are millions more. We belong to a great household of believers.

My mother said that in the early twentieth century most of the farm families wanted many children to help with the farming. Most farm homes had long tables with benches on each side. A husband and wife felt very fortunate if both benches were well filled.

As Christians we should feel a part of a great family. We should want to see that family grow larger and larger.

> He drew a circle and shut me out,
> Heretic, rebel, a thing to flout.
> But love and I had a wit to win;
> We drew a circle that took him in.
>
> — Edwin Markham

Prayer: Father, may we know and be glad that we are members of the household of God. Help us to conduct our lives as children of Thine should. We pray in the name of Jesus. Amen.

October 8

"If we walk in the light, as he is in the light, we have fellowship with one another, and the blood of Jesus his Son cleanses us from all sin." — I John 1:7

The man who knows and understands Jesus is the man who walks in the light of his love. If we love Christ and are loyal to him we grow in knowledge and his truth is revealed to us.

In our family there is a blind lady. She has not always been blind and her trouble came on gradually. It fascinated the children when she would reach for something on the cabinet, or table. She would feel very gently. Then when her hand touched the object she would confidently pick it up. If we know Christ

we should not grope but be confident as we walk in the light of
his way.

> Dream not too much of what you'll do tomorrow,
> How well you'll work perhaps another year;
> Tomorrow's chance you do not need to borrow
> Today is here.

> Boast not too much of mountains you will master,
> The while you linger in the vale below;
> To dream is well, but plodding brings us faster —
> To where we go.

> Swear not some day to break some habit's fetter,
> When this old year is dead and passed away;
> If you have need of living better, wiser,
> Begin today!

Prayer: Lord, help us to see thee better. Amen.

October 9

*"The Spirit of the Lord is upon me, because he hath anointed
me to preach the gospel to the poor; he hath sent me to heal
the broken-hearted, to preach deliverance to the captives, and
recovering of sight to the blind, to set at liberty them that are
bruised."* — Luke 4:18, 19

When I was a little girl my mother sent me on an errand. My
baby sister was seriously ill. I had to walk sixteen blocks to
town and get some medicine prescribed by the doctor. I loved my
sister very much and I returned home as rapidly as possible. My
sister was soon resting well.

The Lord sends us on an errand too. The world is desperately
sick. God asks us to bring the good tidings that there is a remedy
for the world's ills. May the Spirit of the Lord make us willing
and able to carry out his mandate.

> We've a story to tell to the nations,
> That shall turn their hearts to the right,
> A story of truth and sweetness,
> A story of peace and light.

> For the darkness shall turn to dawning,
> And the dawning to noonday bright,
> And Christ's great kingdom shall come on earth,
> The kingdom of love and light.

248

Prayer: Father, may we feel thy call to us. May we answer thy commission and serve thee aright. We pray in Jesus' name. Amen.

October 10

"The earth is the Lord's and the fulness thereof, the world and those who dwell therein." — Psalm 24:1

Isn't it wonderful to know that the universe belongs to God. What a sad thing it would be for us if the universe belonged to a landlord who would not wait past the first of the month for the rent. We all owe so much and are so slow with our payments.

Some people went off the deep end and tried to make the world believe God was dead. How foolish! I know he lives because I feel him in my own heart. I know he lives because he patiently waits for us to turn to him and trust. If God turned the world over to the devil for just a moment chaos would destroy us.

> This is my Father's world,
> And to my listening ears,
> All nature sings, and round me rings;
> The music of the spheres.
>
> This is my Father's world
> I rest me in the thought,
> Of rocks and trees, of skies and seas;
> His hands the wonders wrought.

Prayer: Our God, whose greatness is revealed in all creation, we thank thee for our world so great. We thank thee for letting us live in such a marvelous age. Make us worthy of thy many blessings. We pray in the name of Jesus. Amen.

October 11

"Mine age is departed, and is removed from me as a shepherd's tent: I have cut off like a weaver my life; he will cut me off with pining sickness; from day even to night wilt thou make an end of me." — Isaiah 38:12

The life of the believer should be interesting. Have you ever been walking in the woods in the fall of the year? As one goes along there are so many interesting things to see. There are nuts to be picked up and bright colored leaves to gather.

The believer who is not finding his walk with God interesting is not looking about at life and taking a part in it.

The life we live will show to those about us in what we believe. If we walk with God it shows. Men may doubt what you say but they will believe what you live.

If we do not have the life of God dwelling within us, we are constantly growing more selfish and ugly. If Christ dwells within we grow more like him each day.

Life is uncertain, we must make the most of each day.

> True religion is more than doctrine,
> Something must be known and felt.

Prayer: Heavenly Father, may our conduct today contribute to thy glory and to our spiritual life and welfare. We ask in the name of Jesus. Amen.

October 12

"The heart of the prudent getteth knowledge; and the ear of the wise seeketh knowledge." — Proverbs 18:15

We like to remember Columbus because we think of him as being the one who discovered our country. He had no idea how large the world was, how round it was, or how far the ocean stretched but he was willing to seek and discover.

It isn't the work that tries us, but the sights we have to see;
The children bowing to idols, the slaves who cannot be free,
With those who of evil spirit spend all their lives in fear,
And women toiling in bondage, no hope of heaven to cheer.

It isn't the work that wears us; at least, not what we do,
But that which is left undone when our busy day is through;
It's turning away the scholars who want our schools to share,
And saying "No" to the people who beg for a teacher's care.

It isn't the work that kills us; but the strange, indifferent life
Of those who, too, are Christians, but stand aloof from strife;
It's keeping up the struggle that we abroad must live
Without the friendly backing which you at home could give.

— By a Missionary

Prayer: Father, if we are not willing to go to other lands, make us willing to hold the ropes in order that others may carry the Word. We pray in Jesus' name. Amen.

October 13

"The law of the Lord is perfect, converting the soul: the testimony of the Lord is sure, making wise the simple."

— Psalm 19:7

In recent years we have heard much talk about the laws of our land often seeming to protect the criminal. We read and hear of cases that seem in our eyes to be unfair and unjust to the victim of wrong. God's law is perfect. We cannot hope to keep it without the help of Jesus Christ.

> When some fellow yields to temptation
> And breaks a conventional law,
> We look for no good in his make-up
> But oh! how we look for the flaw!
>
> No one will ask, "How tempted?"
> Nor allow for the battles he fought;
> His name becomes food for the jackals —
> For us who have never been caught.
>
> "He's sinned!" shout we from the housetops;
> We forget the good he has done;
> We center on one lost battle
> And forget the times he has won.
>
> "Come; gaze on the sinner!" we thunder,
> "And by his example be taught
> That his footsteps lead to destruction,"
> Cry we who have never been caught.
>
> I'm a sinner, O Lord, and I know it;
> I'm weak and I blunder and fail;
> I'm tossed on life's stormy ocean
> Like ships embroiled in a gale.
>
> I'm willing to trust in Thy mercy,
> To keep the commandments Thou'st taught;
> But deliver me, Lord, from the judgment
> Of the "saints" who have never been caught.

Prayer: Father, keep us from being unkind in our judgment of others. We ask in Jesus' name. Amen.

October 14

"The fame of him went out into every place of the country round about." — Luke 4:37

Lillian is not famous outside her own community but mention her name in her own town and people will say, "Oh, yes, I know her." She is not young and beautiful, nor is she rich in worldly goods. Lillian is a Christian. During an epidemic when she was just a young bride she went from house to house taking care of the sick. She paid people's bills and ran their errands; took care of the children. All the years since people have kept calling on her for help. The youth has left her face, her body is older and more frail, but she is known as a good woman.

> No matter what others are doing, my friend,
> Or what they are leaving undone,
> God's counting on you to keep on with the job
> 'Till the very last battle is won.
> He's counting on you to be faithful:
> He's counting on you to be true.
> Yes, others may work, or others may shirk,
> But remember — God's counting on you.

Prayer: O God, make thyself known to us, show us the works Thou would'st have us to do. Bow our wills to thine, yield our spirits to the influence of the Holy Spirit. We pray in the name of Jesus. Amen.

October 15

"He said, Abba, Father, all things are possible unto thee; take away this cup from me: nevertheless not what I will, but what thou wilt." — Mark 14:36

One time we were visiting in the country. Two boys in the home had caught some birds and had cages built for them. The owl just sat in his cage and blinked. He was content with his lot. Not so the young eagle. He beat against the wire with his wings and pecked with his beak. He wanted freedom and in a few days would have beat himself to death trying to break the bondage. The boys being gentle fellows turned the young eagle loose and he was soon away in the woods.

> Oft we judge each other harshly
>   Knowing not life's hidden force,
> Knowing not the fount of action
>   Is less turbid at its source,

252

Seeing not amid the evil
  All the golden grains of good,
Oh, we'd love each other better
  If we only understood.

Could we but draw the curtain
  That surrounds each other's lives,
See the naked heart and spirit
  Know what impulse, the action gives,
Often we should find it better,
  Purer than we judged we should,
We would love each other better
  If we only understood.

Prayer: Almighty God, our Father in Heaven, we appreciate the freedom from sin thou hast provided for us through Christ Jesus. Make us worthy of thy love. We ask in Jesus' name. Amen.

October 16

"And make straight paths for feet, lest that which is lame be turned out of the way; but let it rather be healed."

— Hebrews 12:13

There was a family with four children. They were like all children, full of life and mischief. One day as they played one of the boys accidently threw a stick and it seriously injured his brother's eye. In fact, he lost the sight in the eye. For weeks the injured brother had to wear a patch over his eye, and sometimes he was cross and ill. The other children did his work and in every way tried to make up to him for what had happened.

Long years ago I blazed a trail
  Through lovely woods unknown till then,
And marked with cairns of splintered shale
  A mountain way for other men;

For other men who came and came:
  They trod the path more plain to see;
They gave my trail another's name,
  And no one speaks or knows of me.

The trail runs high, the trail runs low,
  Where wildflowers dance, or columbine;
The scars are healed that long ago
  My ax cut deep on birch and pine.

253

Another's name my trail may bear,
    But still I keep, in waste and wood,
My joy because the trail is there,
    My peace because the trail is good.
                    — Arthur Guiterman

Prayer: Lord, show us what paths you would have us make for those who come after us. Help us make the pathway straight. We ask in the name of Jesus. Amen.

October 17

"And in those days there was no king in Israel: every man did that which was right in his own eyes." — Judges 21:25

What a world we would live in if every man went by his own law. No one would be safe for a moment from the ones who feel it is safe to rob and kill. We would be in a state of utter confusion.

God knowing our condition gave us laws to abide by and lawmakers to enforce them.

I was the oldest child in my family. Often my mother would entrust me with the care of my younger brother and sister. When she left she would say, "Now you mind Amy until I return."

God left us a world that is not perfect and our laws are often disappointing in the way they are enforced but one day he will return. If the laws have not been kept he will make a perfect judgment.

My soul is but the battle ground between the base and pure:
What though today I sound sin's depths its miseries endure,
And walk down the valley way of sorrow and despair
With want as my companion and hand in hand with care,
Tomorrow I will climb the heights that lead to realms above,
And comprehend the mystery of Life . . . of Death . . . of
    Love.

                    — Jeanne Breton

Prayer: Father, give us the love in our hearts to obey thy laws. We pray in the name of Christ. Amen.

October 18

"Are you not behaving like ordinary men?"
                    — I Corinthians 3:3 (Moffatt translation)

"We are children of the minister, so we can't act like

that." How often as a child I have said this or had my mother say it to me.

Our own pastor's little girl was near a boy at a ball game when he said an ugly word.

"You shouldn't say that," she said to him.

"Who are you?" he asked her.

"I'm a preacher's kid," she replied proudly.

"Oh, I'm sorry. I will not say that again," said the boy. He was on his best behavior the rest of the ball game.

As Christians we are children of a King. We should always remember this and act accordingly.

> The little birds that fly in air;
> The sheep that need the shepherd's care;
> The pearls that deep in ocean lie;
> The gold that charms the miser's eye;
> All from his lips some truth proclaim,
> Or learn to tell their Maker's name.

Prayer: Lord, make us ever proud to own thee as our Maker, our Lord, and King. Keep us from acting like ordinary men. We pray in the name of the one who was of all men most extraordinary. Amen.

October 19

"And Elijah came unto all the people and said: How long halt ye between two opinions? If the Lord be God, follow Him, but if Baal, then follow him." — I Kings 18:21

We face questions every day, Where is our life going? What purpose do we have in life? Will we live for God or for the world?

How we face these questions determines whether we will be happy or disgruntled, whether we will be useful or just a wasted piece of driftwood on the sea of life.

> Work hard today and pray,
> Be resolute and say,
> "I will not fail in work of mine
> Though I must toil till bright stars shine
> And midnight falls."
>
> Tomorrow when the sun
> Shines on thy duty done,
> Thou wilt rejoice and gladly sing;

To thee thy task sweet peace will bring
And rest complete.

And finished work abides,
Thy toil doth crystallize
The thoughts of brain, thine acts of will,
Thy very life continuing still,
Beyond life's span.

— Charles E. Earle

Prayer: Dear Lord, we pour our hearts out to thee. We want our choice in life to be of service for thee. May we meditate daily on thy Word and will. May we lead others to make the right choices, also. We ask in Jesus' name. Amen.

October 20

"Train up a child in the way he should go: and when he is old, he will not depart from it." — Proverbs 22:6

Sherri was expecting a new baby in her family. Her mother often talked to her about how she must be kind to the baby and that she would have to share her toys.

One day as they talked she said to her mother, "I will make it be a good baby."

Sometimes we are hungry for children and when God blesses us with them we forget to train them to be good. We indulge them in extravagances and whims and they do not grow up in the way they should.

I took a piece of plastic clay
And idly fashioned it one day,
And as my fingers pressed it still
It moved and yielded to my will.

I came again when days were past,
The bit of clay was hard at last
The form I gave it still it bore
And I could change that form no more.

I took a piece of living clay
And gently formed it day by day,
And molded with my power and art
A young child's soft and tender heart.

I came again when years were gone,
It was a man I looked upon,

256

He still that early impress bore,
And I could change him — nevermore.

Prayer: Give us a sense of responsibility as we train our children, we ask in Jesus' name. Amen.

October 21

"In my Father's house are many mansions: if it were not so, I would have told you. I go to prepare a place for you."

— John 14:2

To every hungry soul He gives from out His bounteous store
Its needs — its lessons — Who would ask for more?

How many times in life when things seemed scarce here on earth have I thought of the mansion my Lord is preparing for me. I have never thought of it in terms of beauty; just in terms of peace and quiet. Yet Jesus wants us as Christians to know an inner peace and tranquility here.

Promises are so nice when the one making the promise plans to keep that promise. Jesus is busy now getting that mansion ready for his children. We must get ready to occupy it.

Prayer:

Dear Lord! kind Lord!
Gracious Lord! I pray
Thou wilt look on all I love,
Tenderly to-day!
Weed their hearts of weariness;
Scatter every care
Down a wake of angel-wings
Winnowing the air.
Bring unto the sorrowing
All release from pain;
Let the lips of laughter
Overflow again;
And with all the needy
O divide, I pray,
This vast treasure of content
That is mine to-day!

— Riley

October 22

"And it came to pass, that, when Jesus was returned, the people gladly received him: for they were all waiting for him."

— Luke 8:40

When I left home as a bride we moved to a distant city and I could not go back for three months. Those were such long months because I had never been away before — and I was homesick. My home looked like a mansion at the end of three months when I returned. My family all waited at the door for me and seemed glad to see me.

What a joy it must have been to Jesus to return from a country where the people begged him to leave, to a place where they welcomed him and waited his coming.

> I have a longing in my heart for Jesus,
> I have a longing in my heart for Him;
> I have a longing just to see His face.
> Although I know His presence lingers near me,
>
> Longing, longing for Jesus,
> I have a longing in my heart for Him;
> Just to be near Him, to feel His presence,
> I have a longing in my heart for Him.
>
> I have a longing just to walk with Jesus,
> I have a longing just to hold His hand:
> To know He's there forever near to guide me,
> To know His love will never let me go.
>
> To you who do not know this man named Jesus,
> You've never lived or found life's greatest joy;
> Oh, won't you now take Him as Lord and Saviour,
> And know the fullness of His matchless love.
> — Richard D. Baker

Prayer: As we wait for the return of our dear Saviour may we seek to live for him each day. In his name we pray. Amen.

October 23

"And she had a sister called Mary, which also sat at Jesus' feet, and heard his word." — Luke 10:39

When we think of sitting at someone's feet we think of listening to him as he speaks. We should always be listening for the words of Jesus. We should always listen with an attitude of worship and lowliness. When we sit at the feet of Jesus we must be aware of his love for us and we must ask him to take possession of our lives.

When we give ourselves over to sitting at Jesus' feet we find satisfaction and assurance in life.

At the feet of Jesus, list'ning to His word;
Learning wisdom's lesson from her loving Lord;
    Mary led by heavenly grace
    Chose the meek disciple's place.
At the feet of Jesus is the place for me;
There a humble learner would I choose to be.

Prayer: Father help us ever to sit humbly at thy feet and learn of thee. Make us meek and mild, and help us always to choose the better part of service. We pray in the name of our dear Saviour. Amen.

October 24

"And when Jesus came to the place, he looked up, and saw him, and said unto him, Zacchaeus, make haste, and come down; for today I must abide at thy house." — Luke 19:5

Jesus invited himself to Zacchaeus' house because he had a gift for Zacchaeus. He had the gift of eternal life to bestow upon his new friend.

Jesus could see the good in Zacchaeus and he wanted to claim him for his own kingdom.

Several things worked together that day. God put it in the heart of Zacchaeus to want to see Jesus. He had to overcome the obstacle of being a short man, so he climbed a tree. Jesus, as he walked along, could feel a longing heart nearby. So he looked up into the tree and called to Zacchaeus.

I remember one time when I was a little girl and a girl in school told me she was going home with me. I felt so excited because she was a little older than I and we did not often play together. She invited herself but I was happy.

Prayer: Almighty God, our dear Father, we rejoice that you will come into our hearts and dwell with us. We are grateful for thy love. We pray in the name of Jesus. Amen.

October 25

"Then said Jesus, Father, forgive them; for they know not what they do." — Luke 23:34

Prayer is the greatest power we have on earth. What a pity this power is often used the least. When we pray we link ourselves with God who is all powerful.

When Moses prayed, Israel prevailed and gained great victories. When Elijah prayed God locked the heavens and it did not rain for three years. When Paul and Silas prayed the doors of the jail opened. What a power! When we pray believing today we can still see the miracles of God. Why not use the power of prayer more often?

> Nobody knows the power of prayer,
> But somebody must be listening there
> With a friendly ear for the heart that calls,
> Someone who knows when a sparrow falls.
> Miracles lie in the power of prayer;
> Faith that can banish the soul's despair!
> Hope that shines like a holy light!
> That brightens the spirit's darkest night!
> When earthly help is of no avail
> There is one Friend who will never fail;
> Just lift your eyes — the answer is there
> For nobody knows the power of prayer!

Prayer: Loving Father, life is sweet and precious when we rest in the assurance of answered prayer. Teach us more and more to implicitly trust in thy answer to our prayers being the right answer. We pray in Christ's name. Amen.

October 26

"Are not two sparrows sold for a farthing? and one of them shall not fall on the ground without your Father."

— Matthew 10:29

How wonderful to know that God takes notice of all the small things happening on the earth! If he knows when a small sparrow falls, how much more does he take notice and care when his children are having trouble and are in need of his care.

Sitting in the waiting room of a large railway station, I watched as crowds of people swiftly passed by. "Can it be," I thought, "That God knows each one in this mass of people; knows what burdens and joys each carries in his heart, and cares about the problems?"

Yes, if God cares for the birds and the flowers he cares much more for his children.

> Why should I feel discouraged?
> Why should I feel so sad?
> For His eye is on the sparrow
> And I know He watches me.

I sing because I'm happy,
I sing because I'm free,
For His eye is on the sparrow,
And I know He watches me.

Prayer: Jesus our Saviour, give calm and sweet repose to the weary. Give thy tenderest blessings to those in want or pain. May thy angels spread their wings over those in need. We pray for Jesus' sake. Amen.

October 27

"Harken to me, ye that follow after righteousness, ye that seek the Lord: look unto the rock whence ye are hewn, and to the hole of the pit whence ye are digged." — Isaiah 51:1

Knowledge of history is essential to proper appreciation and evaluation of the present. As parents it is our duty to teach our children about their forefathers. It is the duty of our children to listen.

Often our parents and grandparents had many difficulties in making a place for themselves in the world, but we have profited by a place already established for us.

Americans have a wonderful heritage. Our heritage is principles which have made our land better, our laws greater, and our economy more affluent. When we know more of our heritage we are prouder of it and more ready to uphold the traditions.

So much the dear Saviour had done for my soul,
I want to help other's to find Him;
To tell how His love can a sinner make whole,
I want to help others to find Him.

'Tis thus I can praise Him, my gratitude prove,
I want to help other's to find Him;
In leading sad hearts to the light of his love,
I want to help others to find Him.

For this let me toil till the close of the day,
I want to help others to find Him;
For this is the work that abideth for aye,
I want to help others to find Him.

— Maud Jackson

Prayer: Our Father, we have found Jesus to be a friend ever true. May we be true to him by telling of his love. We pray in the name of Jesus. Amen.

October 28

"Go out into the highways and hedges, and compel them to come in, that my house may be filled." — Luke 14:23

When my husband was a very young minister he was pastor of a church in a rural community where most of the farmers kept a dairy herd. When he would ask some of them to attend services they would give the milking as an excuse. Not many had electric milkers and it was a task to milk twenty or thirty cows, bathe and dress for church, and drive several miles.

One week the young minister decided to show some of them how much he wanted them to attend the services. He went to the home of one man and helped him milk; then he went to the home of another and helped him. He was suffering the next day from sore hands but the people knew how much they were wanted and after that they managed to attend.

> To me that bleeding love of his
> Shall ever precious be;
> Whatever He to others is,
> He is the same to me.

Prayer: Our Father, renew in us again a desire to see people come to the house of the Lord. Stirred by compassion may we go out to compel the lost to come in. We pray in the name of one who said, "Whosoever will may come." Amen.

October 29

"And thou shalt teach them [God's words] diligently unto thy children, and shalt talk of them when thou sittest in thine house, and when thou walkest by the way, and when thou liest down, and when thou risest up." — Deuteronomy 6:7

We are to examine the truth of the things we read in the Bible. We are to teach those truths to our children.

Christianity demands belief. It demands fair examination. The man who says he is an infidel may feel differently if he reads and studies God's Word. Pride sometimes prevents people from studying and making a fair decision.

Some fail to make the proper decision toward God because they do not take the Word of God seriously.

A man walking along a sidewalk in front of a cafe was asked by another man to come in and eat. The man was very hungry but he thought the invitation was not sincere. Another begger

262

walking along the same sidewalk was invited to come in and eat.
He went in and had a sumptuous meal.

> Within this awful volume lies
>   The mystery of mysteries;
> Oh, happy they of human race,
>   To whom our God has given grace
> To hear, to fear, to read, to pray,
>   To lift the latch, to force the way;
> But better had they ne'er been born,
>   Who read to doubt, or read to scorn.

Prayer: We thank thee, our Father, for thy Holy Word, may we
ever teach its precepts to our children and abide by them ourselves.
We ask in the name of Christ our Lord. Amen.

October 30

*"Hath the Lord as great delight in burnt offerings and sacrifices,
as in obeying the voice of the Lord? Behold, to obey is better
than sacrifice."* — I Samuel 15:22

A young man went to travel in the Alps. He hired a guide.
The guide told him, "If you obey me I will see that you make
your trip and return safely."

The young man said that he tried in every way to obey his
guide. Afterwards he said his feeling for the guide was one of
deep respect and love.

Jesus said, "If ye keep my commandments, ye shall abide in my
love."

Obedience is the key that unlocks the door to many things; to
safety, to love, to respect, to the indwelling of Christ in our hearts.

> He does not always lead in pastures green.
> Sometimes, He who knows all
> In kindness leads in weary ways
> Where heavy shadows fall.
>
> Not always by peaceful waters soft and slow,
> My wandering steps he leads,
> Ofttimes the heavy tempest round me blows
> And darkest gloom surrounds the way.
>
> But when the storm beats loudest
> And I cannot find my way,
> His hand always directs my course
> To realms of brighter day.

263

Prayer: God, help us to be more obedient to thy will and direction. We pray in the name of Jesus Christ. Amen.

October 31

"Everyone that is proud in heart is an abomination to the Lord: though hand join in hand, he shall not be unpunished. By mercy and truth iniquity is purged: and by the fear of the Lord men depart from evil." — Proverbs 16:5-6

I once read, "Turning green with envy has a way of making you ripe for trouble."

A woman was in the hospital dying with cancer. "If only she had submitted to surgery two years ago we could have saved her life," the doctor told her husband.

Jealousy and envy are like cancer. Unless they are cut out and thrown away at the beginning they are apt to spread and destroy us completely.

> God moves in mysterious ways
> His wonders to perform;
> He plants his footsteps in the sea,
> And rides upon the storm.
>
> Deep in the unfathomable mines
> Of never failing skill,
> He treasures up his bright designs,
> And works his sovereign will.
> — Cowper

Prayer: Our Father, take from our hearts envy and jealousy. Help us to look only to thee for right and justice. We praise thee for the good things thou hast given us and if someone else had a little more, help us to be glad, not filled with envy. We pray in Jesus' name. Amen.

November:

Thanksgiving Thoughts

November 1

"Our Father which art in heaven, Hallowed be thy name. Thy kingdom come. Thy will be done in earth, as it is in heaven.

Give us this day our daily bread. And forgive us our debts, as we forgive our debtors.

And lead us not into temptation, but deliver us from evil; For thine is the kingdom, and the power, and the glory, forever. Amen." — Matthew 6:9-13

One Sunday we were far from home and very lonely. As is our custom, we went to services in a nearby church. No one spoke to us and we felt more lonely than ever. Then came the time in the service when the congregation repeated the Lord's Prayer. We joined in and soon were so busy worshiping we forgot to be homesick.

> You cannot pray the Lord's Prayer, and even once say "I."
> You cannot pray the Lord's Prayer, and even once say "my."
> Nor can you pray the Lord's Prayer and not pray for another,
> For when you ask for daily bread, you must include your brother.
> For others are included in each and every plea;
> From the beginning to the end of it
> It does not once say "me."

Prayer: Father, make us humble, as we pray thy prayer today. Help us to think of others and their problems more each day. As Jesus was so kind and good to blot out all our sins, help us ever to be quick to forgive, and anxious to make amends. We pray in Jesus name. Amen.

November 2

"And Enoch walked with God: and he was not; for God took him." — Genesis 5:24

Isn't this a beautiful story. Enoch went walking with God. Wouldn't it be nice to know what they talked about! Perhaps Enoch talked of his family, maybe some problems. Maybe they talked about crops or herds of cattle. At any rate it became late and God must have said, "Come Enoch, and go home with me; it is closer to my house than yours."

267

We should all live so close to God that when he is ready for us to go home with him it will be easy just to keep on walking.

> The Master has gone to a distant country
>> And left me a charge to keep.
> A place in His vineyard,
>> A field of labor
> A shepherd to guard his sheep.
> May I be faithful to the work
>> He assigned me,
> Loyal in service, earnest in all
>> That I do.
> May I be faithful,
>> Out in the field may he find me.
> When He returneth,
>> Faithful and loyal and true.

Prayer: Father, help us to remember, "Ye are not your own, ye are bought with a price, even the precious blood of Christ." Make us willing to serve in every way possible the Master who left us a charge to keep. We pray in the name of Jesus. Amen.

November 3

"Behold the fowls of the air: for they sow not, nor gather into barns; yet your heavenly Father feedeth them. Are ye not much better than they?" — Matthew 6:26

This story is told of Carlyle. One day he stopped in the middle of a busy street and picked up a piece of bread that had been carelessly thrown down. He took the bread to a protected place and tenderly laid it down. "That is only a crust of bread but to a hungry dog or a bird it may mean nourishment and help."

How much more thoughtful of us is our Heavenly Father.

> All nature a sermon may preach thee;
>> The birds sing thy murmurs away —
> The birds which, nor sowing nor reaping,
>> God fails not to feed day by day;
> And He, who the creature doth cherish,
> Will He fail thee, and leave thee to perish?
>> Or are thou not better than they?
>
> God gives to each flower its rich raiment,
>> And o'er them His treasures flings free,
> Which to-day finds so fragrant in beauty,
>> And to-morrow all faded shall see.

Thus the lilies smile shame on thy care,
And the happy birds sing it to air:
Will their God be forgetful of thee?
— tr. by Mrs. Charles Spegel

Prayer: O God, we adore thee. Thou hast made the world so beautiful for us to enjoy. We thank thee that thou carest when we wander away and thou wilt call us back and forgive our mistakes. We pray in the name of Jesus. Amen.

November 4

"For we are laborers together with God: ye are God's husbandry, ye are God's building." — I Corinthians 3:9

Have you ever watched two little boys playing on the floor with blocks. One child carefully stacks each block and works to make something which looks to him like a house. When he has his house just about finished the other child rushes over and kicks it down.

Life is like that. There are those who work hard to build worthwhile things. Then there are the ones who seem to get joy from being destructive. We all do well to ask ourselves the question, What type of person am I?

I watched them tearing a building down,
A gang of men in a busy town,
With a ho-heave-ho and lusty yell.
They swung a beam and the side wall fell.

I asked the foreman, "Are these men skilled,
And the men you'd hire if you had to build?
He gave a laugh and said, "No indeed!
Just common labor is all I need.
I can easily wreck in a day or two
What builders have taken a year to do."

I thought to myself as I went away,
Which of these roles have I tried to play?
Am I a builder who works with care,
Measuring life by the rule and square?
Am I shaping my deeds to a well-made plan,
    Patiently doing the best I can?
Or am I a wrecker, who walks the town,
Content with the labor of tearing down?

Prayer: Father, make us builders of thy kingdom. We ask in the name of Jesus. Amen.

November 5

"Take heed therefore unto yourselves, and to all the flock, over the which the Holy Ghost hath made you overseers, to feed the church of God, which he hath purchased with his own blood."
— Acts 20:28

One Sunday I attended a church and read the following on the bulletin; "Thou art welcome, whosoever thou art that enterest this Church. It is thy Father's house: Come in the Spirit of reverence; worship in the spirit of humility; and leave it not without a prayer to God for thyself, for those who minister, and for those who worship here; then go thy way to live Christ in thy daily conduct."

> I want it to be a church that is
> A lamp to the path of pilgrims,
> Leading them to Goodness, Truth
> And Beauty. It will be good, if I am.
>
> It is composed of people like me.
> We make it what it is.
> It will be friendly, if I am.
> Its pews will be filled, if I
> Help to fill them.
>
> It will do a great work, if I work.
>
> It will make generous gifts to many causes,
> If I am a generous giver.
>
> It will bring other people into
> Its worship and fellowship,
> If I bring others.
>
> Therefore, with the help of God,
> I shall dedicate myself to the
> Task of being all of the things
> That I want my church to be.

Prayer: Father, make us worthy of our church. In the name of one who gave himself for the church. Amen.

November 6

"Blessed is the man that trusteth in the Lord, and whose hope the Lord is." — Jeremiah 17:7

270

I rejoiced a great deal when a letter I had sent was returned to me. It was a letter to my Chaplain husband stationed in Italy. The letter had been stamped; "Returning to the states." In great rejoicing I hastened to tell all my friends and neighbors.

> If what I wish is good,
> And suits the will divine,
> By earth and hell in vain withstood
> I know it shall be mine.
> Still let them counsel take
> To frustrate His decree;
> They cannot keep a blessing back
> By heaven designed for me.
> If what my soul requires
> Evil to me would prove,
> His love shall cross my fine desires,
> His kindly-jealous Love.
>
> — Charles Wesley

Prayer: Our heavenly Father, give us the secure knowledge that where thou leadest we may safely go. Teach us to trust in thy wisdom. We pray in the name of our Saviour. Amen.

November 7

"As the hart panteth after the water brooks, so panteth my soul after thee, O God. My soul thirsteth for God, for the living God: when shall I come and appear before God?"

> — Psalm 42:1, 2

Group worship is fine, but there are also times when we need to take time to worship alone. The means and the methods of worship are not all that is important. A person can worship at times when he is the very busiest.

Sometimes when we see some of God's beautiful handiwork in nature, on land or in the sky, we want to worship. What wonderful dividends we reap from worship. It brings a calmness of soul and spirit.

> By all means use some times to be alone;
> Salute thyself; see what thy soul doth wear;
> Dare to look in thy chest, for 'tis thine own,
> And tumble up and down what thou find'st there:
> Who cannot rest till he good fellows find,
> He breaks up house, turns out of doors his mind.
>
> — George Herbert

Prayer: Our Lord and Saviour, we pray today that we will make such desposits in thy Kingdom that we will reap dividends. Help us make preparation for a life to come. Make us friends to the friendless. Guide us in our worship to think first of others. We pray in Jesus' name. Amen.

November 8

"We must all appear before the judgment seat of Christ; that every one may receive the things done in his body, according to that he hath done, whether it be good or bad."

— II Corinthians 5:10

God is still in control and in due time people will reap what they have sown.

A popular cafeteria in our city put a large number of diamond-looking stones in a jar. There were supposed to be a few real diamonds in the group. When a lady dined in the cafeteria she was allowed to pick one stone from the jar. I never heard of anyone getting a real diamond.

We sometimes think we can fool God if we look like good Christians. God looks on the heart, not appearances. He can look at the people in the world and tell the pure diamonds from the glass.

> Say where is life? It is not here I know,
>> Oh! who hath power the priceless boon to give?
> All here is sorrow, sin and death and woe;
>> Say where is life? for surely I would live!
> Be still, my soul, a sweet voice speaks to thee:
>> "I am the Life, look up and follow Me."
>
> All that I sought, Lord, I have found in Thee,
>> Thou art the way, the truth, the life.
> All that I ask for Thou hast given me.
>> Well may I trust Thee, trust Thy loving heart;
> Low at Thy feet adoring do I fall,
>> Own Thee my Lord, my best Beloved, my all!

Prayer: Show us the way to follow thee. We ask in the name of Jesus. Amen.

November 9

"Having the understanding darkened, being alienated from the life of God through the ignorance that is in them, because of the blindness of their heart." — Ephesians 5:18

The lounge was crowded. All the ladies were trying to get to the wash basins and some were almost fainting from exhaustion. A small boy was pushing about between the women, and they were becoming annoyed and impatient.

"Why should that boy be in here?" one woman asked in a rude tone of voice.

"He is blind and must stay near me," the mother spoke up in the child's defense.

First there was perfect silence. Then every woman in the room felt a burst of pity and love for the child. The women almost fell over each other to give him nickles, chewing gum, and trinkets.

We had been blind in heart!

> If you had been living when Christ was on earth,
> And had met the Saviour kind,
> What would you have asked Him to do for you,
> Supposing that you were blind?"
>
> The child considered and then replied,
> "I suppose that without a doubt
> I'd have asked for a dog and a collar and chain
> To lead me safely about."
>
> And how often thus, in our faithless prayers,
> We acknowledge with shamed surprise,
> We have asked for only a collar and chain
> When we might have had our eyes!

Prayer: Our Father, give us faith to ask for the greatest things. Give us kindness of heart for those who are handicapped. We thank thee for our blessings. Our prayer is in the name of Jesus. Amen.

November 10

"The Lord is my strength and song, and he is become my salvation: he is my God, and I will prepare him an habitation; my father's God and I will exalt him." — Exodus 15:2

Faith in God gives us strength for the responsibilities of life.

Long ago in England there lived a man who wanted to be a missionary. Many opposed his project, but he was determined. When he made his appeal for help from the home churches he said, "Expect great things from God; attempt great things for God." We would all do well to make this our motto.

> If you are impatient, sit down and quietly talk with Job.

If you are just a little strongheaded, go and see Moses.
If you are getting weak-kneed, take a good look at Elijah.
If there is no song in your heart, listen to David.
If you are a policy man, read Daniel.
If you are getting sordid, spend a little while with Isaiah.
If you are getting chilly, get the beloved disciple, John, to put his cloak around you.
If your faith is below par, read Paul.
If you are getting lazy, watch James.
If you are losing sight of the future, climb up the stairs of Revelation and get a glimpse of the promised land.

Prayer: Our Father, give us the secret strength that comes only from thee. We ask in Jesus' name. Amen.

November 11

"Salt is good: but if the salt have lost his saltness, wherewith will ye season it? Have salt in yourselves, and have peace one with another." — Mark 9:50

This is Veterans Day.

We all love our country. We want it to be blessed and prosperous. We are willing to sacrifice for it. Yet we often complain when things are not run just as we imagine we would run them.

If we truly want peace we must love all men, regardless of color or creed.

Is this love — the love I've taught?
Will this carnage come to aught?
Down the ages men have died.
In these crusades — crucified!
Ignoring in their greed for self —
"Love thy neighbor as thyself."
And the God of good above
Pitied them, in his great love!

Came the Armistice — and peace,
From the hell of hate surcease.
"Peace on earth good will to men" —
Brothers, will we war again?
— James Edward Hungerford

274

Prayer: Our Father, who rules all nations, we would ask thy blessing on our nation today. May good will be restored on earth and there be peace in the nations. Often we have been selfish and obstinate. Make us gentle and kind. Bless our national leaders and lead them aright. We pray in the name of Christ our Lord. Amen.

November 12

"Remember now thy Creator in the days of thy youth, while the evil days come not, nor the years draw nigh, when thou shalt say, I have no pleasure in them." — Ecclesiastes 12:1

We often think of youth as the golden age of life. We should make each stage of life a golden age.

When we are children we think, "Oh, I will do great things when I am grown." When we are youths we think, "I will do wonderful things when I am away from the discipline of my parents." Then we are grown up and out of school, and we find life has more problems than we thought — but we enjoy working them out. When we are middle aged we feel it will be grand to reach retirement and have days of rest. When we are old we look back and think, "Oh, if I had my life to live over I would not make so many mistakes."

Each age is golden! We should treasure every moment.

> Does not heaven begin that day
> When the eager heart can say,
> "Surely God is in this place.
> I have seen Him face to face
> In the loveliness of flowers,
> In the service of the showers,
> And his voice has talked to me
> In the sunlit apple tree."
>
> — Bliss Carmen

Prayer: We need thee, O loving God and Father. We are often discontent and feel defeated. Make us love life as thou doth give it to us each day. Help us appreciate all good things. We ask in the name of Jesus. Amen.

November 13

"I know whom I have believed, and am persuaded that he is able to keep that which I have committed unto him against that day." — II Timothy 1:12b

Tom was lost on a hunting trip. When he first realized he was lost he became frantic. Then he caught himself going in circles. When he realized this he sat down and began to repeat aloud all the verses of Scripture he could remember. He also quoted the verse above. When he had calmed himself and restored his faith he asked himself the question, "Have I tried all the ways I know to find the camp?"

"Climb a tree," seemed to come to him. Without delay he climbed the nearest tree and found he could see smoke in the distance. He was careful to mark the direction, and started walking that way. In an hour he was back with his companions.

> He leadeth me! O blessed tho't!
> O words with heavenly comfort fraught!
> What'er I do, Where'er I be,
> Still 'tis God's hand that leadeth me.
>
> And when my task on earth is done,
> When, by thy grace, the vict'ry's won,
> E'en death's cold wave I will not flee,
> Since God through Jordan leadeth me.

Prayer: Loving heavenly Father, give us the assurance of thy love and presence today. Help us to rest in the contentment of thy love and grace. We pray in the name of Jesus. Amen.

November 14

"Enter into his gates with thanksgiving, and into his courts with praise: be thankful unto him and bless his name." — Psalm 100:4

One day when I felt especially rushed and discouraged I went to bring in the mail. There among the papers and advertisements I found a letter from a friend. It was a letter thanking us for a very small favor we had given her sometime in the past. Suddenly I didn't feel rushed at all. I wasn't so busy after all. Someone appreciated the things I was trying to do each day and had taken time to express thanks. That made the difference. What had seemed like a day of chores had suddenly become a day of opportunity.

> Not long ago when my skies were gray,
> And the smile of fortune seemed far away.
> I chided the fates that took my store
> And left me naught to be thankful for.

Came another day with a fairer sky,
As I saw my boys go tearing by —
They seemed to shout through the open door
"Say dad you have us to be thankful for."

I have the moon and the stars above
I have a home that is blessed with love
I still can smile as I did before
And that's a lot to be thankful for.

The morning sun brings another day
A time for work, a time for play
I have all these and a great deal more
Say — you have as much to be thankful for.

— Albert Roswell

Prayer: Our Father, teach us to express thankfulness for thy many blessings. We pray in Jesus' name. Amen.

November 15

"When I remember these things, I pour out my soul in me: for I had gone with the multitude, I went with them to the house of God, with the voice of joy and praise, with a multitude that kept holyday." — Psalm 42:4

The following passages are parts of the proclamation made by President Lincoln, October 3, 1863.

"The year that is drawing to a close has been filled with the blessings of fruitful fields and healthful skies.

"To these bounties, which are so constantly enjoyed that we are prone to forget the source from which they come, others have been added, which are of so extraordinary a nature that they cannot fail to penetrate and soften the heart which is habitually insensible to the ever watchful providence of almighty God.

"No human counsel hath devised, nor hath any mortal hand worked out these great things. They are the gracious gifts of the most high God, who, while dealing with us in anger for our sins, hath nevertheless remembered mercy.

". . . and fervently implore the interposition of the almighty hand to heal the wounds of the nation and to restore it, as soon as may be consistent with the Divine purposes, to the full enjoyment of peace, harmony, tranquility and union."

This message is still timely, is it not?

Prayer: Father, today, over a hundred years later than President Lincoln's proclamation, may we still know and honor the one God who gives us our blessings. In Christs' name. Amen.

November 16

"And call upon me in the day of trouble: I will deliver thee, and thou shalt glorify me." — Psalm 50:15

Soon after we moved into a new home we made a trip to visit my father-in-law. He was ninety-five years old at that time. He asked all about the house and, of course, we made it sound just as nice as we thought it was. Last of all I told him about the dishwasher. He sat for a few seconds saying nothing. Then he spoke: "I wish I could have gotten one for mamma."

How well I remembered the farm kitchen with a family of six children, a mother, a father, a maiden aunt and often a hired hand. That meant piles of dishes. How wonderful it would have felt just to have a hot water heater and running water — let alone a dishwasher. I bowed my head and offered a silent prayer of thanksgiving for all our modern conveniences.

> O bless the Lord my soul!
> Nor let His mercies lie
> Forgotten in unthankfulness,
> And without praises die.

Prayer: Almighty God, our heavenly Father, help us to be ever thankful for thy multitude of blessings. For health and happiness. We pray in the name of Jesus. Amen.

November 17

"The blessing of the Lord, it maketh rich, and he addeth no sorrow with it." — Proverbs 10:22

We get so used to our everyday blessings we forget to be thankful for them. How sad God must be at times when we seem so ungrateful! Let's try to cultivate gratitude.

> Oh Lord, I thank Thee for this day
> For your great love and grace
> And for the glow of health I see
> Upon my baby's face!
>
> I thank Thee for my garden small,
> For flowers now growing there,
> It makes me mindful of my heart
> That's lost it's deep despair!

For smudges on my boy's pants
That I can wash today.
I thank Thee, Lord, most heartily.
You've washed my smudge away!

And when I sew a button on
My husband's one white shirt
I thank Thee for thy robe so white
That covers up my dirt!

Oh thank you Lord! I am not poor!
I'm rich in life and love
My home is rented here below,
But I've a mansion up above!

Prayer: Our Father, take away our preoccupation with worldly things. Make us mindful of the wise blessings thou showerest upon us each day. Give us joy in thy presence. We pray in the name of our Saviour Jesus Christ. Amen.

November 18

"Hitherto have ye asked nothing in my name: ask, and ye shall receive, that your joy may be full." — John 16:24

Life, whether long or short, is a marvel of creation, an opportunity for service. The glorious experience called life comes our way but once. Are we grateful for it? Do we deliberately plan to make it count for the most in service and love to others.

While we are young and energetic we often fail to realize how precious life is. Then when the bloom is gone and we cannot call it back, we wish for a second chance.

There's something in the atmosphere
Around this magic time of year,
    That thrills the hearts of men,
And sort of sets the blood astir,
And makes the pulses fairly purr,
From which no doubt you will infer —
    Thanksgiving's here again!
                        — J. E. Hungerford

Prayer: Father, with thankful and humble hearts we bring our lives before thee today. We are grateful for the measure of health thou hast given us. We thank thee for all the benefits we have received from thy hand. We ask thee to take our lives and make them worth while in thy service. For we pray in the name of Jesus. Amen.

November 19

"For what thanks can we render to God again for you, for all the joy wherewith we joy for your sakes before our God."

— I Thessalonians 3:9

During a severe earthquake a few years ago the neighbors were surprised to see an elderly lady going calmy about helping the children, the young mothers, and just anyone she could find to whom she could render service.

"Grandma, aren't you afraid?" one of the children asked.

"No, if the God I worship can shake this old earth like this he certainly can take care of me."

The people hearing her took courage and their faith was strengthened.

> Help us remember
> That serving our neighbors
> Is gratitude offered
>   To Jesus, our Friend.
> For every day's blessings,
> Great without measure,
> We thank Thee and praise Thee,
>   Our Father. Amen.

Prayer: Our Father, we would thank thee that every day we have so many things for which to be thankful. We thank thee for opportunity to serve others and do good each day. Give us the wisdom to lead others in the way of thankfulness. We pray through Christ our Redeemer. Amen.

November 20

"O give thanks unto the Lord, for he is good, for his mercy endureth forever." — Psalm 107:1

When we think of Thanksgiving Day we often think of a picture so commonly seen of Pilgrims on their way to church. We see mothers and fathers and little children walking in the snow to attend worship services.

When we think of that picture and of the ways we have to travel today we should be so thankful. If our children leave home and go thousands of miles away they can still call home and talk in a matter of seconds. If there is an urgent need to get to the bedside of a loved one we can board a plane and be many hundreds of miles away in a few hours.

We give thanks to the same Lord the Pilgrims worshiped. The same Lord supplies our every need.

> Give thanks for your life as you find it;
> Thanks that there's work you can do,
>   Thanks for your health, for
>   The wealth of your strength, and
> The courage to battle things through.

Prayer: Oh God of Hosts, thou hast opened the windows of heaven and poured out untold blessings upon our generation. We offer thanks to thee. We thank thee for the things that make life sweet and happy. Make us worthy of thy mercies. We pray in the name of the giver of all good gifts. Amen.

November 21

"I will remember the works of the Lord: surely I will remember thy wonders of old. I will meditate also of all thy work, and talk of thy doing." — Psalm 77:11, 12

In memory we store joys and pains, pleasures of the past and experiences shared with loved relatives and friends.

> Sitting in a lovely church
> Looking at the ceiling high,
> Thinking of Thanksgiving Day
> Coming so near by.
>
> Our clothes are plentiful and warm
> Life seems happy
> Life seems gay
> In our own American way.
>
> Turkeys on our tables
> Cranberry sauce and candied yams,
> But for other things than these
> I am more thankful, if you please.
>
> Thankful for a home above,
> Thankful for a bit of love
> Thankful for the sky and sun
> Thankful for the friends I've won.

Prayer: Our Father, we are grateful for past Thanksgivings. For those who made the way before us and gave us the opportunities of this land. In Jesus' name we pray. Amen.

281

November 22

"I will strengthen thee; yea I will help thee; yea, I will uphold thee with the right hand of my righteousness." — Isaiah 41:10

Making a purchase in a downtown store I started talking with the clerk. "Are you going to have a nice Thanksgiving?"

"No," she replied, "I lost my husband nine months ago. So, I cannot be very thankful on Thanksgiving."

I felt sorry for her. I could appreciate her feelings. Yet, I thought, she could still find many things for which to be thankful. She had two fine sons, a number of grandchildren, a job, a home — and a loving heavenly Father.

> These to be thankful for: a friend,
> A work to do, a way to wend,
> And these in which to take delight:
> The wind that turns the poplars white.
>
> Wonder and gleam of common things,
> Sunlight upon a sea gull's wings,
> Odors of earth and dew-drenched lawns,
> The pagentry of darks and dawns;
>
> Blue vistas of a city street
> At twilight, music, passing feet,
> The thrill of spring, half joy, half pain,
> The deep voice of the autumn rain.
>
> Shall we not be content with these
> Imperishable mysteries?
> And jocund-hearted take our share
> Of joy and pain and find life fair?

Prayer: We thank thee Father, for our beautiful world. For rich harvest and plenty of food. We thank Thee for the kind and good people who make up a majority of our population. We thank Thee for thy love and patience with our mistakes. We pray in the name of Jesus. Amen.

November 23

"In the morning sow thy seed, and in the evening withhold not thine hand." — Ecclesiastes 11:6

How fine it is when we are young to sow good seed — seeds of helpfulness and kindness; seeds of sharing and improving the world about us.

A man I knew worked very hard as a young man trying to invent machinery that would make the farmer's work easier. In a measure he succeeded. When he was old his health was very poor, but he had plenty to live on because the royalties from his inventions kept coming in.

> We dropped the seed o'er hill and plain,
>   Beneath the sun of May,
> And frightened from our sprouting grain
>   The robber crows away.
>
> And now, with autumn's moonlit eves,
>   Its harvest time has come,
> We pluck away the frosted leaves,
>   And bear the treasure home.
>
> Then shame on all the proud and vain,
>   Whose folly laughs to scorn
> The blessing of the hardy grain,
>   Our wealth of golden corn!
>
> Heap high the farmer's wintry hoard!
>   Heap high the golden corn!
> No richer gift has Autumn poured
>   From out her lavish horn!
>
> But let the good old crop adorn
>   The hills our fathers trod;
> Still let us, for his golden corn,
>   Send up our thanks to God!

Prayer: Our Father, we thank thee for our new age, for new visions of feats to accomplish. We thank thee for fresh opportunities to gather harvest from seed sown by our fathers. Amen.

November 24

"Giving thanks unto the Father, which hath made us meet to be partakers of the inheritance of the saints in light."

— Colossians 1:12

A missionary was growing very discouraged and homesick. He tried harder to witness for Christ. When things looked the blackest and he thought he would have to give up as a failure, the worst man in the village came to him and told him that he now trusted Christ. Seeing the man on his knees begging God for forgiveness and salvation, the missionary cried out, "Thank you God, for the privilege of preaching to people in this village."

As Thanksgiving Season nears
And all thoughts are centered 'round
Home and happiness of family,
Health, and all the joys we've found,
Mem'ries of my childhood linger —
Of my Mom and Dad and kin,
And each precious bygone moment
I relive with them again.

Oh, the scenes that flash before me,
(Ah, those meals my Mom could cook!)
How my Dad would show he loved me
With each word and act and look!
How I pray that the Tomorrows
Of my Sons may, too, unfold
Precious mem'ries of Thanksgivings
As I in my heart now hold!

— Jewel Alice McLeod

Prayer: Father, we thank thee for the seasons and the joy each brings. Most of all we thank thee that thou hast made a way for us to be partakers of the inheritance of the saints. We pray in the name of Christ our Saviour. Amen.

November 25

"We walk by faith, not by sight." — II Corinthians 5:7

A ten-year-old boy was lost in the woods. One minute he had been with his father and brother; the next he had wandered away and could not find them again. He called and called but the rustle of the leaves drowned out his calls. All night long he wandered around. He was very cold but he kept walking, shaking his arms and legs. Early the next morning he put his ear to the ground as he had heard about Indians doing. He thought he heard the sound of a big truck. Sure enough as he walked and listened he soon found a road. A short time later a car picked him up and he was soon re-united with his loved ones.

Often we come to a place when we want to give up. If we just keep walking, working, and listening for the voice of God we will come to a place of safety.

God has given you His promise,
That He hears and answers prayer:
He will heed your supplication,
If you cast on Him your care.

Prayer: Thou who didst redeem us, hear our call today. Make us true followers of thine. Give us courage to keep walking when the way is rough. We pray in the name of Jesus. Amen.

November 26

"In everything give thanks: for this is the will of God in Christ Jesus concerning you." — I Thessalonians 5:18

A little child went to visit some friends. At the table the family she was visiting started noisily passing the food. Noticing the little visitor was not eating, the mother in the home asked, "Aren't you hungry, dear?"

"Oh, yes, I am hungry, but I always wait for the food to be blessed."

The children of the home looked at her, ashamed; the parents were aghast. "Will you bless the food for all of us?"

The little child said the little verse her mother had taught her;

> Father we thank Thee for the night,
> And for the pleasant morning light;
> For rest and food and loving care,
> And all that makes the world so fair.
>
> Help us to do the things we should,
> To be to others kind and good;
> In all we do, in work or play,
> To love Thee better day by day.
>
> — Rebecca J. Weston

Prayer: How shall we thank thee, Lord, for all thy abundant mercies; for friendships, homes, true kindness of friends. Be near to guide us today, we pray in the name of Christ our Lord. Amen.

November 27

"Blessed is he that considereth the poor: the Lord will deliver him in time of trouble." — Psalm 41:1

There were two stores in a small town. One store had an easy-going owner who was always trying to serve his customers better. If he could help someone by going a few blocks out of the way he didn't mind. The other storekeeper was just the opposite. Every aim and plan was to make more profit. One year, times were very hard and more and more people had come to the easy-going storekeeper and asked for credit. People said, "He will surely have to go out of business if he doesn't stop helping people." But the kindly man managed to keep his doors open and he was happy to be able to help others.

> Great God of Nations, now to Thee,
> Our hymn of gratitude we raise;
> With humble heart and bending knee
> We offer Thee our song of praise.

> Thy name we bless, Almighty God,
> For all the kindness Thou has shown
> To this fair land the Pilgrims trod —
> This land we fondly call our own.

> We praise Thee that the Gospel's light
> Through all our land it's radiance sheds
> Dispels the shade of error's night,
> And heavenly blessings around us spreads.

> Great God, preserve us in Thy fear;
> In danger, still our Guardian be;
> O spread Thy truth's bright precepts here;
> Let all the people worship Thee.

Prayer: Our God, help us to have assurance of thy love and care. We ask in Jesus' name. Amen.

November 28

"It is a good thing to give thanks unto the Lord." — Psalm 92:1

"Let us come before his presence with thanksgiving, and make a joyful noise unto him with psalms." — Psalm 95:2

The Bible admonishes us to be thankful. As Americans we set aside a certain day in which to proclaim our thanks to God for his goodness.

We should always give thanks to God. He does not confine his blessings to just one day each year but pours them out each day we live.

Dr. Torrey, a minister, told the story of a young university student who saved seventeen men from drowning. When he became exhausted and could swim no longer the boy kept saying, "Did I do my best?"

Later, in a revival service, Dr. Torrey was told that the boy was in the services. He asked him to come forward and testify. Asked if any one thing stood out in the experience, the young man replied, "Not one of the seventeen thanked me."

Grave on thy heart each past "red-letter day"!
Forget not all the sunshine of the way
By which the Lord hath led thee: answered prayers,
And joys unasked, strange blessings, lifted cares,
Grand promise-echoes! Thus thy life shall be
One record of His love and faithfulness to thee.

— F. R. Havergal

Prayer: Lord, we thank thee for the Thanksgiving heritage. Make us worthy of the example of our forefathers. We pray in the name of Jesus. Amen.

November 29

"If a man love me, he will keep my words: and my Father will love him, and we will come. unto him, and make our abode with him." — John 14:23

My son had just returned from two years of military service, much of which had been spent in Germany. He found things at home changed and strange. He decided to go to a religious retreat in the mountains. The second day he returned home.

"It is lonely in a crowd when you do not know any of the people," he explained.

If we love God he will abide with us and we will always have a precious companion.

Pray, don't find fault with the man who limps,
    Or stumbles along the road,
Unless you have worn the shoes he wears
    Or struggled beneath his load.
There may be tacks in his shoes that hurt
    Though hidden away from view,
Or the burdens he bears placed on your back
    Might cause you to stumble, too.
Don't sneer at the man who's down today,
    Unless you have felt the blow
That caused his fall, or felt the shame
    That only the fallen know.
You may be strong but still the blows
    That were his, if dealt to you
In the selfsame way at the selfsame time,
    Might cause you to stagger, too.
Don't be too harsh with the man who sins,
    Or pelt him with words or stones,

287

Unless you are sure, yea, doubly sure,
That you have not sins of your own.

Prayer: Help us to see that all things work together for good to them that love thee. In Christ's name. Amen.

November 30

"Gracious is the Lord, and righteous; yea, our God is merciful."
— Psalm 116:5

A little girl walking around the block with her father noticed the moon and stars shining very brightly.

"Look, daddy, God has washed his windows. See how bright his lights are."

We should feel as near to God and that God is as real at all times, as the little one felt on that clear night.

Let him who would deny that God is real
Out into the night with heart uplifted steal.
And see the wonders of the heavens above,
To be convinced of God's eternal love.

The moon and stars proclaim His wondrous power
And all of nature sings of Him each hour.
Dear God, teach us that Thou hast made Thy plan
An everlasting benediction to man.

Teach us to glorify Thy name
Through worship of This only Son
The wonders of Thy love proclaim
Each day as victory is won.

Prayer: Dearest Lord, help us to feel the comfort of thy presence. May we always know that thou art real and very near. Give us joy in this knowledge. We ask in the name of Jesus. Amen.

December:

Getting Ready for Christmas

December 1

"When he giveth quietness, who then can make trouble? and when he hideth his face who then can behold him? whether it be done against a nation, or against a man only." — Job 34:29

The year had been long and we were physically exhausted. For our vacation we drove up into the mountains and enjoyed the quiet of nature. On Sunday we attended a small country church where we heard a good sermon. God gave rest and quietness to our souls as well as to our bodies.

> I needed the quiet, so He drew me aside
> Into the shadows where we could confide;
> Away from the bustle where all the day long
> I hurried and worried when active and strong.
>
> I needed the quiet, though at first I rebelled,
> But gently, so gently, my cross He upheld;
> And whispered so sweetly of spiritual things;
> Though weakened in body, my spirit took wings
> To heights never dreamed of when active and gay,
> He loved me so gently, He drew me away.
>
> I needed the quiet, No prison my bed,
> But a beautiful valley of blessing instead:
> A place to grow richer, in Jesus to hide,
> I needed the quiet, so He drew me aside.

— A. H. Mortenson

Prayer: Our Father, when we turn aside and spend a quiet time with thee, our hope and courage are renewed. We ask thee to grant us grace to face life's problems. Fill us with a desire to be alone with thee some part of each day. Through Jesus Christ we pray. Amen.

December 2

"And when he had given thanks, he brake it, and said, Take, eat: this is my body, which is broken for you: this do in remembrance of me. After the same manner also he took the cup, when he had supped, saying, This cup is the new testament in my blood: this do ye, as oft as ye drink it in remembrance of me."
— I Corinthians 11:24, 25

Baptism and the Lord's Supper belong together. They have to do with the same event, the resurrection of Christ.

Several years ago my husband and I bought some cemetery

lots and paid them out by the month. We did not want our children burdened with making that choice after we were gone. We always planned we would also buy a headstone but never have had time for that. People just want some way to be remembered when they are gone from this earth.

Jesus planned a Supper for us to remember him by. How precious the observance of that supper is to his redeemed children.

> Could we with ink the ocean fill,
>> And were the sky of parchment made
> Were every blade of grass a quill,
>> And every man a scribe by trade;
> To write the love of God with ink
> Would drain the ocean dry;
>> Nor would the scroll
>> Contain the whole,
> Though spread from sky to sky.
>>>> — Written by a blind girl

Prayer: Father, may we often examine our hearts and see if we are keeping the right memory of our Lord and Saviour. Keep us by thy love and guidance close to thee. We pray in the name of Jesus. Amen.

December 3

"But God commendeth his love toward us, in that, while we were yet sinners, Christ died for us." — Romans 5:8

Two friends of mine just back from a trip to twelve foreign countries told me the following story.

Just a few days before they were to leave for home Lou became ill. She knew she must have help or she could not start home. They found their way to a doctor's office in West Berlin. The doctor was very efficient and quickly located a kidney infection. As the doctor worked he said several times, "Ah, in America you have the good life."

As they winged their way home a few days later they looked down from the plane on the beautiful clouds and thanked God for letting them live in America. They had not realized before how good God had been to them.

> For the love of God is broader
>> Than the measure of man's mind,
> And the heart of the Eternal
>> Is most wonderfully kind.

If our love were but more simple,
We should take him at his word,
And our lives would be all sunshine
In the sweetness of our Lord.
                            — F. W. Faber

Prayer: Loving heavenly Father, teach us to love as thou hast loved. Make us willing to think of others first. Fill us with a desire to serve mankind. We pray in the name of Jesus. Amen.

December 4

"Behold thou hast instructed many, and thou hast strengthened the weak hands. Thy words have upholden him that was falling, and thou hast strengthened the feeble knees." — Job 4:3, 4

When I was twenty-five years old we lived in an apartment attached to a store. We took turns running the little store and going to school, the Southwestern Baptist Seminary at Fort Worth, Texas. To many, I am sure, it looked as if we were having a hard time. We had three small children, only one old enough for kindergarden. My husband's youngest sister also lived with us and she also went to school part time.

One day a young minister came into the store. A church he had felt sure would call him, had called another man. He was so blue he had decided to give up and quit school. I talked very earnestly to him about how God upholds those who follow him. He soon left but I think the picture of three young people and three children making out as best they could with the pennies and dimes from milk and bread sales helped him. He went back to school and later was called to serve a church. Sometimes a word of encouragement is worth a great deal.

Yet I argue not
Against Thy hand or will, nor bate a jot
Of heart or hope, but still bear up and steer
Right onward.
                            — John Milton

Prayer: Father, fill us with words of courage, In Jesus' name we pray. Amen.

December 5

"Thou shalt worship the Lord thy God, and him only shalt thou serve." — Matthew 4:10

None of us like to taste the humiliation of defeat. We like to have our children win when they are in contest. We like to have our team win in games. Our heavenly Father likes to have us win a victory over temptation. He is there on the side line watching and pushing for us to be victorious. Perhaps if we remember he is for us it will help us turn aside temptation and win a victory.

> Never a trial that He is not there;
> Never a burden that He doth not bear;
> Never a sorrow that He doth not share.
> Moment by moment I'm under his care.
>
> Never a heart-ache, and never a groan,
> Never a tear-drop, and never a moan,
> Never a danger but there, on the throne,
> Moment by moment, He thinks of his own.
>
> Never a weakness that He doth not feel;
> Never a sickness that He cannot heal.
> Moment by moment, in woe or in weal,
> Jesus, my Saviour, abides with me still.
>
> — Daniel W. Whittle

Prayer: Almighty God, our heavenly Father, we confess that we are often tempted to sin. We often forget to pray before we make decisions. Help us to turn to thee and find strength to resist temptation, peace in our hearts and the light of hope. We ask in the name of Christ. Amen.

December 6

"He shall not be afraid of evil tidings: his heart is fixed, trusting in the Lord." — Psalm 112:7

In the mountains of a foreign land some men and boys were standing near a precipice. A climber had become lost and was stranded down below. The men were talking of a way to get a rope to the man below and lift him out.

"You are light and small, Jack. Will you let us tie a rope around you and send you down?"

The shepherd lad drew back in fear, "Oh no!" he cried. Then he saw his father coming across the field. "I will gladly go if my daddy holds the rope."

We need not be afraid in this world of evil and trouble so long as our Father holds the rope.

> This is my Father's world,
> And to my listening ears,

All nature sings, and round me rings
    The music of the spheres.

This is my Father's world,
    I rest me in the thought
Of rocks and trees, of skies and seas
    His hand the wonders wrought.

This is my Father's world,
    O let me ne'er forget
That though the wrong seems oft so strong,
    God is the ruler yet.

— Maltie D. Babcock

Prayer: Most Gracious Father, we feel that thou art never far from us. We count it a dear privilege to be able to call thee Father. May we ever trust in thy care. Amen.

December 7

"And they came to Jericho: and as he went out of Jericho with his disciples and a great number of people, blind Bartimaeus, the son of Timaeus, sat by the highway side begging." — Mark 10:46

Little Bobby took two nickles and held them over his eyes. "Look mommie, I can't see."

"Bobby I wouldn't do that. You should be so happy you are able to see," his mother replied.

Do we as Christians sometimes hold things of the world over our eyes and make ourselves blind to the joys and beauties around us? Do we let a little bit of jealousy keep us from enjoying the blessings of friendship with some people? We should seek to keep our spiritual eyes so bright we can enjoy all the wonders and beauties about us.

Broken-hearted? No, you're not.
You've too many blessings still
That you know cannot be bought.
See the good, forget the ill —
Joy will come to you unsought,
And abide with you until
Earth becomes a beauty spot!

Prayer: Our Father, help us to realize there is a cure for spiritual blindness. There is the same cure the blind begger found beside the highway, the belief and love of Jesus Christ. May we like Bartimaeus call upon thee, Lord, for help and healing. We ask in the name of Christ. Amen.

December 8

"If ye then, being evil, know how to give good gifts unto your children, how much more shall your Father which is in heaven give good things to them that ask him?" — Matthew 7:11

> These are the gifts I ask
> Of thee, Spirit serene:
> Strength for the daily task,
> Courage to face the road,
> Good cheer to help me bear the traveler's load,
> And for the hours of rest that come between,
> An inward joy in all things heard and seen.
> These are the sins I fain
> Would have thee take away:
> Malice, and cold disdain,
> Hot anger, sullen hate,
> Scorn of the lowly, envy of the great,
> And discontent that casts a shadow gray
> On all the brightness of a common day.
> — Henry Van Dyke

Sometimes we pray for our loved ones and we ask God to give them certain gifts. Oftentimes they are selfish requests. We should always remember to ask that God's will be done in the matter of gifts.

Linda was used to her father leaving on Monday mornings for business trips. One Monday when he was going to a foreign land he asked her what she would like to have him bring her. She thought of all the things she had heard about foreign countries and her little heart trembled with fear.

"Just bring back my daddy to me," she told him.

Her father was so pleased at this request made from a heart of love that he took special pains on his trip to select Linda a beautiful doll dressed in native costume.

Prayer: Dear Lord, if our prayers are selfish, forgive us. May our requests be made subject to thy will. Amen.

December 9

"The woman then left her waterpot, and went her way into the city, and saith to the men, Come, see a man, which told me all things that ever I did: is not this the Christ? Then they went out of the city, and came unto him." — John 4:28, 29, 30

When Jesus met the woman at the well and she trusted and believed him to be the Christ, he did not send her to some distant city to witness. She went into her own city where people knew all about her sinful life. There she told the men about Jesus and brought them to him.

There is a Samaria for each child of God; a place where he especially wants us to witness for him. Are we finding our Samaria, or are we waiting for a chance to go to some far away place and tell the story?

We have a friend who wanted very much to become a minister when he was a young High School student. For some reason he never studied theology, nor did he make an effort to become a minister. Often he told friends how he felt called. When a new minister came to the church he told him about his desire to become a minister. The new minister immediately led the church to start a mission to a minority group. He appointed this man to fill the pulpit on Sundays until the mission grew strong enough to hire a pastor. That frustrated man soon was happy serving in his own Samaria. He had not really looked for it before.

We must each search for a place to serve. Christ will lead us to the right Samaria.

Prayer: Father, may we be zealous in our search for a place of service, if it be thy will. Amen.

December 10

"And he saith unto them, Follow me, and I will make you fishers of men. And they straightway left their nets, and followed him." — Matthew 4:19, 20

We can picture James and John as they go to their father Zebedee, "Father we are going to follow Jesus and be fishers of men."

I am sure Zebedee hated to see his boys go. They had worked so closely together on the boat, to make a living. Yet I cannot think they left without first winning their father to Christ. Perhaps he was proud that the Master had called his fine young sons to be followers.

> As God leads I am content;
>   He will take care!
> All things by his will are sent
>   That I must bear;
> To him I take my fear,
> My wishes, while I'm here;
> The way will all seem clear,
>   When I am there!

As God leads me so my heart
    In faith shall rest.
No grief nor fear my soul shall part
    From Jesus' breast.
In sweet belief I know
What way my life doth go —
Since God permitteth so —
    That must be best.

— L. Gedicke

Prayer: O Lord, direct us in all our following. Give us favor and grace as we seek to be fishers of men. May we glorify thy Holy name. We ask in the name of Jesus. Amen.

December 11

"Simon Peter saith unto them, I go a fishing. They say unto him, We also go with thee. They went forth, and entered into a ship immediately; and that night they caught nothing."

— John 21:3

Peter and the disciples seemed to have lost sight of the fact that they had twice seen the risen Lord. They had forgotten there was a kingdom to be expanded for the Lord, and that they were the ones he had selected to build that kingdom on earth. They gave up and decided to go fishing.

How often we lose sight of our goal in serving Christ and just go fishing after worldly pleasures and activities. Next morning the sight of the Lord on the sea shore brought them back to their task.

Whether you'll try for the goal that's afar
Or be contented to stay where you are.
Take it or leave it. Here's something to do,
Just think it over. It's all up to you!
What do you wish? To be known as a shirk;
Known as a good man who's willing to work,
Scorned for a loafer or praised by your chief,
Rich man or poor man or begger or thief?
Eager or earnest or dull through the day,
Honest or crooked? It's you who must say!
You must decide in the face of the test
Whether you'll shirk it or give it your best.

Prayer: Our Gracious heavenly Father, keep us from going astray after things of the world. Give us strength of character to decide on the path of service for thee. We pray in the name of our Great Redeemer. Amen.

298

December 12

"For ye were sometimes darkness, but now are ye light in the Lord: walk as children of light." — Ephesians 5:8

Sin leaves a mark on all of us. A woman was brutally murdered on the campus of a great school. A feeling of fear went over the whole town because no one knew who the murderer might be. Some perverted mind in the school took delight in writing ugly things on waste baskets and walls. When at last the criminal was caught tensions relaxed and people acted more normal.

> Someone started the whole day wrong —
>   Was it you?
> Someone robbed the day of it's song —
>   Was it you?
> Early this morning someone frowned;
> Someone sulked until others scowled;
> And soon harsh words were passed around —
>   Was it you?
>
> Someone started the day aright —
>   Was it you?
> Someone made it happy and bright —
>   Was it you?
> Early this morning, we are told,
> Someone smiled and all through the day —
> This smile encouraged young and old —
>   Was it you?

Prayer: Our Father, direct our paths today. Give us a gracious attitude toward all we meet. Make our words pleasing to thee. May we glorify thy name by our deeds. We pray through Jesus Christ, our Lord. Amen.

December 13

"I shall see him, but not now: I shall behold him, but not nigh: there shall come a Star out of Jacob, and a Sceptre shall rise out of Israel, and shall smite the corners of Moab, and destroy all the children of Sheth." — Numbers 24:17

God fulfilled his promise by sending Christ from among the ranks of the children of Israel.

Two girls were promised a nice gift by their mother. There were some strings attached to the gift. They were to clean the house each Saturday until Christmas. Then they would receive the gift, some money for their own use in shopping.

Sometimes the girls wanted to run and play, or sit and look at television on Saturday but they would remember the promise of their mother and first clean the house.

> O Word that broke the stillness first,
>   Sound on! and never cease
> Till all earth's darkness be made light,
> And all her discord peace.
> Till selfish passion, strife and wrong,
> Thy summons shall have heard,
> And thy creation be complete,
> O thou Eternal Word.

— Longfellow

Prayer: Our Infinite Father, give us busy hands to help forward the time when all promises shall be fulfilled. Give us a spirit of love and gladness as we think of the prophecies given and fulfilled. Make us willing to serve thee more. We pray in Jesus' Name. Amen.

December 14

"And he shall judge among many people, and rebuke strong nations afar off; and they shall beat their swords into plowshares, and their spears into pruning-hooks; nation shall not lift up a sword against nation, neither shall they learn war any more."

— Micah 4:3

The Scripture above really deals with the second coming of Christ. Yet as Christmas time draws near we should think of peace on earth and in our hearts.

When Jesus returns he will solve the problem of peace. In the meantime we must think what we can do to make the world more peaceful. We can be at peace with our friends and neighbors.

> Have you any old grudge you'd like to pay?
> And wrong laid up from a bygone day?
> Gather them all now, and lay them away
>   When Christmas comes.
>
> Hard thoughts are heavy to carry, my friend,
> And life is short from beginning to end;
> Be kind to yourself, leave nothing to mend
>   When Christmas comes.

— William Lytle

Prayer: Father, we thank thee for the season of Christmas. A season when we think of joy and peace. Fill our hearts with forgiveness and love. Give us generous impulses and thoughts toward others. We pray in the name of Jesus. Amen.

December 15

"For mine eyes have seen thy salvation, which thou hast prepared before the face of all peoples. . . . And his name shall be called . . . Prince of Peace. Of the increase of his government and of peace there shall be no end."

— Luke 2:30, 31; Isaiah 9:6-7

The meaning and the message of our Christian faith remain the hope of the world.

Fifty years ago Christmas was celebrated with a cedar tree cut in the woods and decorated with red berries and pop corn strung on strings.

Families met at Grandmother's house and often the children slept on beds made on the floor. Near each little head would be a stocking borrowed from an older and larger person. Fresh fruit was used to fill the stockings, along with some peppermint sticks of candy.

Christmas morning the story of the birth of Christ was read and prayer service conducted before the day's festivities started.

> Some good old-fashioned customs
> Go out of style, no doubt;
> But sending Christmas greetings
> We couldn't do without.
> And so the custom lingers —
> Let us hope it always will —
> For the same old-fashioned friendship
> Prompts the same old greetings still.

Prayer: We thank thee Father, for all our Christmas' past, for health and home and happiness. We pray in the name of Jesus. Amen.

December 16

"Through the tender mercy of God: whereby the dayspring from on high hath visited us, To give light to them that sit in darkness and in the shadow of death, to guide our feet into the way of peace." — Luke 1:78, 79

George was especially happy as Christmas drew near. During

301

the past year he had received the gift of salvation. Now he wondered what he could do for Jesus at Christmas time to show his love. Mother suggested he make a gift to the Christmas mission offering at church. He planned to do that but it did not seem enough. Then he thought of Mr. Fields down the street. Mr. Fields did not know Jesus as his Saviour. On the way home from school George stopped to see him. From among his school books he took a New Testament. He read the story of Christ's birth to Mr. Fields and asked him to come to church next Sunday.

"Now I have really tried to give a gift to Jesus."

> Not what you get, but what you give,
> Not what you say, but how you live;
> Giving the world the love it needs,
> Living a life of noble deeds.
> Not whence you came, but whither bound;
> Not what you have or whither found,
> Strong for the right, the good, the true —
> These are things worthwhile for you.

Prayer: Help us our Father, to make a frank evaluation of our lives. Help us to determine to live more effectively for thee. Fill our hearts with the joy of the Christ Child at this time. We pray in Jesus' name. Amen.

December 17

"And when they were come into the house, they saw the young child with Mary his mother, and fell down, and worshiped him: and when they had opened their treasures, they presented unto him gifts; gold, and frankincense, and myrrh." — Matthew 2:11

Sometimes we feel Christmas has lost its meaning because it is so commercialized. Christmas will never lose its meaning as long as we put Christ first. We must never forget that it is the season for giving gifts. Our greatest gift is to give ourselves to Christ.

A friend of mine has four grandchildren. She gave each child some money and then took them to the home of a missionary home on furlough. They listened to the missionary tell about the need on her mission field, then each child gave her some money and asked that she use it in a foreign land.

> Then let every heart
> Keep Christmas within.
> Christ's pity for sorrow,
> Christ's hatred for sin,

Christ's care for the weakest,
Christ's courage for right.
Everywhere, Everywhere,
Christmas tonight!

— Phillips Brooks

Prayer: Our Father, thy great gift to our needy world has set us an example of giving. As the first act of worship at the manger was one of giving, help us to give at the Christmas season, that others may have enough. We pray in Jesus' name. Amen.

December 18

"And he sent them to Bethlehem, and said, Go and search diligently for the young child; and when ye have found him, bring me word again, that I may come and worship him also."

— Matthew 2:8

Who do we put at the head of our list? Herod put Jesus' name, but not for worship. He wanted to kill him. The wise men wanted Christ's name first in order to worship. All through life some are selfish and pretend to put Christ at the head of their list when it is only for personal gain. The people who put Christ at the head of their list are happy people.

Polly was always ill by Christmas day because she wore herself out trying to buy each friend and relative a gift that cost exactly what she thought they had spent on her the year before. Could we ever repay God for the great gift He gave to us?

> On Christmas day the Child was born,
> On Christmas day in the morning;
> He trod the long way, lone and lorn,
> He wore the bitter crown of thorn,
> His hands and feet and heart were torn,
> He died at last the death of scorn.
> But through his coming Death was slain,
> That you and I might live again.
> For this the Child of the Maid was born,
> On Christmas Day in the morning."

Prayer: Father, fill us this season with a more worshipful spirit. We have indeed had good tidings of great joy. Help us to share them with others. For his name's sake we pray. Amen.

December 19

"And suddenly there was with the angel a multitude of the heavenly host praising God, and saying, Glory to God in the highest and on earth peace, good will toward men."

— Luke 2:13, 14

A few years ago at Christmas time my Sunday School class received a letter from the pastor of a small church in the mountains of Colorado. The letter asked if we would give an offering to help the little mountain church buy a chime system. The women were enthusiastic and soon we shipped to them all the necessary equipment for them to play hymns over a loud speaker. The system was installed in time for the little town to hear Christmas music. People who had grown to take Christmas for granted heard the beautiful music and were drawn back to remember the meaning of Christmas.

> I heard the bells on Christmas day
> Their old familiar carols play,
> And wild and sweet the words repeat
> Of peace on earth, good-will to men.
>
> And in despair I bowed my head:
> "There is no peace on earth," I said.
> "For hate is strong and mocks the song
> Of peace on earth, good-will to men."
>
> Then pealed the bells more loud and deep:
> "God is not dead, nor doth He sleep;
> The wrong shall fail, the right prevail,
> With peace on earth, good-will to men:"
>
> Till, ringing, singing on its way,
> The world revolved from night to day,
> A voice, a chime, a chant sublime,
> Of peace on earth, good-will to men!
>
> — Longfellow

Prayer: We thank thee, God, for beautiful music at Christmas time. We pray through Jesus. Amen.

December 20

"And when they had seen it they made known abroad the saying which was told them concerning this child.

And all they that heard it wondered at those things which were told by the shepherds." — Luke 2:17, 18

A young girl, who won a prize in a contest at school, went up and down her block telling all her friends and neighbors, "I won, I won!"

When we hear of a friend having a new baby we like to tell someone else the good news. People say bad news travels faster than good news but most of us like to bring good tidings to our friends. What greater tidings could we publish than the tidings of Jesus birth!

> Christmas is a time of secrets,
> So I'll whisper one to you;
> Grandpa says that all who try it
> Find that every word is true:
> "Would you have a happy day?
> Give some happiness away."
>
> Grandpa says this little secret
> Should be carried through the year,
> And if all would try to heed it
> Earth would soon be full of cheer.
> "Would you have a happy day?
> Give some happiness away."

Prayer: Our Father, thou hast indeed sent us glad tidings of great joy. May we in turn give those tidings to others. As we think of the manger of the new-born babe, may we not think of mere decorations but of the wonder of the gift of salvation. In Jesus' name. Amen.

December 21

"Peace I leave with you, my peace I give unto you: not as the world giveth, give I unto you. Let not your heart be troubled, neither let it be afraid." — John 14:27

The gifts of this world are trivial, but the gifts of Christ are beyond price. We can live without most of the superfluous things we get at Christmas but Christ is indispensable. Often people give to us because we gave to them. Christ gives to us because he loves us.

> Who profits most? 'Tis not the man
> Who, grasping every coin he can,
> Unscrupulously crushes down
> His weaker neighbor with a frown.
> He is not worthy of his trust,

And friendless, knows his gold is dust.
He loses what he sought to gain,
And finds instead of pleasure, pain.

Who profits most? It is not he
Of life's great opportunity.
He is not mourned — why should he be?
Who shirks responsibility;
Who, hermit like, himself withdraws
To live apart from human flaws;
To scoff at mortal frailties?
He turns away — no vision sees.

Who profits most? It is the man
Who gives a boost where'er he can;
Who's on the square in all that's done,
And trusts and helps the others on;
Who puts his task above mere self,
And values friends, and counts them wealth.
Who profits most? Is that your quest?
It is the man who serves the best.

Prayer: Oh, God, may we this Christmas learn the art of giving ourselves. We pray in the name of one who gave all for us. Amen.

December 22

"There is that maketh himself rich, yet hath nothing: there is that maketh himself poor, yet hath great riches."
— Proverbs 13:7

I knew a woman who had very little money, yet she always had a small Christmas gift for all her friends. After getting home from her job she would prepare the evening meal for her invalid husband; then she would start on her Christmas gifts. She made candy and filled small boxes for friends. She became so famous for her candy people began asking her to make some to sell and soon she had a thriving business.

A surgeon brings a laughing lad
    With twisted limbs made strong —
A teacher brings brave visions,
    A singer a silver song.

An engineer brings bridges,
    A mason a temple wall —

A mother brings a trembling prayer,
   And love illumines all.

I wonder what the Christ-Child did
   With myrrh the magi bore,
And gold and frankincense! These gifts
   He uses evermore!
                                    — Earl Brown

Prayer: We thank thee Father, for the love and good-will abroad
in our land at Christmas time. Make our lives and deeds beautiful in these days. We ask in the name of Jesus. Amen.

December 23

*"When they heard the king, they departed; and, lo, the star,
which they saw in the east, went before them, till it came and
stood over where the young child was."* — Matthew 2:9

For each person Christmas brings a different message. Most of
us feel a message of hope and love. Wouldn't it be wonderful if
we could live each day as though it were Christmas.

The pure, the bright, the beautiful
   That stirred our hearts in youth,
The impulse of wordless prayer,
   The streams of love and truth,
The longing after something lost,
   The spirit's yearning cry,
The striving after better hopes —
   These things can never die.

The timid hand stretched forth to aid
   A brother in his need;
A kindly word in grief's dark hour
   That proves a friend indeed;
The plea for mercy softly breathed,
   When justice threatens high,
The sorrow of a contrite heart —
   These things shall never die.

Let nothing pass, for every hand
   Must find some work to do,
Lose not a chance to waken love —
   Be firm and just and true.
So shall a light that cannot fade
   Beam on thee from on high,

And angel voices say to thee —
"These things shall never die."
— Charles Dickens

Prayer: Father, are we making Christmas as you would have us to? Make us controlled with thy love. Let us look about and help the needy at our door. We pray in the name of Jesus. Amen.

December 24

"And so it was, that, while they were there, the days were accomplished that she should be delivered. And she brought forth her firstborn son, and wrapped him in swaddling clothes, and laid him in a manger; because there was no room for them in the inn." — Luke 2:6, 7

The shepherds were afraid the night they heard the angels sing, but the sheep and the flocks and herds were quiet. They were trusting in the same shepherd as always, and saw no change. Herod was afraid. He saw not a tiny babe in a manger but pictured a king who would take his place. He heard not a song of joy but only felt hate.

The tidings were brought to all people but only a few heard.

I dreamed I saw Christ come again
Across the snowy Christmas plain,
With gifts and blessings in His hand
For every heart in every land;
But he brought not a painted toy,
Some little superficial joy,
A dole a moment's need to cure,
A Christmas dinner for the poor.

He brought to all men everywhere
The right to do, the right to share,
The right to think, the right to learn,
The right to labor and to earn,
Courage to walk with head erect.
In peace of mind and self-respect.
The right to face life unafraid.
Oh, what a Christmas Day it made.
— Ilion T. Jones

Prayer: Father, we are filled with tender memories on this eve of our Saviour's birth. We ask that you will fill our hearts with the presence of the King of kings. Give us generous hearts and may the star shine brightly and the angels sing more beautifully today because our hearts are right. In his name. Amen.

December 25

"And, behold, thou shalt conceive in thy womb, and bring forth a son, and shalt call his name JESUS. He shall be great, and shall be called the Son of the Highest: and the Lord God shall give unto him the throne of his father David."

—Luke 1:31, 32

Mary was just a sweet young girl, engaged to be married. She loved her betrothed and looked forward to a happy life. When the angel told her she was to become the mother of a child called Jesus, she did not know what sacrifice she would have to make. Perhaps Joseph would make her a public example and forsake her. Yet she was submissive to God's will. God in turn worked out her problems.

> Seems to me the stars shine brighter
> Christmas night;
> Seems to me the snow lies whiter,
> Christmas night;
> That the solemn trees stand straighter,
> And the frosty moon sets later,
> And the hush is stiller, greater,
> Christmas night.
>
> Seems to me sad things are fewer
> Christmas night;
> Seems to me glad things are truer
> Christmas night;
> Seems to me the bells ring clearer
> From their steeples louder, nearer;
> Seems to me the whole world's dearer
> Christmas night.

Prayer: May the message of peace and brotherhood fill our souls at this Christmas season. Use our lives and our money to bring joy to those in need. We pray in the name of the King of kings, Amen.

December 26

"And the Word was made flesh, and dwelt among us."

—John 1:14

309

When Jesus came to dwell in our hearts he brought some permanent gifts — gifts which go on day after day.

The greatest gift is that of eternal life, the secure knowledge that we will live on throughout the ages in heaven. He brings us the gift of a sense of his abiding presence ever with us. He gives us the gift of holiness. He gives us a gift of power to overcome sin. He brings to our hearts a gift of joy and gladness, a knowledge that his storehouse is full and we can call upon him in time of need.

> A twinkling star can never be
> Mere symbol of eternity;
> It is a beacon, clear and strong,
> To guide the race of men along.
>
> The sailor lost on pathless sea
> Finds comfort in its symmetry;
> The wanderer who strays afar
> Is oft led home by friendly star.
>
> It was a star that blessed night,
> That led the Wise Men to the light;
> So when the way seems steep or far,
> Re-chart your course by guiding star.
>   — Donovan Marshall

Prayer: Accept our deepest gratitude for all the joys we have experienced this Christmas. Fill our hearts with the love of Christ in such a way that we will continue Christmas all the year. We pray in the name of Jesus. Amen.

December 27

"And we know that all things work together for good to them that love God, to them who are the called according to his purpose." — Romans 8:28

William was determined to make a minister. He felt sincerely in his heart that God had called him. His parents were very poor and could not help him go to school. He borrowed a few dollars and with all he possessed tied in a pasteboard box he went to a college. It happened that the very day he arrived someone had resigned in the maintenance department. He was given the job. Often during the years that followed William was tired but always he pushed on because he felt God was with him.

Never, not since the world began
Has the sun ever once stopped shining.
His face very often we could not see,
And we grumbled at his inconstancy,
But the clouds were all to blame, not he,
For, behind them, he was shining.

And so, behind life's darkest clouds
There's something always shining.
We veil it at times with faithless fears,
And dim our sight with foolish tears,
But in time the atmosphere always clears,
For there's something always shining.

Prayer: Our Father, who hast declared thy love to all men, may
we ever rest in the knowledge that all things do work together for
good; that thou art ruling the world and art our friend. We ask
in the name of Jesus. Amen.

December 28

*"For he saith, I have heard thee in a time accepted, and in the
day of salvation have I succored thee: behold, now is the day of
salvation."* — II Corinthians 6:2

The year is rapidly drawing to a close. Time is always speeding
on. No one can promise you another day of life. We must trust
God for that. We should finish any tasks we feel important today.
Most of all we must see that we are right with God. It is always
later than we think. We should be ready at all times for the end
of life for us.

Dream not too much of what you'll do tomorrow,
How well you'll work perhaps another year;
Tomorrow's chance you do not need to borrow —
Today is here.

Boast not too much of mountains you will master,
The while you linger in the vale below;
To dream is well, but plodding brings us faster
To where we go.

Talk not too much about some new endeavor
You mean to make a little later on;
Who idles now will idle on forever
Till life is done.

Swear not some day to break some habit's fetter,
When this old year is dead and passed away;
If you have need of living wiser, better,
Begin today!

Prayer: Father, make us conscious of the time of our lives fleeting away. May we prepare for all tomorrows. We ask in Christ's name. Amen.

December 29

"A new commandment I give unto you, That ye love one another; as I have loved you, that ye also love one another."
— John 13:34

Some things seem strange to us at the time they happen but God always sees what is best in accordance with his will.

Sometimes we are tempted to take the easy way out and give our love only to those who love us. We want to tell the story of Jesus only to the clean and pretty people of the world. If we follow the new commandment we will love all people.

> The camel at the close of day
> Kneels down upon the sandy plain
> To have his burden lifted off
>   And rest again.
> My soul, thou too shouldst to thy knees
> When daylight draweth to a close,
> And let thy Master lift thy load
>   And grant repose.
> Else how couldst thou the morrow meet,
> With all tomorrow's work to do,
> If thou thy burden all the night
>   Dost carry through?
> The camel kneels at break of day
> To have his guide replace his load,
> Then rises up anew to take
>   The desert road.
> So thou shouldst kneel at morning's dawn
> That God may give thee daily care
> Assured that He no load too great
>   Will make thee bear.

Prayer: Father, we would pour ourselves out in thy service. Use us today. For we ask in Jesus' name. Amen.

December 30

"He left nothing undone of all that the Lord commanded Moses." — Joshua 11:15

As the year draws to a close we think of the many thing we have left undone during the past twelve months. We seriously promise ourselves to do better during the next year.

As each day passes we do not notice the wasted minutes, but if all were added up and presented to us at one time we would be shocked to see how much time we had spent in careless idleness — time we could have spent accomplishing the tasks we omitted.

> Although some seeds are wasted and some work destroyed by gale,
> Some crops yield unexpectedly, while others seem to fail.
> Yet there must be a harvest, the fulfillment of our toil,
> The goodness will be gathered after patience from the soil.
>
> And life, too, has a harvest for the aims that we pursue,
> Although some good deeds planted do not flourish it is true.
> Some plans are disappointing, sown too early or too late,
> While impulses of kindness might grow friendships that are great.
>
> In nature and in life we plan our way and sow our seeds,
> But in God's time and season reap the harvest of our deeds.

— Kathleen Partridge

Prayer: May the harvest we reap from this past year be fruitful. Forgive us the omissions we have made. In Jesus' name. Amen.

December 31

"The Lord hath done great things for us; whereof we are glad." — Psalm 126:3

"I will remember the years of the right hand of the Most High." — Psalm 77:10

We do not understand some of the errors we have made these past twelve months. This is a busy age. Perhaps we made some mistakes because we did not take time to think and meditate. We cannot undo the past, but we can ask God to help us make the future better. All of life is hastening to fulfill its mission. Let us go our way with enthusiasm. Make today a grand and glorious end of a wonderful year.

> Only a day of life, soon to be done,
> 'Tis passing now to die at set of sun.
> Only a day, but fraught with vital things;
> Issues of Life and Death each hour brings.

> Only a Day! But as each moment flies
> Some earth-worn pilgrim folds his arms and dies.
> Only a Day! Only a breath of time,
> Yet filled with opportunities sublime.

> If this one day shall thus be spent for him,
> New joy shall come to saint and seraphim;
> In earth and heaven the choirs of God will sing,
> As to the cross the lost ones we shall bring.

> Then count each day a part of God's great plan;
> Use well its hours to help your fellow man;
> Time is the stuff of which our lives are made,
> And when 'tis lost all mankind are betrayed.

Prayer: At the end of this year, our Father, we come with deepest gratitude to thank thee for the many great things thou hast done for us. In the name of Christ we pray. Amen.